Case Studies for Teaching Social Psychology

Second Edition

We dedicate this book to

- *Alexandra Rutherford for uniting scholarship, humor, and an eye for the telling detail*
- *Jane Halonen for keeping students laughing, learning, and engaged*
- *Scott Lilienfeld for his calm, compelling advocacy for psychological science*
- *The informal "brain trust": Amber, Tay, Ann, and Meara*

Case Studies for Teaching Social Psychology
Critical Thinking and Application

Second Edition

Thomas Heinzen
William Paterson University

Wind Goodfriend
Buena Vista University

Los Angeles | London | New Delhi
Singapore | Washington DC | Melbourne

FOR INFORMATION:

SAGE Publications, Inc.
2455 Teller Road
Thousand Oaks, California 91320
E-mail: order@sagepub.com

SAGE Publications Ltd.
1 Oliver's Yard
55 City Road
London, EC1Y 1SP
United Kingdom

SAGE Publications India Pvt. Ltd.
B 1/I 1 Mohan Cooperative Industrial Area
Mathura Road, New Delhi 110 044
India

SAGE Publications Asia-Pacific Pte. Ltd.
18 Cross Street #10-10/11/12
China Square Central
Singapore 048423

Library of Congress Cataloging-in-Publication Data

Names: Heinzen, Thomas E., author. | Goodfriend, Wind, author.

Title: Case studies for teaching social psychology : critical thinking and application / Thomas Heinzen, William Paterson University, Wind Goodfriend, Buena Vista University. Description: Second edition. | Thousand Oaks, California : SAGE, [2022] | Includes bibliographical references and index.

Identifiers: LCCN 2020037218 | ISBN 9781544393520 (paperback) | ISBN 9781544393537 (epub) | ISBN 9781544393544 (epub) | ISBN 9781544393551 (ebook)

Subjects: LCSH: Social psychology. | Critical thinking.

Classification: LCC HM1033 .H4558 2022 | DDC 302—dc23

LC record available at https://lccn.loc.gov/2020037218

Acquisitions Editor: Lara Parra
Editorial Assistant: Elizabeth Cruz
Content Development
    Editor: Chelsea Neve
Production Editor: Bennie Clark Allen
Copy Editor: Lana Todorovic-Arndt
Typesetter: Hurix Digital
Proofreader: Jen Grubba
Indexer: Integra
Cover Designer: Gail Buschman
Marketing Manager: Katherine Hepburn

This book is printed on acid-free paper.

21 22 23 24 25 10 9 8 7 6 5 4 3 2 1

Contents

Preface: To Students and Their Teachers

> "This a strange book full of even stranger stories."
>
> Rolls (2015, p. 1)

Geoff Rolls was right about case studies and strange stories.

This collection of case studies uses the strangeness of human (and other animal) behaviors to demonstrate how you can observe behavior, collect and organize data, and then analyze and interpret your results. Each case study connects to social psychological concepts and theories. For example, you will experience social psychology through reading about

- altruistic vampire bats,

- social cooperation among whales,

- the fall and rise of self-esteem during pregnancy,

- using the fear of death to market diamonds,

- violence in the world's first story-telling film,

- a baseball umpire who let the catcher call balls and strikes, and

- the aroma of bacon inspiring a cease fire in war.

WHY CASE STUDIES?

This collection of case studies will introduce you to social psychology.

You will see familiar social behaviors through the lens of science—and that changes how you think. Case studies are also memorable—and that means you will carry some of these stories with you for the rest of your life. Case studies also play a distinctive role in science—and that will make you a more critical thinker about everything you experience in your social world.

Case Studies Probe the Future and Learn From the Past

Watch the concrete being poured at a construction site.

You will notice the iron rods or steel mesh sticking out from the walls as the concrete is poured into the frames. Case studies are the steel mesh embedded in the concrete of psychology's broad experimental foundation. Case studies are the network of memorable observations that hold all that hard research together. When they work, case studies are a sign of a healthy science (Flyvbjerg, 2006). Case studies can have two general purposes: *research* and *teaching*.

Case Studies for Research

Case studies can inspire research that develops our scientific future.

The case study of Pittsburgh Steeler football player Mike Webster started as a single autopsy. However, his brain damage became the case that signaled a larger issue and penetrated the troubled future of the National Football League. Puzzling out that marquee, difficult case had medical and social consequences that are still unfolding. For example, there appears to be greater reluctance among parents to encourage their children to play American football (FiveThirtyEight, 2020).

In psychology, the case study of Phineas Gage (Case 3.1) helped to connect brain damage to personality. Furthermore, the case of facilitated communication exposed a bogus therapy for people with autism (Case 2.1). Fernald's (1984) comparison case studies of Little Hans (Sigmund Freud) and Clever Hans (Oskar Pfungst) clarified the gap between clinical speculations and hard-won psychological knowledge (Case Study 1.3; see also Yin, 2009, p. 18, for a summary of the elements of a research case study).

Case Studies for Teaching

Case studies can also inspire memorable teaching and learning.

Case studies for teaching are typically brief and designed to provoke discussion and critical thinking. Harvard MBA students will study about 500 fictional and nonfictional case studies because "we believe the case study method is the best way to prepare students for the challenges of [future] leadership" (Harvard Business School, 2014). The same technique can be used in psychology, to help students see theories and concepts all around them, to facilitate discussion, and to show how abstract ideas are clarified in real people's lives.

CASE STUDIES AND GUIDELINES BY THE AMERICAN PSYCHOLOGICAL ASSOCIATION FOR THE PSYCHOLOGY MAJOR

Learning from case studies matches the five goals for the undergraduate psychology major created by the American Psychological Association (APA).

Goal 1: Knowledge Base in Psychology

Social psychology is a connective course, and case studies make connections.

The content of social psychology draws on knowledge from every chapter of a standard general psychology textbook. For example, psychology's history is prominent in the case studies of cognitive dissonance (see Case Studies 6.1 and 6.2). "Phineas Gage" (Case Study

3.1) could be the poster case study in at least four chapters. We also highlight less prominent histories by describing the group processes that connected Ada Lovelace, Grace Hopper, and the "Sensational Six" women who invented computer programming (Case Study 8.3).

Goal 2: Scientific Inquiry and Critical Thinking

Case studies ask difficult questions; difficult questions require critical thinking.

Learning through case studies happens through the discussion questions at the end. They are designed to get under the skin of automatic, binary, or multiple-choice type responses. These case studies justify social psychologists' passion for experiments (facilitated communication; Case Study 2.1) but sample widely from other methods, including archived data that challenge our own history (e.g., the Milgram experiment; Case Study 7.1).

Goal 3: Ethical and Social Responsibility in a Diverse World

Case studies address large social issues and private ethical dilemmas.

The connections between stereotypes, prejudice, and discrimination become a sympathetic face in Doloreisa's story of sex trafficking (Case Study 11.1). We also learn how social contagion produced a moral panic that forcibly deported US citizens during the Great Depression (Case Study 9.1). Wesley Autrey had to make a swift ethical decision when a young man having a seizure stumbled onto the tracks as the approaching "1 train" entered the stop at 137th Street in New York City. It is a vivid way to ask deep questions about the origins of human goodness (Case Study 10.3).

Goal 4: Communication

Case studies make it easy for students to practice their communication skills.

The specific APA goal is clear: "Students should demonstrate competence in writing and in oral and interpersonal communication skills" (Halonen et al., 2013, p. 30). Our best lectures won't help our students practice their communication skills. If nothing else, students will remember *their* presentations. A well-managed discussion gently coerces reluctant students and restrains louder voices. In large classes, you might try rotating students as leaders of small discussion groups or assigning a different student to summarize each case to the rest of the class in only 100 words.

Goal 5: Professional Development

Most of our students will not attain doctorates in social psychology.

Academic culture somehow suggests that this represents a failure. We object! There are 44 case studies in the second edition, and each could suggest multiple career opportunities. "The Rock in the Coffin" (Case Study 5.4) demonstrates the importance of social influence in marketing. The case study of school shootings (Case Study 8.2) demonstrates social roles for teachers, police, researchers, and journalists. "Health Detective"

(Case Study 2.3) demonstrates how well psychology skills align with opportunities in public health.

GUIDELINES FOR TEACHING ONLINE

Higher education is changing quickly.

In the middle of the coronavirus pandemic, *The Chronicle of Higher Education* tried to anticipate its effects on higher education (see "How Will the Pandemic Change Higher Education?" 2020). Their 23 interviews reached a consensus that the movement toward online courses was accelerating.

For now, we suggest only three general principles because they fit well with teaching and learning from case studies.

Principle 1: Early and Easy Engagement

Engage with students early and often.

First impressions produce halo effects that are not easily dispelled, and folk wisdom reminds us that you never get a second chance to make a first impression. You may want to practice the interface with your institution's learning management system. Moreover, Henry and Meadows (2008, p. 4) emphasize that "A great web interface will not save a poor course, but a poor web interface will destroy a potentially great course."

Then, put your most engaging material (as images, questions, slides, or links) at the front of your presentations.

Principle 2: Less Is More

It is easy to get carried away with the bells and whistles of online instruction.

However, less is often more in online environments. Even the online syllabus has a sensitive influence on perceptions of the professor and the course. Too many hyperlinks, for example, is not necessarily a good thing (see Grigorovici et al., 2003). You have several practical decisions that will influence how students experience your course. Simple is good.

Principle 3: Communication

Reviews of best practices for online teaching emphasize communication.

Students don't want uncertainty about the rules that will govern an online course. Neither do faculty. Communication between students and faculty should be

- Early and clear at the beginning of the course
- Structured during the course
- Perceived as fair throughout the course

As teachers, try thinking of yourselves as curators of the museum of social psychology.

CHANGES IN THIS EDITION

While we were pleased with the first edition, two major changes were made, and we hope they will make this edition even better.

First, we've expanded the content. There are now a total of 44 cases, compared to only 39 in the first edition. The new cases emphasize subjects of interest to today's students, including the influence of culture, technology, and intersectionality. Second, we reconsidered the andragogy of how each case is presented. Now, every case follows the same format. Each starts with a section called "The Social Situation," which frames the subject and why it's important. Next, each case has a middle section: "Theory and Method." Students learn about the specific ideas being testing and how researchers chose their particular methodological approach. Finally, every case ends with "Results and Discussion," helping students see the big picture and start critical analysis. This is a nice, informal introduction to the basics of APA writing, offering a comforting consistency throughout the book.

We hope these changes will help both instructors and students see the meaning of each case, the development of social psychological ideas over time, and the remaining questions. We also welcome comments and feedback, as we hope that each edition will offer an increasingly better experience. We can only achieve that with your help, and we appreciate it very much.

Tom Wind

How Do Social Psychologists Think?

1

1.1 TO WEAR OR NOT TO WEAR AN INEFFECTIVE MASK: THAT WAS THE QUESTION DURING THE CORONAVIRUS PANDEMIC

The Social Situation

It will happen again.

Social psychologists can help to prepare the public for the next pandemic. Steven Taylor's (2019) book, *The Psychology of Pandemics: Preparing for the Next Global Outbreak of Infectious Disease*, provides specific guidance. Taylor's book was published just prior to the coronavirus disease of 2019 (COVID-19) pandemic. But you can practice your social psychological skills now by searching for the dangerous, one-word assumption in the next sentence about recommended behavior from the World Health Organization (WHO, 2019, p. 1):

> This document summarizes WHO's recommendations for the rational use of personal protective equipment (PPE) in healthcare and community settings.

The early WHO advice was offered on February 17, 2020, right as COVID-19 was ramping up in the United States. Their still useful advice described specific ways to avoid becoming infected with the virus:

- washing hands frequently with soap and water for at least 20 seconds, or using an alcohol-based hand rub if soap and water are not available;

- avoiding touching your eyes, nose, and mouth;

- practicing respiratory hygiene by coughing or sneezing into a bent elbow or tissue and then immediately disposing of the tissue;

- wearing a face covering if you have respiratory symptoms and performing hand hygiene after disposing of the covering; and

- maintaining social distance (a minimum of 2 meters or 6 feet) from individuals with respiratory symptoms.

This life-saving advice changed only slightly as the situation changed and scientific understanding grew. However, that lifesaving, medical advice was sure to be sabotaged because the communicators at the WHO were not thinking like social psychologists. The most dangerous assumption about human behavior is hidden from the reader's attention in the middle of the first sentence: rational.

We can't assume that humans will behave rationally. Figure 1.1 describes how COVID-19 (and similar infections) found its way to your doorstep, and possibly into your body. The rational way to stop the spread of influenza (and many other infectious diseases) is to block the transmission at any point in the process. But which behavior has a greater chance of success: Asking people to wash their hands more, or asking them to touch their faces less?

The rational way to stop the spread of influenza (and many other infectious diseases) is to block the transmission at any point in the process. If only we humans were rational. But we're not. Which do you think is easier: Asking people to wash their hands more, or asking them to touch their face less?

Theory and Method

This case study relies on **naturalistic observation** of medical students in a classroom.

Many of our baseline behaviors tend to be founded on emotions and **intuition** rather than reason and **logic**. We are emotional and reactive when we experience unexpected, health-threatening events, such as the COVID-19 virus (see Chen et al. 2019; De Las Cuevas & de Leon, 2019; Whitehead & Russell, 2004). It's also hard for us to use logic

FIGURE 1.1

Spread of Coronavirus Disease

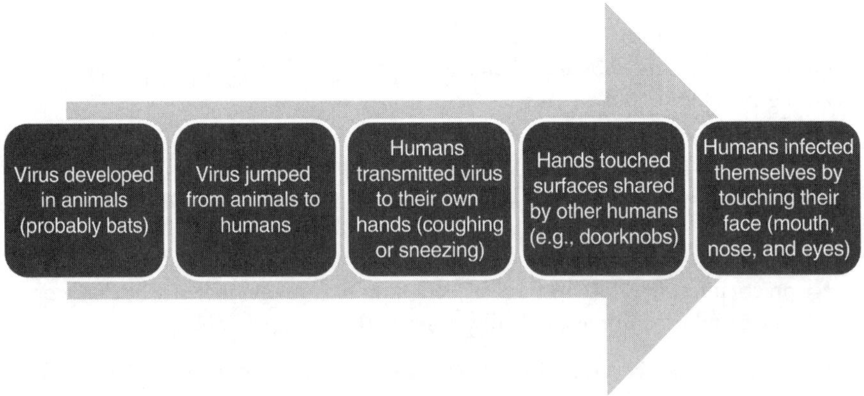

Virus developed in animals (probably bats) → Virus jumped from animals to humans → Humans transmitted virus to their own hands (coughing or sneezing) → Hands touched surfaces shared by other humans (e.g., doorknobs) → Humans infected themselves by touching their face (mouth, nose, and eyes)

Source: World Health Organization.

to break automatic, routine, habitual behaviors. The second piece of advice on the WHO list is *avoiding touching your eyes, nose, and mouth*. Social psychologists understand why this advice is doomed to failure. You can tell humans not to touch their faces. But that isn't going to stop them because face-touching is an automatic behavior.

An Australian research team told a group of 26 medical students that they were going to be part of an observational study (see Kwok et al., 2015). They knew they were being videotaped, but they did not know why. The class was videotaped so that the research team could count the frequency of hand-to-face contacts and where they occurred on the face: either with mucosal or non-mucosal areas. You might want to make your own prediction about the average number of facial touches per hour—and their location—after the research team counted how often these 26 medical students touched their own faces.

Results and Discussion

The numbers were probably higher than you anticipated.

There were a total of 2,346 facial touches in this class of 26 students. On average, each student touched their face 23 times per hour. Almost half (44%) touched an area with a mucous membrane. This provides a convenient pathway for viruses such as influenza or COVID-19, or the new viruses that emerge every year. The mucous membrane touches were almost evenly divided between the mouth (372 touches; 36%), the nose (318 touches; 31%), and the eyes (273 touches; 27%). There were combinations of touches to multiple mucosal areas (61 touches; 6%). The remainder (1,322; 56%) were contacts with non-mucosal areas.

As an intervention, it appears to be easier to increase hand washing rather than to reduce face touching. This hypothesis found support in a review of 100 relevant studies (Lunn et al., 2020). Why? Because face touching is an automatic behavior and therefore resistant to change. More hand washing can be encouraged by reminding people that it helps both them and their loved ones by slowing spread of the disease. Behavior, as the social psychologist understands it, is a function of a person interacting within an environment.

In addition to more hand washing and less face touching, the debate about how best to reduce the COVID-19 transmission included whether non-infected persons should cover their face. It could be a scarf, shop mask, or anything other than the carefully designed medical mask. At first, the WHO insisted that non-medical masks were irrelevant because they don't screen out the virus.

They emphasized that our first commitment regarding masks must be to the health care workers who routinely intubate or work with patients who are coughing, sneezing, or gagging on them. We need healthy health care workers for selfish reasons, if nothing else. We want them to be able to (a) treat us when our turn comes, and (b) not infect the rest of the population.

However, the debate grows more complicated when we consider using ineffective masks that do not actually screen out the virus. At first, public health workers were concerned that encouraging the public to make and wear their own masks would lead to a false sense of security. People wearing masks might feel like it was safe to ignore social distancing or go to public events just for something to do. Either would increase rates of disease transmission. On the other hand, any mask or scarf would limit the distance that contaminated droplets would be distributed from people sneezing, singing, shouting, or coughing.

Another view is that encouraging people to wear even an unsafe mask would limit their access to their own face and break the chain of contamination. In other words, they might not touch their nose and mouth as frequently, especially when out in public. Therefore, even a homemade mask could limit or reduce those habitual 23 touches per hour. Wearing the mask might also remind people of the possible danger of approaching other people too closely.

Finally, homemade masks might not be useful at all from a medical point of view— unless you also factor in the psychology of how they affect behaviors based on both intuition and logic.

DISCUSSION QUESTIONS

1. During the COVID-19 pandemic, there were lots of reminders not to touch your face. Some people complained about this, noting that each reminder just made them want to touch their face! Why do you think this seemingly ironic experience occurred?

2. Some people took COVID-19 very seriously, while others seemed to think it was no big deal. At the same time, some people watched the news obsessively, while others tried to ignore it. What variables (personality traits, previous experiences, professions, family situations, etc.) might differentiate one type of person from another? How could you test your hypothesis?

3. Now that the world has experienced COVID-19, do you think people will act any differently if another pandemic arises? Why, or why not?

KEY TERMS

- **Naturalistic observation:** Watching and recording people's behaviors where they would have happened anyway, but for research purposes
- **Intuition:** The ability to know something quickly and automatically; "gut feelings"

that take little mental effort and can occur habitually.
- **Logic:** The ability to use reason, think systematically, and carefully consider evidence when making a decision

1.2 AN EXERCISE ABOUT SEX AND SOCIAL INTERACTIONISM

The Social Situation

Consider this thought experiment.

A young heterosexual couple find themselves in an unplanned romantic situation. No condoms are available. Both are familiar with the need for birth control and the dangers from sexually transmitted infections. As they become aroused, the power of the immediate situation exerts increasing pressure.

What happens next?

People sometimes make solemn promises to themselves about sex, such as "no unprotected sex." To say that this is a matter of life and death is more than playing with words. Sex without protection could produce a new life or transmit a deadly disease.

Social psychology influences this decision through the interaction between the individual (personality, attitudes, values, hopes, knowledge) and their environment (presence of others, circumstances, social norms, physical cues). There probably isn't anyone else nearby as the couple makes this decision. However, several social psychological variables are present and influencing what happens next.

Theory and Method

This theoretical case study is a mental exercise in thinking like a social psychologist.

The fairly common sexual situation described here is teeming with social psychology. Here are five social psychological influences likely to affect the couple's decision on what to do next:

- **Social norms** are unwritten rules of expected behavior of people within your group. Social norms about sexuality may differ if the couple is on a religious retreat compared to a spring break in Florida.

- **Individual differences** indicate how you usually differ from others in your group. It's factors such as your personality and values. Individual differences influence behavior if you, for example, are a free-spirited rebel or a self-disciplined student.

- **Socialization** is how your behavior is shaped by others' expectations, including your culture. The couple may have internalized strict religious teachings intended to control sexual behavior. But they also may have rejected those teachings, thinking them old-fashioned. In addition, men and women feel different pressures and are subject to different stereotypes about their expected sexual behaviors.

- **Attributions** are explanations of your own and others' behavior—often biased in self-serving ways. If one person wants to go ahead and the other does not,

TABLE 1.1

Examples of Social Influences on Social Situations

Social Influence	Social Situation
Social norms	A low-achieving high school student earns straight As in college.
Individual differences	A politically active first-year student joins a religious cult.
Socialization	A third-grade "troublemaker" is later sent to prison at 19.
Attribution	Large groups gather in crowds during a virus contagion.

then they may each interpret the other person's motives in ways that make them feel good about themselves.

- **Interactionism** identifies how these individual influences combine to shape behavior. Interactionism, for example, recognizes that romance is less appealing for most people in an environment of a filthy apartment compared to a beautiful bedroom with a fireplace, but that some personalities will feel the opposite, or that other factors may become more important than the environment.

A thought experiment relies on your imagination. Play a Mix-and-Match game by using Table 1.1 to demonstrate how any social influences (on the left) can explain any of the social observations (on the right). Remember, if you can apply more than one idea from the left column to the situations in the right column, you're seeing interactionism at work.

Results and Discussion

Social psychology's founder, **Kurt Lewin**, was a foot soldier in the trenches of World War I.

On a very cold night, he observed soldiers burning fine furniture taken from a house. He wondered why they would behave in such an uncivilized way. Lewin recognized that their decision to behave was the product of two factors: (1) their immediate experience (they were cold) and (2) how people construed, or understood, the immediate situation (a cold night could be life-threatening). The situation led them to do things they normally wouldn't have done. Lewin famously observed that behavior is the result of the interaction between the situation and the person. His point was that we're all capable of behaviors that might surprise us, if the situational factors are strong enough.

Consider an interactionist perspective as you imagine how each social psychological factor might specifically apply to the romantic couple and their immediate situation:

- Social norms
- Individual differences
- Socialization
- Attributions

For each of these four concepts, what would likely lead to the couple moving forward with a sexual encounter anyway (despite protection)? What would likely lead them to decide to stop or wait?

DISCUSSION QUESTIONS

1. Lewin's famous prediction (i.e., behavior is a function of both the individual person and the social environment or situation) is a well-known foundational idea in social psychology. Does this question—"personality versus the situation"—seem as important or interesting as another classic question, "nature versus nurture"? What are the similarities and differences between the two questions?

2. When you consider your own decision making, identify two specific instances when your personality or self-concept mattered more than situational pressures (you went against what most other people seemed to be doing) and two specific instances when you went along with the crowd, despite doubt on some level that it was the "right" decision. Can you identify what differentiates when you follow your personality versus when you follow demands of the situation?

3. People sometimes conform to a situation despite their inner nature (e.g., engaging in a riot). In other cases, sometimes people conform to a situation by *not* engaging in a behavior (such as not sticking up for a bully victim because no one else is doing so). Which type of situation—action versus inaction—leads to more regret, and why?

KEY TERMS

- **Social norms:** Unwritten rules of expected behavior of people within your group
- **Individual differences:** How you usually differ from others in your group, such as your personality and values
- **Socialization:** How your behavior is shaped by others' expectations, including your culture
- **Attributions:** Explanations of your own and others' behavior (they can often be biased)

- **Interactionism:** How individual influences, such as personality, culture, and the immediate environment, combine to shape behavior
- **Kurt Lewin:** The founder of social psychology, who believed that all behavior is a function of both the individual person and their environment

1.3 THE NEIGHS HAVE IT: TESTING THEORIES WITH EXPERIMENTS

The Social Situation

Clever Hans was always hungry.

Horses are food motivated. Clever Hans knew it was feeding time whenever his owner, Mr. Wilhelm von Osten, appeared in his wide-brimmed hat. The retired school teacher was coming with food and a plan to teach his horse the fundamentals of mathematics. First it was addition, then subtraction, followed by multiplication and division.

Mr. Wilhelm von Osten was thrilled whenever Clever Hans tapped his right hoof to communicate correct numerical answers. "Clever Hans, what's one plus two?" Three hoof taps. Amazing! And the questions could be even more complicated. "Clever Hans, if the fourth day of the month is a Saturday, what is the date of the following Wednesday?" Eight hoof taps!

The international excitement over Clever Hans began in Germany around the year 1900. The local children thought the old man was ridiculous, but they stopped their taunting when the famous General Zobel entered their modest courtyard. He was followed by an actual Duke, and then Germany's most famous scientist, the zoology Professor C. G. Schillings. The children were also questioned by reporters. The man they had mocked made them mini-celebrities.

Schillings tested Clever Hans in private and then sent an enthusiastic, affirmative report to an international congress of scientists. This horse could do math! It was gaining credibility from experts. The crowds grew larger, and von Osten toured the country with Clever Hans, never charging for people to see this amazing animal. Clever Hans usually got the answers to questions right, even when strangers asked them.

Believers, doubters, philosophers, theologians, the curious, and the hustlers—they were all interested in Clever Hans. At last, a commission was formed, made up of several learned men who were trying to figure out how von Osten was tricking his audiences. They each were assigned to carefully observe different parts of Mr. von Osten's body during a performance. The commission included a circus animal trainer, someone who knew how to get animals to do tricks. Like the others, he could not find any cues. The word went out: Clever Hans really could think like a human.

Clever Hans became an international sensation, and the story was picked up by the *London Standard* and the *New York Times*. One headline read: *CLEVER HANS AGAIN. Expert Commission Decides That the Horse Actually Reasons.* There were poems about Clever Hans, and his name was sung on the vaudeville stage. The image of Clever Hans appeared on post cards, liquor labels, and children's toys.

Clever Hans was certainly learning—but it wasn't the lesson Mr. von Osten thought he was teaching.

Theory and Method

This case study demonstrates how experiments peek below the surface of behavior.

The theoretical stakes in the Clever Hans affair were higher than Mr. von Osten imagined. Charles Darwin's book *On the Origin of Species* had just been translated into German (originally published in 1859). The clergy were trying to make sense of what those disturbing ideas meant for their theology. What were humans supposed to believe about themselves if they shared common ancestors with apes, and horses were as smart as many humans? A smart horse seemed to knock humans off their self-appointed perch of specialness.

But teaching math to a horse was not easy. The lessons had started simply. "Two," the old man would say as he leaned forward to help Clever Hans paw the ground twice. "Plus three" was followed by three more assisted taps. "Equals five" he told the horse as he looked up and finally gave Clever Hans something to eat. Clever Hans seemed to understand that von Osten wanted him to tap his hoof. But did he understand much more than that?

Competing Hypotheses

Wilhelm von Osten believed many different hypotheses about what was happening.

For example, he had saved the skull of a previous horse. He believed that analyzing the horse's head bumps, **phrenology**, would reveal its particular kind of intelligence. Phrenology was a popular idea at the time to explain human intelligence, personality, and mental illness. It was believed that certain bumps on your head reflected parts of your brain that were bulging out, causing various problems. If it worked for humans, why not horses? Animal intelligence seemed to be Mr. von Osten's favorite **hypothesis**: Clever Hans was simply clever!

The existence of Clever Hans also seemed to support Darwin's theory of evolution by means of natural selection. The problem with this hypothesis was that the existence of a horse as smart as Clever Hans seemed more like a giant leap within a species, as opposed to the very gradual evolution that Darwin had proposed.

A third hypothesis came from the famous Austrian psychologist Sigmund Freud. Even though Freud never saw Clever Hans himself, he had heard about him and favored the idea of **thought transference**—a fancy way of saying that van Osten and Clever Hans actually had some kind of telepathic connection (see Fernald, 1984). Freud's idea probably seems the most outlandish to you, and plenty of people had their doubts. One of those skeptics was Oskar Pfungst.

Testing Hypotheses

Oskar Pfungst had a strategy when he started testing Clever Hans.

He wanted to test Clever Hans under various conditions to see if his rate of correct responses would change. Pfungst called his strategy the **process of elimination.** Namely, he systematically ruled out various competing explanations for what was happening until there was only one remaining hypothesis. He also wanted to eliminate **experimenter bias,** or subtle ways in which the researchers might be influencing the results to support their own ideas.

For example, Pfungst personally supported the telepathy explanation. He discovered that when he concentrated very hard on the numerical answer to a mathematical question, Clever Hans would tap out the correct number. That seemed to support the idea that Clever Hans could read his mind. But Pfungst wasn't convinced, as this kind of test wasn't scientifically valid.

A **spurious correlation** occurs when two things happen at the same time. We are tempted to interpret one as causing the other, when really there's something else going on. Fortunately, unbiased, scientific testing revealed a spurious correlation between intense concentration in a questioner and Clever Hans tapping out a correct answer.

Results and Discussion

Experiments can help us see past our own biases.

Pfungst noticed that questioners always leaned forward to watch Clever Hans' hoof after asking him a question. They also raised their heads when Clever Hans had tapped out the correct response. Leaning forward was something people seem to do naturally whenever they are concentrating.

Leaning forward in his broad-brimmed hat was how the old math teacher had trained his horse. Then he would look up to give him a bit of food when Clever Hans had tapped out the correct number. Looking up was the signal that Clever Hans could stop tapping and expect some food.

So Clever Hans wasn't really doing math at all. He was just stomping his hoof until someone raised their head, because he knew a treat was coming—and remember Clever Hans was always hungry. The apparent mathematical magic of Clever Hans wasn't due to his cleverness; it was due to food conditioning.

With that new hypothesis, Pfungst set up some experiments. First, he asked the horse a series of questions with a specific answer (let's say it was five hoof taps). But this time, as Clever Hans approached five, Pfungst kept leaning forward, looking down. Clever Hans kept tapping. As soon as Pfungst lifted his head, the tapping stopped.

To gather more scientific evidence for the idea that Hans was simply looking for cues, Pfungst added blinders to the horse's head. For the first time, Clever Hans started twisting about when questioned. He was apparently trying to see the questioner. When he settled down but was still unable to see his questioner, Clever Hans' remarkable mathematical abilities disappeared.

Another experiment tested whether Clever Hans was telepathic. This time, Pfungst arranged for people to hold up a card with a number and ask Clever Hans to tap out the number on the card. Clever Hans could do it, but only when the person holding the card had looked at the number first. If they didn't know the number, Hans just kept tapping.

The questioners were surprised at these results. They too had come to expect and believe in the mathematical abilities of Clever Hans. Pfungst concluded that the questioners did not realize that they had been sending subtle nonverbal signals to the always-hungry horse.

A book titled *The Horse That Won't Go Away* (Heinzen et al., 2015) describes the many ways that the Clever Hans effect has infiltrated our lives with false beliefs. This effect occurs when an animal or another person senses what we want, even when we don't realize we're sending out signals. Applied to animals, the list includes dogs, artistic elephants, and several horses that have been credited with almost magical powers.

In addition to Clever Hans, a horse named Beautiful Jim Key was a main attraction at the 1904 World's Fair in St. Louis. Lady Wonder was a crime-solving horse, consulted sometimes by the police in the 1920s. More recently, a horse named "Velvet" has told her owner about her many previous lives. But Velvet is only one of many horse psychics on You Tube. They usually are sites hosted by people happily deceiving themselves for attention or hoping to deceive you for money.

Clever Hans passed away many years ago. However, the Clever Hans effect continues to demonstrate why experiments are so important to social psychologists. We need experimental truth-tellers such as Oskar Pfungst, who use science to demonstrate when the emperor is naked and when our hypotheses are simply wrong. Physicist Richard Feynman warned us that the first principle of science is that you must not fool yourself—and you are the easiest person to fool.

DISCUSSION QUESTIONS

1. Many people claim to have psychic powers of one type or another (e.g., communicating with the dead, the ability to sense the location of lost objects, or mind reading). Identify one specific form of "psychic" powers and explain how you might use the process of elimination to test these powers.

2. People around the world were extremely excited to see Clever Hans and believe he was capable of doing math. Why are humans motivated to believe in magic, superpowers, alien visits, or other such fantastical phenomena? What is it about our psychology that causes us to be excited about this kind of idea?

3. If you have a pet, do you think it is capable of some form of Clever Hans effect? Does your pet exhibit signs of trying to read your body or voice signals and then do what it thinks you want? Provide some specific examples.

KEY TERMS

- **Hypothesis**: A specific statement made by a researcher about the expected outcome of a study

- **Phrenology**: Non-scientific theory that the bumps on your head reveal your intelligence, personality, and mental illness

- **Thought transference**: Telepathy or mind reading

- **Process of elimination**: Systematically ruling out various explanations until there is only one left

- **Experimenter bias**: Subtle ways a researcher influences the outcome of a study or interprets the results

- **Spurious correlation**: When two things occur at the same time, but neither causes the other (e.g., a third thing might influence both)

- **Clever Hans effect**: When an animal or person senses what we want without us realizing we're sending signals

1.4 A PAINFUL INTUITION: BLOODLETTING

The Social Situation

The pain woke him up on the day he died.

The previous night's morphine mixture (laudanum) had helped him sleep. But now Dr. Benjamin Rush's pain was so intense that he demanded another bleeding (Fried, 2018). Two physicians recommended against it, but they would not overrule their friend and mentor. The compromise was to drip only four ounces of blood from Rush's side, where the pain was most acute.

There is a lot to admire about Benjamin Rush. He was a signer of the U.S. Declaration of Independence and is considered the father of modern psychiatry. In addition, Rush "served tirelessly as an advocate for many social reforms including temperance, women's rights, and humane treatment of the mentally ill . . . women's education and the abolition of slavery" (Toledo, 2004, pp. 61–62). He was a product of the Enlightenment and a believer in social activism (see Shryock, 1971).

However, he also believed in bloodletting.

Theory and Method

This case study demonstrates why social psychologists emphasize **critical thinking**, objective analysis, and application of ideas.

Benjamin Rush believed in a hypothesis. He believed so strongly in his medical hypothesis that he had never bothered to test it (see Shryock, 1971; Toledo, 2004). Why no experiments? Because his idea was intuitively obvious.

Why bother with critical thinking about something that is so obviously true? If something inside your body is causing you illness, then the best chance for a cure is to get that something outside of your body. Disease is caused by an imbalance of substances in the body, he reasoned, so the cure was to rebalance the body through **bloodletting**. Get that blood out, and you'll feel better.

Leeches were a common method. But cutting was also popular, or "cupping," which was creating suction through well-placed glass cups on the skin. Toledo (2004) described Rush's usual approach: "Typically, Rush would 'relieve' his patients of eight pints of blood over two or three days." And if that did not work, Rush would administer "another round of bleeding and purging." Purging involved inducing vomiting and elimination. It's easy to understand why Rush thought this would work; many of us have vomited and immediately realized we actually feel better. If there's poison in the system, it seems obvious that the poison should come out.

Results and Discussion

To Benjamin Rush, the evidence for success seemed obvious: Many patients did not die.

Their survival was proof (from his perspective) that his hypothesis was sound, and his intuitive application of bloodletting was effective. His biggest test was when he administrated his methods to the sick people struggling through Philadelphia's contagious yellow fever epidemic in 1793. Many of his patients lived, so Rush experienced a **confirmation bias** that his ideas were valid. He interpreted what he saw around him as evidence that his hypothesis was a good one.

However, an intuitively appealing hypothesis combined with this kind of evidence still did not make bloodletting effective. He certainly didn't have a **control group** of people with yellow fever, who were randomly assigned *not* to receive bloodletting so he could compare outcomes. This lack of experimental evidence in favor of confirmation bias almost certainly caused more harm than good. "Without doubt," Toledo (2004) concluded, the "brand of heroic medicine initiated and propagated by Rush cost thousands of Americans' lives including his own." Benjamin Rush was *the* medical expert of his day, but his intuition about bloodletting was dead wrong. Modern medical science has shown that bloodletting simply doesn't work and usually makes things worse.

Intuition and logical reasoning anchor opposite ends on the spectrum of how humans think. Your intuition, knowing without knowing how you know, is wonderful, even thrilling when it works. But Benjamin Rush's story demonstrates why trusting our intuition can be so hazardous when it fails. Benjamin Rush's hunch about medicine had life-and-death consequences. Our intuition also has major life consequences as we make big decisions about our careers, marriage, children, buying a house, and much more.

We can't avoid using our intuition. However, we need to practice **healthy skepticism**, especially when it comes to psychology. Bogus interventions, even if they are innocent, might cost individuals and taxpayers millions of dollars and sometimes harm participants.

For example, the Scared Straight program sounds like it should work. Having anti-social teenagers visit hardened prisoners should help keep them away from criminal activity, but it sometimes has the opposite effect (see Lilienfeld, 2007). A meta-analysis of the Drug Abuse Resistance Education (DARE) program came to a similar

TABLE 1.2

Warning Signs That Psychological Therapies May Not Be Valid

Substantial exaggeration of claims regarding treatment effectiveness
Excessive appeal to authorities labeled as "gurus" or "experts"
Uses of a slick sales pitch and extensive promotional "deals"
Tendency of advocates to be defensive and dismissive of critics
Extensive reliance on anecdotal evidence to claim validity
Tendency of treatment followers to insulate themselves from criticism
Extensive use of made-up but scientific-sounding terms or "psychobabble"

conclusion (Pan & Bai, 2009). There are other popular therapies that don't help and sometimes harm people. The list includes Critical Incident Stress Debriefing (CISD), Eye Movement Desensitization Reprocessing (EMDR), Facilitated Communication (FC), and Recovered Memories of Sexual Abuse (see Barlow, 2010; Lilienfeld, 2007; Otgaar et al., 2019).

Above is a partial list of "tells" or features that will help you spot social psychological therapies that sound too good to be true and may be harmful (see Meichenbaum & Lilienfeld, 2018).

DISCUSSION QUESTIONS

1. Bloodletting was a popular trend to make people feel better for years. Identify other trends you think might be occurring in your society or culture right now, which you suspect might not be scientifically valid. Why are these trendy ideas so appealing to so many people?

2. Find an advertisement for a product that claims to have medical or physical results (e.g., diet pills, exercise equipment, hair loss treatments, toothpaste). Design an experimental study that makes use of (1) a control group and (2) random assignment to test the product's claims.

3. Bloodletting was popular for hundreds of years. Several famous people may have died because of bloodletting, or more quickly because of it, including Lord Byron and George Washington. Investigate at least one historical example of someone who was treated through bloodletting and describe the circumstances. What is the evidence that bloodletting either helped or hurt their condition?

KEY TERMS

- **Critical thinking**: Objective analysis and application of ideas
- **Bloodletting**: A formerly popular medical technique in which blood was removed from the body, often through cuts or leeches
- **Confirmation bias**: Selectively paying attention to or remembering information that supports what you already believe to be true, while ignoring or explaining away contradictory information

- **Control group**: A comparison group in a scientific study that provides a way to know whether an intervention causes changes in a given outcome
- **Healthy skepticism**: Constructive doubts about claims if they are presented without scientific evidence to support them

The Social Psychologist's Toolbox

2

2.1 CRUCIAL EXPERIMENTS: WHO'S TALKING NOW?

The Social Situation

Ouija boards are spooky stuff, right?

No one seems to be in charge, yet fingers slide a pointing device toward letters that form words and then sentences. It is as if the Ouija board has a mind of its own. Many believe those messages are coming from the "great beyond," "the other side," or departed ancestors.

The Ouija board evolved out of the spiritualist movement in the United States. Spiritualists tried to connect the dead with the living, but it had the strangest beginnings, supported by the confessions of the Fox sisters who started it. The oldest sister Leah (age 33 at the time) discovered her younger sisters Margaret (age 13) and Kate (age 10) had a unique ability:

> [They] could make weird noises by cracking the joints in their toes, and used this ability to trick their superstitious mother into believing that a ghost was present. . . . Leah took her two younger sisters to Rochester, New York, where they set up shop . . . bringing forth spirits of the deceased to communicate with the paying customer . . . mediums added a board (the planchette, a forerunner of the Ouija board) that could be used to spell out the messages of the spirits. (Benjamin & Baker, 2014, p. 18)

So now you know the origins of the Ouija board: two toe-cracking teenagers.

The Ouija board experienced a wave of popularity during and after World War I, when many families desperately wanted to communicate with the sons, fathers, and brothers who had vanished into the fog of war. However, the most interesting question about the Ouija board is where the words and sentences are coming from. If dead people are not directing movements on a letter board, then who is communicating?

Theory and Method

This case study demonstrates the value of crucial experiments when testing new therapies.

Answers to the Ouija question arrived from an unexpected source. **Facilitated communication** (FC) was a technique intended to help people with disabilities communicate, now part of the renamed Institute on Communication and Inclusion (ICI, 2020). FC became popular in the late mid- to late 1990s, when many families desperately wanted to communicate with their sons—and daughters—who had vanished into the mysterious disease called autism (and other developmental disabilities).

FC offers a seductively simple solution to complex neurological problems. A trained "facilitator" physically supports the hand, arm, sleeve—whatever seems to work—of a person who cannot verbally communicate. As that person's hand hovers over an alphabet board, the facilitator senses the individual's intended movement toward a letter and guides his or her pointed finger to that letter. Those single letters became connected to words that formed sentences that, over time, were structured into paragraphs: Just like a Ouija board.

The central question about FC is the same as the Ouija board question: Who is communicating? The first research tool that most social psychologists reach for is the **controlled experiment**. Controlled experiments require at least two conditions that can be compared, and (ideally) random assignment of participants into one of those conditions. As you will see, social psychologists have many other research tools available to them. But they favor experiments because, with a little ingenuity, they can create a **crucial experiment** that will provide an unambiguous answer to a relevant question. A crucial experiment decisively concludes whether a hypothesis is valid and/or whether an intervention is effective.

The central danger of FC is the warning credited to the philosopher Sir Francis Bacon in the 1600s: We humans "prefer to believe what we prefer to be true." Could the small army of sincere, hard-working, well-educated facilitators be deceiving themselves about the effectiveness of FC? In the case of FC, there were just two questions:

1. Is FC real?

2. Who is communicating?

FC: The Movement

FC was more than a revelation; it was a revolution with a small "army of believers."

The army included social workers, loving parents, academics, and mid-level professionals. According to the American Psychological Association (APA, 2003), FC soon "was spreading like wildfire all over the U.S. and Canada." With the help of FC, individuals once labeled as unintelligent and unteachable "scored well on standard IQ tests, wrote brilliant essays, and even composed poetry."

FC was a revolution in how we thought about and helped care for people with so-called disabilities. Their communication problems were *motor* difficulties, not *mental* disabilities (Biklen, 1990). What a discovery! The passion among advocates for people with disabilities has always been to treat people with the same dignity and respect as so-called normal people. Their motives were pure, even noble. Now they were the leading edge of a humanitarian revolution (APA, 2003).

FC: Trouble in Paradise

"Dear Mom and Dad. I could never tell you what was in my heart. Now I can: 'Thank you.'"

Messages expressing profound love and gratitude weren't the only facilitated messages being sent to parents. An FC facilitator with just one hour of training had facilitated an important message to the Wendrow family in Bloomfield, Michigan. Their daughter Aislinn had been diagnosed with autism at the age of two.

"My dad gets me up. . . . He puts his hand on my private parts," the adolescent Aislinn supposedly had typed, with the help of her FC facilitator. And just like that, Julian Wendrow became labeled as a sexual predator. The Wendrow family previously had been strong believers in FC, but now they *knew* that—at least in their case—it couldn't be true.

Two days later, Aislinn met with investigators at a county facility—but with the same facilitator at her side. Things got worse. Now Aislinn, through her facilitator, reported that the sexual abuse had been chronic, involved photographs, and that her 13-year-old brother Ian had been forced to participate.

Julian was sent to the county jail for 80 days. Solitary confinement gave him time to consider a possible 75-year sentence. Aislinn's mother, Tali, was released on bail, but with a tracking device. Ian was interviewed (without parental consent) by zealous police. They badgered him until he finally admitted that sometimes his father showered with Aislinn—something not uncommon for children with severe developmental difficulties.

The two children were shuffled around foster homes until Ian finally was placed in a juvenile facility. "I was moved in with kids who were like at the time 17, 18," Ian reported. People "who had actually been abused . . . it was scary" (Berman & Balthaser, 2012).

The Wendrow family slowly discovered that they were not the only family victimized by FC.

FC: Crucial Experiments

Crucial experiments can be disturbing.

In the crucial experiments for FC, the experimental procedures were simple, direct, and friendly. The whispering test arranged for an experimenter might say the word *baseball* to the person with autism, then "Please type out the word I just whispered in your ear." If the facilitator had not heard the word baseball, but the person with autism could be facilitated to type baseball, then FC must really work.

The results would be crucial for facilitators, too. What would it do to *your* sense of self to discover that your good intentions had divided a family and imprisoned innocent parents? Most of the facilitators were well-educated individuals; certainly most of them were well meaning. Critical thinking probably had been taught in their college classes. But it might have been no more than an abstract idea, quickly forgotten after passing some multiple choice test.

Now critical thinking really mattered.

Results and Discussion

Why would anyone want FC to fail if it really worked?

And who would want FC to succeed if it were not real? If autistic children are being sexually abused, then we all need to know about it and make it stop! But we also don't want to separate innocent, loving, dedicated parents from the children who desperately need them. FC failed one crucial experiment after another, and the more tightly controlled the experiment was, the worse that FC performed.

Failure 1. The Message-Passing Test

The whispering test was a version of the message-passing test.

Both tests asked two crucial questions: (1) Is FC real? (2) Who is communicating? The message-passing test required only three brief stages.

1. Show a familiar object, such as a key, to the person with a disability.

2. Allow the facilitator either to (a) see the key, or (b) not see the key. (Do this several times, randomly changing back and forth between the two conditions.)

3. Ask the person with a disability to name the object each time, with the help of their facilitator.

If the person with autism is not able to type out the word *key* unless the facilitator already knows the answer, then FC is not real, and the communication is coming from the facilitator. In one experiment (Wheeler et al., 1993), the researchers tested "the 12 most competent producers of facilitated communication." The researchers loaded the dice in favor of FC being real. But the only correct responses (e.g., typing the word *key*) occurred when the facilitator also had seen the key.

Failure 2. The Naming and Description Tests

FC failed other crucial experiments.

Montee and colleagues (1995) asked seven clients with moderate to severe mental retardation to name pictures and describe activities they had just engaged in. These seven particular clients had been communicating fluently using FC for 6 to 18 months. Once again, the experimenters were loading the dice in favor of FC—but they still couldn't get FC to work. This time, they used pictures and activities.

When both facilitator and client saw the same picture, FC seemed to work with a success rate of about 75%. But when the facilitator did not see the same picture, the success rate was 0%. When both facilitator and client saw the same activity, FC seemed to work with an 87% success rate. But when the facilitator did not know about the activity, the success rate was 0%.

The American Psychological Association reviewed all the evidence regarding FC (or what is now called "supportive typing") and concluded that "there was no scientifically demonstrated support for its efficacy" (APA, 2003). The American Academy of

Pediatrics (1998), through a committee on children with disabilities, issued a similar statement:

> In the case of FC, there are good scientific data showing it to be ineffective. Moreover, as noted before, the potential for harm does exist, particularly if unsubstantiated allegations of abuse occur using FC. Many families incur substantial expense pursuing these treatments, and spend time and resources that could be used more productively. (p. 432)

Did crucial experiments, official medical authorities, and scientific societies convince the hardcore believers in FC that it was bogus? Would they have convinced you? If the case study of the Wendrow family wasn't enough to make you skeptical, maybe the case of disability scholar Anna Stubblefield (summarized by Sherry, 2016) may persuade you to be cautious.

Stubblefield was a professor and believer in FC. She received a 12-year sentence for sexually assaulting a disabled man who, she claimed, had given her permission via FC. Sherry (2016) wrote that

> The (conscious or unconscious) power of the person guiding the hands to manipulate the other person is the key flaw in facilitated communication. Critics liken this process to a Ouija board. Even with the best of intentions, the person who "facilitates" the conversation directs the conversation; they are the authors, rather than the disabled person.

So, who is doing the talking? The facilitators. But just like a Ouija board, they didn't know it was coming from a self whose judgments had been compromised by a group-supported, passionate belief in FC and their own good intentions.

DISCUSSION QUESTIONS

1. FC is enjoying a mild resurgence in popularity. Explain why, in the face of crucial experiments and formal objections from multiple professional societies, people continue to believe in FC.

2. Design a crucial experiment that could test who is doing the talking in a Ouija board. How could you test whether the spirits of dead people were really moving the pointing device on the Ouija board?

3. What do you imagine that the believers in FC thought about themselves at different stages of this case study: during their training, after experiencing its apparent effectiveness, and after learning that it was bogus? Even on an unconscious level, what would motivate an FC facilitator to accuse a client's parents of sexual abuse?

4. Consider other trendy medical or psychological treatments, such as essential oils, crystals, and so on. Choose one example and design an experiment to test whether any positive effects (1) actually exist and (2) are caused by the treatment itself or by a placebo effect.

KEY TERMS

- **Facilitated communication**: A technique intended to help people with severe disabilities express themselves through a helper and a keyboard; scientific evidence indicates it does not work.
- **Controlled experiment**: A research method involving at least two conditions that can be

compared; ideally, participants are randomly assigned to one of those conditions.
- **Crucial experiment**: A study that definitively provides evidence that a hypothesis is valid or that an intervention is effective

2.2 ETHNOGRAPHY: GANG LEADER FOR A DAY

The Social Situation

"How does it feel to be Black and poor?"

Sudhir Venkatesh (2008) looked at his clipboard and continued reading: "Your answer options are: Very bad, somewhat bad, neither bad nor good, somewhat good, very good." Born in India but raised in Southern California, Sudhir Venkatesh is the son of a professor and an academic product of the beautiful beachfront campus of the University of California, San Diego.

He had moved from there to work with a University of Chicago professor studying the lives of young Black men from urban areas. He took his **survey** to Chicago's soon-to-be-demolished Lake Park housing. He arrived as drug buyers were moving in and out of the area, on foot and by car. Would a survey work in this neighborhood?

Someone grabbed him by the shoulder. Another took his clipboard.

"Who do you represent?"

They suspected a rival Mexican gang on a scouting trip, preparing for an attack on their drug territory. One showed Venkatesh his gun; another waved a knife in front of him. They kept asking him if he spoke Mexican. He tried to explain that he was there to conduct a survey. They returned his clipboard, and Venkatesh pressed forward. He asked, "How does it feel to be Black and poor?" Pause. "Very bad, somewhat bad, neither bad nor good, somewhat good, very good."

"F—you. You've got to be f—ing kidding me."

He decided that the survey method was not going to work in this situation.

Theory and Method

This case study demonstrates how ethnography enhances social psychology.

You can see things with **statistics** that you can't see in any other way. You can graph population trends, map voting patterns, calculate probabilities, and observe an epidemic unfolding. However, using *only* statistics hides other critical observations. That's why Venkatesh started hanging out with J. T., the leader of a Chicago drug gang. Venkatesh was becoming an ethnographer.

Most social psychologists are trained to be experimenters. But ethnographic research is one of the many other discovery tools in the social psychologist's toolbox. For example, Venkatesh could have made discreet **naturalistic observations** by having a Harry Potter-like invisibility cloak, planting a hidden microphone, or taking pictures from behind a parked car.

Those all would have been unrealistic and dangerous. **Ethnography** gains knowledge by openly participating in a community and its culture. Statistics, naturalistic observations, and ethnography are all useful tools (in addition to traditional experiments) developed to collect information in particular situations.

On his next visit, Venkatesh left his clipboard behind.

Ethnography was helping Venkatesh understand Chicago race relations in a new way. He got an insider's look at the supportive communities inside housing projects, the self-sacrificing generosity of chronically poor people, the surprising economics of drug dealing, and the organizational structure of street gangs. You can find the complete story of this case study in Venkatesh's (2008) book *Gang Leader for a Day*.

J. T. was surprised to see that he had returned. Instead of survey questions, Venkatesh asked about oil changes, fancy hubcaps, and whatever else was occupying the rotating shifts of drug dealers when they were not transacting business. He wondered at the openness and lack of a police presence. But he let those questions wait for another day.

During one visit, J. T. suddenly came out shouting to the crew, "Okay! They're ready, let's go over there." Venkatesh wanted to go along, but J. T. simply smiled and said, "Why don't you meet me here next week. Early morning, all right?" Then the entire crew jumped into their cars, drove away, leaving Venkatesh standing alone.

It took Venkatesh 4 years and some serious discussions with his professors to realize that what he was seeing as an ethnographer also might create legal trouble for himself and the university (pp. 185–186). He mentioned to a couple professors about

> how J. T.'s gang went about planning a drive-by shooting—they often sent a young woman to surreptitiously cozy up to the rival gang and learn enough information to prepare a surprise attack—my professors duly apprised *me* that I needed to consult a lawyer.

If he learned of a plan to harm someone, then Venkatesh had a legal obligation to tell the police. It was okay to talk with the gang after a fight. However, he could not go to any planning meetings. There was, at least in Illinois at that time, no such thing as a researcher–client privilege such as journalists and lawyers have with their clients.

J. T. introduced Venkatesh to soul food. They began spending long hours in restaurants where J. T. did his version of paperwork, while Venkatesh read textbooks and prepared for class. J. T. ran a large organization, but he didn't want to leave a paper trail of evidence. J. T. "could keep innumerable details straight in his mind: the wages of each one of his two hundred members, the shifts each of them worked, recent spikes in supply or demand." J. T. was smart and had taken some college courses.

Results and Discussion

Stereotypes were being destroyed.

Venkatesh would never be able to think about Chicago gangs and drug dealers in the same way. The gangs were structured like corporations and, like many corporations, the really big money—"if you lived to see it," J. T. cautioned—flowed to the few at the top. J. T. wasn't there yet. But he was getting close.

A Party in the Park

J. T. sent some of his workers to pick Venkatesh up at a bus stop.

They drove him to a park. When he arrived, Venkatesh found himself at a large barbecue of some 50 people there to celebrate a child's first birthday, complete with balloons and a large cake. An older woman put her arm on Venkatesh's shoulder.

"Is this the young man you've been telling me about?" she said to J. T.

"Yes, Mama," J. T. said between bites, his voice as obedient as a young boy's.

"Well, Mr. Professor, I'm J. T.'s mother."

"They call her Ms. Mae," J. T. said.

"That's right," she said. "And you can call me that, too."

Carla, the birthday girl, was a 1-year-old whose father and mother were both in jail for selling drugs. The adults in her building had decided to raise the child. This meant hiding her away from the Department of Child and Family Services, which would have sent Carla into foster care. Different families took turns taking care of Carla. Venkatesh reported that

> Ms. Mae talked about how teenage girls shouldn't have children so early, about the tragedy of kids getting caught up in violence, the value of an education, and her insistence that J. T. attend college.

To Venkatesh, it all sounded so unexpectedly . . . normal: balloons and birthday parties, a community pulling together to help one of their own, proud mothers insisting that their children go to college, peace-building community parties with barbecue, basketball, and card games. Stereotypes that Venkatesh didn't even know he had were smashed with every conversation. At the same time, J. T. was still the head of a drug gang.

Ethnography: Another Tool in Social Psychologists' Toolbox

There are many ways to understand human behavior.

Social psychologists favor experiments. But properly conducted **quantitative studies** are not inherently better or worse than properly conducted **qualitative studies** or purely observational studies. They all require attention to detail, personal integrity, and cautious interpretations. The appropriate research tool depends upon the purpose of the study and the constraints of every situation. We humans are complicated people; we need all of the tools in social psychologists' toolbox.

Some reviewers of *Gang Leader for a Day* have expressed concern that Venkatesh sensationalized parts of the world he entered. However, most social scientists have recognized the added value of Venkatesh's ethnographic approach. Psychologist Robert Sternberg (2008) wrote that "Venkatesh's book is a model for how one can use ethnographic methods to study the practical intelligence of populations that are out of reach for most behavioral scientists" (pp. 730–731).

DISCUSSION QUESTIONS

1. What kinds of information was Venkatesh able to gather and understand because he used an ethnographic approach, instead of a more traditional survey or experimental approach? On the other hand, what are two disadvantages that this study has due to the ethnographic approach?

2. The book *Gang Leader for a Day* is a well-written, entertaining book that is full of both drama and insight. Does the drama mislead the reader by creating sympathies that are really the bias of the writer? In addition, discuss how experimenter bias may have been involved in Venkatesh's writing and conclusions.

3. How does ethnography apply to your life? If an ethnographer were studying you as a case study, what patterns might emerge? What would an observer find most interesting, surprising, and troubling about your life? Which approach would allow the researcher to get to know you better?

KEY TERMS

- **Survey**: A research method in which participants answer set questions, often on scale ranges such as "disagree" to "agree" or "very bad" to "very good"
- **Statistics**: Mathematical analyses of data to find trends and patterns
- **Naturalistic observations**: A research method in which people's behaviors are observed in their authentic settings, often without them realizing they are being observed
- **Ethnography**: A research method in which the scientist openly participates in a community and its social life and culture
- **Quantitative studies**: Research in which the results are represented in numerical form, like scores between 1–10
- **Qualitative studies**: Research in which the results are not numerical, such as interviews or essay questions where participants explain their perspective or experiences

2.3 HEALTH DETECTIVE: THE MISSING PUMP HANDLE

The Social Situation

Superstition and science are fighting over your thoughts.

However, they are not struggling over *what* you think but *how* you think. This case study describes a famous battle that was a turning point in the wars between superstition and science. The battlefield was a cholera epidemic, and the eventual victory was the birth of the public health movement. Social psychology has a role to play in public health. But you have to be able to separate authentic clues from false leads, which is an important part of critical thinking.

Connecting Social Psychology to Public Health

The public health movement saves lives.

It could have saved many more lives during the COVID-19 pandemic. We needed the students partying on Florida beaches to stop partying, religious leaders to stop calling for congregations to gather together in person, and high government authorities to listen to data.

Furthermore, the public health movement needs social psychology students who can do four things:

1. collect meaningful data,

2. listen to the data,

3. communicate data, and

4. use social influence techniques to enact change—even when the audience is not listening.

We'll call this case study the Battle of the Cholera Epidemic of 1854, but it also represents your possible future. Table 2.1 shares only a fraction of the most notable regional epidemics and global pandemics listed on a 5-page spreadsheet in Wikipedia. It probably will take several years before we can accurately insert statistics about COVID-19 in Table 2.1. Prompt public health responses to Ebola and Zika helped limit their tragedies.

The Price of Ignorance

Don't blame Sarah Lewis for not knowing.

Sarah and her husband Thomas, a London police officer, were new parents. Life was good. They felt fortunate to be living at 40 Broad Street, close to the good-tasting water from the Broad Street well in London's Golden Square neighborhood.

For the first time in her short life, the Lewis' baby had gotten seriously ill with diarrhea. While Sarah Lewis waited for the local doctor, she rinsed a diaper in some warm water. Then she emptied the bucket in the cesspool in the cellar and accidentally started an epidemic.

TABLE 2.1

Death From Epidemics and Pandemics From Around the World

Relatively Recent Epidemics and Pandemics	Deaths
1899–1923: Sixth cholera pandemic	> 800,000
1915–1926: Encephalitis pandemic	~ 1.5 million
1918–1920: Flu pandemic	> 17 million
1957–1958: Flu pandemic	~ 2 million
1968–1969: Flu pandemic	~ 1 million
1920–present: HIV/AIDS pandemic	~ 32 million
2002–2004: SARS epidemic	< 1,000
2004–2020: Ebola epidemic	< 15,000
2009: Flu pandemic	~ 500,000
2015: Zika virus	~ 100
2019–present: Coronavirus pandemic	?

Source: Adapted from List of Epidemics via Wikipedia.

Emptying soiled water into the cellar or throwing it out the back window was just how it was done in London, 1854. There was nowhere else to take it. And yes, the stench was terrible. But if you needed to live and work in the big city, then you put up with the stench—and the risks.

Cholera was the biggest public health risk in midcentury England. There had been about 20,000 deaths from cholera in 1833 and another 50,000 in 1848–1849. This 1854 epidemic was headed in the same direction, only worse. The death rates were higher and faster than previous epidemics. Think of the impact of those numbers on a relatively small population.

By comparison, the 1941 attack on Pearl Harbor killed "only" 2500 people and launched the United States into WW II. The 2001 terrorist attacks on 9/11 killed about 3,000 people and triggered the War on Terror that the United States has been fighting for two decades. Shouldn't a terrifying epidemic trigger at least a comparable response to prepare for the next epidemic?

This 1854 cholera outbreak helped launch the public health movement.

If Superstition Wins . . .

Sarah Lewis could not know what she had started.

She did not know that (a) *Vibrio cholerae* was rapidly reproducing in her daughter's small intestine, and (b) the contaminated cesspool in her cellar was seeping into the

Broad Street well. It wasn't her fault, but the epidemic was under way. Cholera causes dehydration as the body eliminates fluids in every possible way. The cure is clean water. Worried family members naturally rushed to the nearest well trying to save the people they loved—usually the Broad Street well.

The cholera epidemic killed Sarah's baby daughter, her husband, three others in their building, and—in just 2 weeks—about 700 of her friends and neighbors. It would kill thousands more before it ended. The diaper that Sarah Lewis had rinsed was only the beginning of the battle over *how* we think about cholera—and superstition was winning.

Theory and Method

This case study celebrates the power of a really good visual display of data.

Cholera creates fear. "Imagine," wrote Stephen Johnson (2006) in *The Ghost Map,* "if every time you experienced a slight upset stomach you knew that there was an entirely reasonable chance you'd be dead in forty-eight hours" (pp. 32–33). Survivors of the COVID-19 pandemic understand that feeling. A few coughs and an ache make you wonder: Do I have it? Cholera was a mysterious disease that spawned superstitious explanations and crazy cures.

The Structure of Superstition

No one knew what caused cholera or how it was transmitted.

It might pass over one building but afflict the next door neighbors. Ironically, the idea of a real but invisible world of tiny germs was beyond the imagination of most people. They believed in angels and demons, but the entire idea of germs just sounded crazy! **Germ theory** would just have to wait for better ways to communicate scientific evidence.

Cholera seemed to strike randomly. We humans respond to apparent randomness with explanations, and they don't have to be very good explanations. Many are merely **superstitions**, an excessive belief in supernatural beings or rituals as the cause of events or human behaviors.

Popular but Bizarre Hypotheses

There were many incorrect hypotheses about cholera.

One was that people would be cured through bloodletting (see Chapter 1); the disease could be released if enough blood were removed. That didn't work. Some people believed that cholera was divine retribution: God was punishing humanity for its sins. But some of the most upstanding citizens developed cholera, and many "sinful" men in a nearby workhouse didn't (they had their own well).

The miasma hypothesis was the most widely accepted explanation: Cholera was thought to spread through the noxious, very stinky air. In a large city where people emptied their waste in their basements and backyards, it just *felt* right to blame cholera on the bad air (as in "mal-aria"). They ignored the evidence that two people could be breathing the same air but only one might develop cholera. Their belief blinded them to alternative explanations, a problem referred to as **confirmation bias**. For example, they somehow never noticed that the "night soil men" who occasionally removed the muck in the cesspools (and thus had plenty of exposure to the bad air) were not getting cholera.

A fourth hypothesis was generally ignored by everyone but the local physician, John Snow (no, not the one from *Game of Thrones*): the waterborne contagion hypothesis. Snow thought that cholera was being spread through exposure to contaminated water. For most people, this was the most bizarre explanation of all. Wasn't water something that would *help* most diseases? Snow had to come up with a way to convince people.

Results and Discussion

Situations can reveal what people really believe.

The revealing situation in this public health crisis was whether you dared to drink water that came from the Broad Street well (see Johnson, 2006). If you believed the waterborne contagion hypothesis, then no. If you favored the miasma hypothesis, then go ahead and swallow.

Correlations Are Clues; Hypotheses Are Specific

Design precedes data.

Tracking down a disease requires specific, testable hypotheses. You have to think first, before you start collecting data. You're not looking for numbers; you're looking for patterns based on meaningful comparisons. In 1854, the source of the contagion was not all water, or even all local water. It was specifically the water from the Broad Street well, the well right next door to the Lewis family.

But no one had any data, no one even knew how to collect such data, and the formula for the **correlation coefficient** that could clarify the association between two variables did not yet exist. They didn't know it, but they were waiting for someone very much like a modern social psychologist.

They didn't have social psychologists, but they did have John Snow, the founder of the public health movement. There was a pattern to the data, but it could only be seen in two ways: on a map and through the lens of statistics. During the Battle of the Cholera Epidemic of 1854, an illusory correlation linked cholera to the foul air. It was wrong, and belief in it killed thousands of people.

Communicating Data: How Science Defeats Superstition

John Snow didn't need the formula for the correlation coefficient.

But he did need a visual display of data. He used the map of the Golden Square neighborhood, shown in Figure 2.1. The *X*s represent all of the nearby wells. Then he added a dot to represent each death of cholera and where the person had lived. The death dots were clearly clustered around one well in particular: the Broad Street well next door to the Lewis family. The map showed data, and anyone could see a strong, positive correlation between how close people lived to the Broad Street well and how likely they were to die of cholera.

FIGURE 2.1

John Snow's Map

Source: Original map made by John Snow in 1854.

John Snow's map communicated this victory of science over superstition. It feels awkward, of course, to think of an event that started out by killing "only" 700 innocent people as a victory. Like the COVID-19 pandemic, many more people died because the authorities would not listen to the wise data coming from public health advocates. Some people also simply didn't believe the data even after they heard them. Even after Snow's warnings about the pump, people kept using it—until he had the handle removed.

The particular viciousness of the 1854 cholera outbreak became the birth pangs of the public health movement. It was a victory that slowly liberated people from the fear of cholera, as well as the actual disease. An upset stomach was no longer cause for existential alarm—but only because of critical thinking and social action that saved countless lives.

DISCUSSION QUESTIONS

1. What do the authors mean by "design precedes data"? Explain this idea in your own words. Include a discussion of why interpreting patterns after they are known (instead of hypothesizing in advance) might lead to hindsight bias.

2. How are scientific findings communicated in psychology? Who are the critical audiences for science communications? How could psychological scientists become better communicators to the general public? John Snow had to convince both government officials and everyday people that his hypothesis was correct. Are social psychologists good or bad at communicating their research findings to the general public?

3. Compare and contrast people's beliefs and behaviors during the cholera outbreak in London and the COVID-19 outbreak around the world, starting in 2019.

KEY TERMS

- **Germ theory**: The currently accepted idea that most diseases are started and carried by microscopic pathogens
- **Confirmation bias**: The tendency to pay attention to evidence that supports existing beliefs and ignores contradictory evidence
- **Superstition**: Belief in supernatural beings or rituals as the cause of events or behaviors
- **Correlation coefficient**: A number between −1.00 and +1.00 that clarifies the association between two variables

2.4 WITCHCRAFT AND FALSE CONFESSIONS: THEN AND NOW

The Social Situation

Don't be surprised when another innocent person is released from prison.

The Innocence Project has used DNA testing and other sources of evidence to help untangle one of the strangest observations in the American legal system: the psychology of false confessions. This case study demonstrates that the social psychology of false confessions began with an iconic American legal case: the Salem witch trials.

John Hathorne was the Salem magistrate usually portrayed as the one person most responsible for the tragedies in Salem Village and Salem Town in 1692. However, the lens of social psychology paints a slightly different picture. Hathorne had doubts, and he tried to resolve those doubts with the kind of experiments that are familiar to every psychology major.

If Hathorne had understood the difference between a **single-blind** and a **double-blind** experiment, then the entire Salem witch trials might have ended with nothing worse than a bad case of social embarrassment. Unfortunately, Hathorne didn't know how to conduct a good experiment, but he was close.

We will never know, of course, whether the power of the situation might have overwhelmed him anyway. The rule of law had been suspended as Salem waited for a new charter to arrive from England. In addition, the Puritans really believed in the powers of Satan promoted by their authoritative, Harvard-trained clergyman, Cotton Mather (see Boyer & Nissenbaum, 1976; Burr, 1914/2002; Hill, 2002; C. Mather, 1693; I. Mather, 1684). The Puritans believed that

a. Satan could give human witches extraordinary powers,

b. Satan had targeted the Puritans because they were so special,

c. Indians were preparing another attack on the Puritans,

d. Salem Town and Salem Village would not resolve their conflicts, and

e. witches grew stronger when faith got weaker.

Theory and Method

This case study demonstrates how an experiment almost stopped the Salem witch trials.

The legal issue came down to psychological tests. Of course, psychology as we know it did not exist in 1692. But John Hathorne recognized that he needed to discover whether the accusing children were honest witnesses, hysterical, making it all up, or deceived by Satan. He needed to find out if the specters that the children claimed were tormenting them were real. And to do that, he needed to find out whether the accusations of witchcraft were valid.

Specters were witches' images of themselves that enabled a witch to be in two places at once. A witch (usually a woman) could be stirring her soup at home while her specter flew about on a stick tormenting people. The alibi that "I was at home stirring my soup" was useless if specters were accepted as evidence. And the preadolescent girls in Salem Village were giving what was regarded as eyewitness testimony to the extraordinary havoc caused by specters.

Hathorne didn't have the words for it, but he was trying to test for the **reliability** and **validity** of their eyewitness testimonies.

Spectral Evidence

The reports of spectral activity were alarming.

Betty Hubbard described seeing the specter of the accused witch Sarah Good lying on a table with naked breasts, feet, and legs. Samuel Sibley tried to kill the specter (visible only to the girls). Betty Hubbard confirmed that Samuel hit Sarah Good's specter across the back hard enough to almost kill her (see Norton, 2002, p. 28). In reality, he was just waving a stick around in the air, but it was pure, intense drama to those who believed.

For example, Abigail Williams and Mercy Walcott saw the specter of Deliverance Hobbs biting another girl on the foot. When Benjamin Hutchinson struck at the apparition with his sword, the two girls declared that he had successfully stabbed the specter of Deliverance Hobbs on the side. But then more and more specters started arriving, so many that "the roome was full of them." Brave Benjamin Hutchinson protected the girls by continually thrusting his rapier in the air.

At last, the girls exclaimed that Benjamin had killed two specters "for the flore is all covered with blod" [the floor is all covered with blood]. Grown men were bravely slashing the air as they battled Satan, their most terrifying enemy. But they could never know whether their blows had landed without the help of two young girls vividly narrating the unfolding battles.

Consider the situation of these preadolescent girls. Even at their tender ages, they already were working hard labor at the lowest rung of the Puritan social ladder. They could only look forward to many more years of hard labor in a cold, harshly disciplined culture. They may have been having the time of their lives manipulating these gallant men into defending them from a terrible fate (see Roach, 2013).

Logic Traps Can Cancel Justice

Lydia Dustin was in a logic trap.

She was 65-years-old and imprisoned on accusations of witchcraft. She was acquitted at trial. However, legal procedures kept her in prison until she could pay her prison maintenance fees. Of course, she could not earn the money needed to pay those maintenance fees because she was in prison accumulating even more fees. Lydia Dustin was still in prison when she died the following spring, murdered by bad procedures.

Trusting spectral evidence presented another logic problem to the Puritans. They were asking liars (the specters speaking through the girls) if they were lying. What can you learn when you ask a liar if she is lying? The Puritans' courtroom procedures had no way to unravel this conundrum.

There was another logical reason to doubt the reliability and validity of spectral evidence. A powerful Satan might send the specter of an innocent person to do his evil bidding. Hathorne could not resolve these logic problems . . . unless there was some test that would reveal who was lying and who was telling the truth.

The Experimental Impulse

The Salem magistrates were trying to use critical thinking.

They didn't get very far but neither have most novelists, playwrights, and filmmakers trying to make sense of the Salem witchcraft trials. Almost every account has misunderstood, avoided, or misled audiences about the presence of doubt during the 1692 Salem witchcraft trials. With the possible exception of the Reverend Cotton Mather, everyone had doubts.

Even the accusers and the magistrates had doubts. They could not tell whether the witches (in the form of specters) were real. But to the social psychologist, those doubts—and how people reacted to their doubts—are the most compelling parts of the story.

Hathorne tried to resolve his doubts with experiments.

Salem's Almost Scientific Touch Test

Imagine the scene.

The pre-adolescent girls are at the front of a crowded meeting house. When an accused witch enters the room, their bodies go into convulsions, their mouths gape open, tongues hang out, and they might not be able to see or hear. They sometimes became trapped in a world of mimicry, compelled to imitate the gestures and words made by the accused witches.

"But I am not a witch," the accused might protest, throwing her hands in the air.

"But I am not a witch," the girls would chant back, also throwing hands in the air.

Some of the accused witches would be brought to the front. Their bodies would be inspected for warts or pimples or other signs that little demon "familiars" were feeding off their bodies. It is one of the most bizarre examples of "correlation does not imply causation": older women tended to be regarded as witches—and they were more likely to have protuberances on their skin. But just having some bumps on your skin didn't really mean you were a witch.

Experiment 1. The Touch Test

The logic of the touch test was simple.

If an afflicted girl were touched by a real witch, then her afflictions would abruptly cease. Why? Because the evil power had been discharged back to its source. The Puritans' understanding of the touch test was exactly opposite to how it had first been used (see Beard, 1882). Originally, a witch touching someone sent their evil powers into the person.

The experimental logic had led those early tests of witchcraft to use a single-blind procedure by taking a supposedly afflicted person and putting "an Apron before her Eyes" to find out if the accuser was faking the symptoms. However, by the time the Puritans got hold of the touch test, its logic had been reversed the same way a whispering game muddles a message as it is passed from one person to the next. The fact that the same test could indicate the presence of a witch using two opposite results is another example of confirmation bias: We believe what we want to believe.

Experiment 2. The Single-Blind Procedure

The importance of a single-blind procedure also occurred to John Hathorne.

The author of *The Scarlet Letter*, Nathaniel Hawthorne, added a 'w' to his name to distinguish him from his embarrassing ancestor. But John Hathorne had doubts, and he tried to resolve them with a controlled experiment. He just wasn't a very good experimenter, and critical thinking would have helped.

And so, on April 22, 1692, such a large crowd of spectators came to the Salem Village meetinghouse that even the window light was shadowed by observers. That critical day's interrogations began with the accusations of witchcraft against Deliverance Hobbs. She did not live in Salem Village, so the tormented girls would not recognize her.

Hathorne and Corwin, the chief interrogators, recognized that this was an opportunity to test whether Deliverance Hobbs was really a witch. If Abigail and Mary could not recognize her when they saw her (even though they had supposedly seen her specter), then the girls must be faking it. When Deliverance Hobbs did enter the room, Abigail Williams and Mary Wolcott could not identify the witch who afflicted them.

However, they quickly created an explanation. Some witch had struck them blind—that's why they couldn't identify her! But they knew she was in the room. In an empty courtroom, a single-blind experiment might have been good enough. But in a crowded courtroom full of eager, gossiping observers, justice required a double-blind experiment that would not allow the girls to hear the whispers that Deliverance Hobbs had entered the meeting hall.

Results and Discussion

Deliverance Hobbs avoided hanging.

She made a **false confession** and named others as witches to avoid being put to death. Those she named who refused to make a similar false confession were hanged. Doubt eventually helped end the Salem witchcraft trials. But those doubts were not expressed early enough or strong enough. The terror only ended after 19 public hangings and perhaps another 11 deaths from neglect in prison. The terror ended when devout Puritans started listening to the stubborn voice of healthy skepticism.

Learning how to conduct experiments on humans is a challenge like no other type of science. Thus, we should not be surprised that in 1692, none of the magistrates had the slightest idea of all the tools in a social psychologist's tool box. Certainly, no one had told John Hathorne about double-blind experiments or random assignment to groups. Hathorne had no way of naming (much less controlling for) confirmation bias, memory distortions, or the effects of having other people in the room when conducting an experiment.

But in 1692, even John Hathorne was trying to do the right thing. So he looked for ways to use preexisting tests and some original experiments to test for the presence of witchcraft. They just weren't very good (reliable or valid) psychological tests. But let's give even the most maligned Puritans, John Hathorne and his fellow magistrates, credit for at least trying. A few of those experiments came tantalizingly close to stopping the Salem witchcraft trials before anyone had to die.

DISCUSSION QUESTIONS

1. Procedures are rules that guide behavior. Following proper procedures is critical to success in surgery, law, experimentation, and even when assembling a bicycle. Identify three other activities or professions whose success depends on following the correct procedures. What happens when procedures are not followed?

2. Imagine that you are a judge in the historic Salem witch trials. Design a valid and reliable way to test for spectral witches.

3. Provide an example of how the word *witch hunt* is used by politicians or other public figures as a way to draw attention away from their own bad behavior. What are the connotations of this term today, and how are those connotations based on the Salem witch trials?

KEY TERMS

- **Single blind**: A study procedure in which participants don't know what condition they are in
- **Double blind**: A study procedure in which neither participants nor experimenters know which condition participants are in until after the results are measured
- **Reliability**: Consistency of measurement or results over multiple testing occasions
- **Validity**: The extent to which claims are really true
- **False confession**: Admitting to a crime you didn't actually commit

The Social Self

3.1 PHINEAS GAGE: THE SELF WITH A HOLE IN HIS HEAD

The Social Situation

Phineas Gage's accident happened on September 14, 1848 (see Bigelow, 1850; Harlow, 1868, 1993; Macmillan, 2000).

Mr. Gage was the outstanding foreman of several railroad construction workers near Cavendish, Vermont. The men were mostly Irish immigrants who had carried some of their ancient regional feuds into America. These were tough men, and an unpopular foreman was subject to "violent attacks . . . some of which ended fatally" (Macmillan, 2000, p. 22).

So, imagine the human-relations skills Gage must have needed to keep the railroad projects moving forward. He had to be fair and be perceived as fair. He had to calm the impulses of violent men yet harness their energies into an effective team.

Phineas Gage was very good at his job, but that was all about to change.

Theory and Method

This case study expands the familiar story of Phineas Gage.

There is a slight variance in the historical records; however, there is a consensus about the primary facts. The customary focus within psychology has been on how Phineas Gage's personality changed after his accident. But Phineas Gage still was able to perform complex tasks, work effectively with horses, drive a six-horse stage coach, tell exciting tall tales to his nephews, and reconnect with his mother shortly before he died.

Phineas Gage's unusual story demonstrates "the wonderful resources of the system in enduring the shock and in overcoming the effects of so frightful a lesion, and as a beautiful display of the recuperative powers of nature" (Harlow, 1868, 1993, p. 279). His story also demonstrates how **social neuroscience** advances our understanding of the brain's role in the development of a social self. People often think of personality, love, and the soul—who we *really* are—as "matters of the heart." They're off by about 12 inches; they are "matters of the brain."

The Accident

The pre-accident Phineas Gage was more than an accomplished foreman.

Dr. John Harlow (Gage's doctor) described the pre-accident Gage as a man "who possessed a well-balanced mind," "a shrewd business man," and a man "of temperate habits and possessed of considerable energy of character." This description represents the baseline **personality** of Phineas Gage, how Phineas Gage consistently behaved over time and across many situations.

On the day of his famous accident, Gage was using a 43-inch, 13-pound iron rod to tamp blasting powder into a hole drilled into some rock. The tamping rod was pointed at one end and flattened at the other. The goal was to explode the rock into small enough pieces so that the workers could cart them away and prepare the ground to lay track for the railroad. The hole was supposed to be covered with sand that would direct the force of the blast deep into the rock rather than back out the hole (see Bigelow, 1850; Macmillan, 2000). Prior to the accident, Phineas Gage was sitting on a rock shelf above the hole. Harlow (1868) reported that

> The powder and fuse had been adjusted in the hole, and he was in the act of "tamping it in", as it is called, previous to pouring in the sand. While doing this, his attention was attracted by his men. . . . Averting his head and looking over his right shoulder, at the same instant dropping the iron upon the charge, it struck fire upon the rock, and the explosion followed. (p. 275)

The pointed end of the long iron rod shot upward, entered Gage's head just below his left cheek, passed behind most of his left eye, continued through the front left portion of his brain, and shot out the top of his head. It landed about 23 meters (about 75 feet) away. The men retrieved his iron rod the next day and reported that, even after rinsing it off in a nearby creek, it was still greasy with some of Gage's brain matter.

The Survivor

Gage was knocked over, of course.

But he may never have lost consciousness, or only briefly. His men "carried him to the road, only a few rods distant, and put him into an ox cart, in which he rode, supported in sitting posture." Some of the men ran ahead while Gage, his back against the front of the oxcart, wrote a note in his foreman's log book (see Bigelow, 1850).

His workers took him to the hotel where he was staying and Gage walked up the steps, again possibly without any help, and sat on the porch. The first physician, Dr. Williams, did not believe him until Gage showed him the hole in his head. He even made a joke, something like, "Well, this should be work enough for you, doctor!"

Another physician arrived, Dr. Harlow, and the two physicians cleaned the wound. Then they shoved remaining pieces of Gage's skull back into place wherever they seemed to fit. When his skull was examined after his death many years later, those chunks of skull were still there, slowly being knit back. Dr. Harlow started recording what would become one of the most famous stories in the history of brain science and psychology.

Results and Discussion

Gage's brain was still working.

He could still recognize his mother and uncle and, only a few days after his accident, made plans to return to work. But his physical and mental health cycled between recovery, infection, and delirium for several weeks. As his condition slowly stabilized, Dr. Harlow noticed some odd features about his patient. Gage's memory was "as perfect as ever" but his patient "would not take $1000 for a few pebbles." That was strange. Had this "shrewd business man" lost his ability to understand money?

Gage Was "No Longer Gage"

Phineas Gage's personality changed, and this is where the story usually stops.

About a month after the accident, Harlow wrote that Gage had become "exceedingly capricious and childish . . . will not yield to restraint when it conflicts with his desires." The change in personality was so great that Gage's friends described the post-accident Gage as "no longer Gage." Apparently, the damage to Gage's left **frontal lobe** was somehow linked to a profound change in his self—but not to all of his self. This man "of temperate habits" and who "possessed of considerable energy of character" had become crude and difficult to work with.

It is easy to imagine Gage's acquaintances saying, "Why doesn't Phineas just get control of himself? Doesn't he know what he's doing?" The answer seems to be no. Gage seemed to have minimal **self-insight** (the ability to self-observe and evaluate our own behavior). In addition, the new Gage was probably less able to **self-monitor** (the ability to notice and adjust our own behavior across different social situations).

Curiously, patients with similar brain damage (usually due to brain surgery) demonstrate a similar story. When Beer et al. (2006) allowed patients with similar brain damage to see themselves on a video recording, they were surprised to discover that they were disclosing personal and inappropriate information. What we call the "self" appears to be connected to particular regions and neural pathways within the brain.

Yet Gage Was Still Gage

But there is more to the story of Phineas Gage.

The most exciting parts of Gage's life, and his contributions to social neuroscience, were still to come. Even though many social restraints had disappeared, Gage could still perform some very difficult tasks—even with a hole in his head!

Phineas Gage got a job working in a horse stable—and appears to have held that job for about 18 months. He must have done good work because the owner of the stable offered Gage a job driving a six-horse stagecoach through the mountain roads in Chile, South America. This employer placed a great deal of trust in Phineas Gage.

Think about what Gage could still do. Managing all those horses on rural mountain roads is surely a complex skill, yet Gage—the man with a large hole in his head—held this difficult job for about 7.5 years. When he began to have seizures, he joined his mother and sister (who were living in California) where, according to letters written by his mother to Dr. Harlow, Gage continued working. He also liked to tell his nieces and nephews hair-raising stories of his adventures in Chile. He worked well with animals, enjoyed a strong work ethic, and could tell great stories—what an uncle!

Yes, Gage's personality was changed after the iron rod removed portions of the left frontal lobe of his brain—but he was not *entirely* changed. Gage still knew who he was and how to get home. He could drive a stagecoach, accommodate passengers, and cooperate with other workers. Gage apparently kept that long iron rod close, even when driving the stagecoach. The tamping rod was buried with him after he died, not long after moving to California to be with his mother. You can see online the actual tamping rod held by Gage in recently discovered photographs. Gage's skull and the iron rod are displayed at the Warren Anatomical Museum in Boston.

Social neuroscience also owes gratitude to Phineas Gage's mother. She agreed to donate Gage's skull, and his iron tamping rod, to Dr. Harlow so that one of the greatest stories in brain science could continue to be told.

The Symphonic Self

We need both poets and scientists.

How else can we describe how beautifully the brain pulls the scattered experiences of life into a coherent self? Fernando Pessoa (2002) wrote in *The Book of Disquiet* that "my soul is like a hidden orchestra; I do not know which instruments grind and play away inside of me, strings and harps, timbales and drums. I can only recognize myself as a symphony" (p. 310).

The self simultaneously draws on each complex layer and region of the brain the same way that a symphony conductor simultaneously draws on multiple sections of an orchestra. But Damasio (2010), who created a computer simulation of Phineas Gage's brain trauma, believes that the brain routinely performs something far more impressive than the music produced by the most beautiful symphony orchestra.

"The marvel," Damasio wrote, "is that the score and conductor become reality only as life unfolds" (p. 24). The self is a symphony orchestra that plays magnificent music only once, without a score, and without any rehearsal—and then flows smoothly into its next performance.

What a magnificent, creative self!

DISCUSSION QUESTIONS

1. People who are high in self-monitoring change how they present themselves to best fit into any given situation. People low in self-monitoring act more consistently, regardless of the situation. After his accident, Gage became extremely low in self-monitoring. What are advantages and disadvantages to being very low in self-monitoring?

2. It is possible that people who experience brain traumas lose at least some of their ability to consent to being studied by scientists. Discuss the ethical considerations that should be in place regarding participants who may lose such abilities.

3. Gage appeared to have a changed personality and to have lost some types of abilities (such as financial reasoning). However, he retained many other important abilities, such as his memory. Which parts of the "self" are the most essential to our understanding of who we are? If you were to experience an accident causing brain damage, which function or ability would you be most concerned about losing, and why?

KEY TERMS

- **Social neuroscience**: The study of how the social environment interacts with the brain
- **Personality**: Enduring patterns of thought or behavior within a given person (e.g., shyness, the tendency to be competitive)
- **Frontal lobes**: Part of the brain at the top and front of the skull responsible for several higher thinking functions

- **Self-insight**: The ability to observe and evaluate our own behavior
- **Self-monitor**: The ability to notice social demands in various situations and to change our behavior to match those demands

3.2 THE CHANGING SELF: IDENTITY OF TRANSGENDER INDIVIDUALS

The Social Situation

March 31 is now the Transgender Day of Visibility.

We all experience changes in our self-concept over the course of our lives. People often find a thrill in changing their names due to marriage or divorce. Sometimes we feel like different people after a promotion at work gives us a different title. New citizenship in a country other than the one of our birth might give us the sense that we're part of a new culture. But perhaps no one feels this kind of change more than **transgender** individuals.

It's not just Caitlyn Jenner, Carmen Carrera, and Chaz Bono. According to a poll from the Williams Institute, about 1.4 million people from the United States identified as trans in 2016; that's 0.6% (Williams Institute, 2016). In 2017, a different poll estimated the number to be more like 3% (GLAAD, 2017). The culture offers more respect and opportunity to LGBTQ (standing for lesbian, gay, bisexual, transgender, queer) individuals than ever before, with "historic achievements achieved for both legal equality and cultural acceptance." This progressive attitude is most prevalent in younger generations.

If transgender people are given the opportunity to live in their true identity (not the one assigned at birth), they often experience a remarkable level of psychological and emotional well-being (Lev, 2004; Riggle et al., 2011). Their public **self-concept** can finally match their private self-concept, resulting in a feeling of personally unprecedented relief and flourishing. Unfortunately, however, trans people are also often subject to negative experiences, including discrimination (e.g., Clements-Nolle et al., 2006), trauma (e.g., Mizock & Lewis, 2006), and more.

While "coming out" can be an emotional roller coaster for anyone in the LGBTQ community, transgender people may have the most extreme changes in their sense of self after they are able to legally change their name, gender, and (if possible) physical body through hormone treatments and surgery. One study (Riggle et al., 2011) interviewed trans people to learn how they felt about their changing sense of self.

Theory and Method

Sixty-one trans people participated.

They were a mix of people; some identified as male-to-female, some as female-to-male, some as queer, and some noted that none of these labels really applied. They were recruited online and responded to a survey asking them about their experience. Two questions were the most important.

First, they were asked, "Overall, how positive do you feel about your current self-identification as a transgender individual?" Happily, 72% reported that they felt extremely or very positive. Another 25% said they were "somewhat" positive, and only 3% said they were "not very" positive. Interestingly, zero participants said they were "not at all" positive about their trans identity.

The second major question in this study was simple and open-ended: "Please tell us below what you think the positive things are about being a transgender identified person. Please describe as many positive aspects as you think are important to your life and in as much detail and with examples if you wish."

What did they say?

Results and Discussion

"Only difficulties."

That sentiment—that there were *no* positive aspects of the transgender identity—was reported by 10% of the participants (Riggle et al., 2011). However, even these people were then able to explain themselves in terms of hard challenges and difficulties in the process that could be seen now as positive. Looking back, the challenges were lessons, and they were overcome.

From the rest of the participants, researchers identified eight separate themes in terms of how people's sense of self changed both in terms of individual identity and connection to the larger LGBTQ community.

- *Congruency*: Almost half the participants celebrated that their inner feelings and outer appearances finally matched. They used words like *honesty*, *truth*, *unity*, and *true peace*. One noted, "You can live the life that you know should be yours, [not] stuck in a foreign body . . . being whole, happy, and peaceful" (p. 150).

- *Personal growth and resiliency*: One-third reported experiences of personal growth, using terms like *more self-confident*, *stronger*, and *more self-aware*. One 57-year-old person wrote, "I wouldn't wish my life on anyone, but if I had the choice to be transgender, I would do it all over again. All the problems have made me a much stronger and better person" (p. 151).

- *Empathy*: About 25% wrote that being transgender allowed them to have greater empathy for minority groups "It has forced me to think about stereotyping, about being and feeling marginalized, and has increased my empathy with others in minority groups or on the margins. I think I have become a more sensitive, thoughtful, and compassionate person" (p. 151).

- *Interpersonal experiences*: Many people (about 17%) discussed positive "coming out" experiences as they told friends and family about their true self-concept. One wrote, "The act of self-disclosure, when done with sensitivity toward the person you are sharing with, is a liberating experience, and while potentially scary because you risk rejection, it is probably the single most important thing you can do towards mental, emotional, [and] physical health" (p. 151).

- *Unique perspective/insight*: One common theme was that by being trans, they understood both the male and female perspective. One participant who described herself as FTM (female-to-male), butch dyke, and lesbian described this unique view, afforded from living between social labels: "Being not 'one or the other' by being 'both and' is a place of privilege that allows me insights into the complexities of gender identities and gender relationships that many people do not experience. Being transgender presents a challenge to accepted thinking and stereotypes and encourages us all to examine our own prejudices and blinkered views" (p. 152).

- *Living beyond the binary*: Over one-third of the people in this study noted that being trans was a positive escape from the socially conforming view that sex and gender only offer two options. Many pointed out that gender is fluid and that labels were pointless; one expressed enjoying the balance of being neither traditionally male nor female.

- *Activism*: About one-fourth of the sample pointed out that they enjoyed a sense of activism in the community, through educating others and serving as a role model. They hoped that their experiences could be inspirational for others.

- *Links to the LGBTQ community*: Finally, several people wrote that their experiences were positive because others were supportive. One eloquent statement observed that, "One positive aspect is my relationship to the trans and queer community. I feel like my gender and sexuality have a home and a unique culture. Having trans and queer space means I always have a place where I can get and lend support, and can have access to activities and events geared toward the community. Whereas in the mainstream culture my identity would be marginalized, in trans and queer spaces, it is celebrated and normalized" (p. 153).

The authors of this study pointed out that these themes are likely going to be important to anyone who is part of the LGBTQ community. Especially when it comes to our sense of self, positive narratives and experiences are essential for a positive **self-esteem** and the feeling that we are accepted for our authentic selves.

DISCUSSION QUESTIONS

1. Think of a transgender celebrity and find an article interviewing them before and after they "came out." Did the way they talk about themselves or their view of the world seem to change? In what ways?

2. This case study points out that younger generations are (in general) more understanding of the LGBTQ community, compared to older

generations. Identify three reasons why you think that is the case.

3. The study discussed in this case study focused only on transgender people's *positive* experiences and senses of self. If a follow-up study were done focusing on challenges and negative experiences, what themes do you think would emerge, and why?

KEY TERMS

- **Transgender**: People with a mismatch between the sex they are assigned at birth and the one they feel is correct, psychologically
- **Self-concept**: The personal summary of who we are, including our positive and negative qualities, relationships to others, group memberships, and beliefs

- **Self-esteem**: Our evaluation or judgment of our self-concept, including both positive and negative aspects of our identity

3.3 THE DISAPPEARING SELF: LOST MEMORY

The Social Situation

Who are you if you have lost your memory?

You don't know if you like peas, cats, or basketball. You don't know if you've ever been on an airplane. You can't recall how old you are. You don't recognize your own family. All of these are real possibilities for people who have Alzheimer's disease (AD).

Such symptoms get worse as AD marches relentlessly through your brain. The disease hacks a destructive trail of neural plaques and tangles across connections that once flowed effortlessly across your brain. In advanced stages of AD, you will look into a mirror and not recognize the person looking back at you (Biringer & Anderson, 1992). Your self-concept and self-insight decline as the self disappears.

The disappearing self is expensive. In addition to the emotional costs, projections from the World Health Organization (WHO) indicate that AD will become so expensive that it threatens to upend established international social and economic structures (see Aajami et al., 2019; Fishman et al., 2019; Rasmussen & Langerman, 2019; Wortmann, 2012). But it is a complicated economic analysis. For example, a caregiver who takes off work represents lost income to the national economy, yet often savings compared to institutionalized care. There also are different expectations in different cultures, different economies in different regions, and different levels of infrastructure able to provide care (Blank, 2019).

However, it is safe to say that the costs associated with AD are (a) enormous and (b) escalating (see Kalamägi et al., 2019).

Theory and Method

This case study uses **archival data** and a case study to illustrate the many costs of AD.

The story of Mrs. R. demonstrates one way that social psychology can limit any **excess disability** that develops when an individual's social psychological environment aggravates the symptoms of AD (Brody et al., 1971). Social psychology can help us understand and improve the intimate social environment around care for people with AD (see Kitwood, 1997).

The Case of Mrs. R: What the Husband Perceives

Steven Sabat's (1994, p. 160) case study of Mrs. R. demonstrates how social psychology can improve care for people with AD.

> Mrs. R. was 64 years old when she was first diagnosed with probable Alzheimer's disease and was now 68. She and her husband had enjoyed a long marriage and continued to display affection and commitment to one another. Her medical records reported that she had severe problems with both short-term and long-term memory, needed assistance with personal grooming, and sometimes wandered aimlessly.

Her spouse demonstrated consistent affection and concern for her well-being. But now he described his wife of many years as someone who was generally helpless, disoriented, and forgetful. He was concerned that his wife

> . . . needed help taking medications, that she no longer cooked or did housework, or any other home repairs, no longer handled money, never wrote or used the telephone, and if left alone, she watched a great deal of television or did nothing. He also reported that she needed assistance when eating. . . . The couple had a history of a strong, loving marriage, and in much of their behavior towards one another that history was still very much manifested in the present.

One notable disagreement between Mr. and Mrs. R. involved an outfit she had picked out for her birthday celebration at the adult daycare. When she wanted to wear it again the next day, he refused. He thought she had forgotten the previous day's celebration. He also put on her makeup for her because he thought she used too much.

The Case of Mrs. R.: What the Staff Reports

Contrast the spouse's report with what the staff observed at her adult daycare.

"Mrs. R. did not require any help whatsoever when eating. Her eye–hand coordination was coherent, and she was able to cut her food and feed herself quite well." The summary of her personal grooming told a similar story. Mrs. R. was happy to pick out her own clothes and did not like her husband doing it for her. She was self-conscious about her facial appearance and used makeup to cover any blemishes.

At her adult daycare, the aimless wandering at home was replaced by purposeful activities. She would help move chairs as needed for new activities, helped others find the bathrooms, and navigated the rooms. She was able to comfort individuals in pain and developed a warm relationship with a woman who was losing her hair. Her only wandering did not seem aimless and only occurred when there was a break in the usual activities.

Results and Discussion

The case study of Mrs. R. demonstrates the power of the situation.

> There was a striking difference in the behaviour shown by Mrs. R. in two different social settings: at home as opposed to the day-care centre. The difference spans the range from functional and competent in the latter setting to dysfunctional and incompetent in the former setting.

Mrs. R. was experiencing **disempowerment** (Kitwood, 1990). Her husband was doing things for her that she was able to do for herself. She could feed herself, but he was doing it for her. This, in turn, produced a decreasing sense of **agency** in Mrs. R. about her ability to manage her own life. This was aggravated as her husband gradually took over the various household chores that Mrs. R. had been completing by herself. So, she did less, and he did more—until he came to regard her as more disabled than she actually was.

Social Psychological Insights

The underlying process between Mr. and Mrs. R. is familiar to social psychologists.

A **self-fulfilling prophecy** begins with the application of a descriptive label. Mrs. R.'s husband assumed lower expectations for her until she was—at least at home—becoming more disabled than her disease actually dictated. Sabat (1994) pointed out another related social psychological feature: stigmatization.

The label of incompetence assigned to Mrs. R. by her husband turned "going for a walk" into "wandering aimlessly." The term for this larger process is confirmation bias. In her husband's sincere, caring perception, everything Mrs. R. did confirmed that AD was stealing her sense of self, and he could not imagine evidence that contradicted what he "knew" must be true.

Kitwood (1997) identified the features that make up a toxic environment for someone with AD. He recognized that a harmful social psychological environment is not composed of malicious acts or deliberate cruelty. Instead, the resulting cruelty comes from good intentions to help someone with a dementia, and their family, cope with a difficult life situation. The characteristics of what Kitwood calls a **malignant social psychological environment** include

1. Treachery: using deception to gain compliance (e.g., to enter a nursing home)

2. Disempowerment: not allowing the person to exercise the skills they have

3. Infantilization: patronizing someone as if they were a child

4. Intimidation: inducing fear through threats and physical punishment

5. Labeling: using a category name as global descriptor (as in "lost their marbles")

6. Stigmatization: treating a person as an undesirable object

7. Invalidation: not recognizing how the other person is experiencing their world

8. Ignoring: behaving as if the person were not present

9. Mockery: pointing out and making fun of odd behaviors

10. Disparagement: sending verbal/psychological messages of incompetence

Career Opportunities for Psychology Students

Personhood.

That single word sums up Kitwood's (1997) antidote for a malignant social psychological environment. **Personhood** is what gerontology nurses call "person-centered care" (see Dewing, 2007); it's essentially acknowledging someone's agency and individual rights. It's not universally embraced, but it appears to resonate within the context of geriatric nursing. If you were experiencing some of the symptoms of AD, wouldn't you want the respect and empowerment of personhood?

There is another one-word antidote for a malignant social psychological environment: *You.* There are levels of career opportunities available to psychology students in what is a fast-growing industry—and make no mistake: Geriatric care is an industry. That's why we want psychology students who can carry and sustain person-centered care into every corner of the industry.

The career opportunities for undergraduate psychology majors range from training to be a recreation therapist to managing a health care facility. The industry often pays for certifications that advance your training and job prospects. For you, gerontology also can be a satisfying, often funny, yet existentially real career. The social costs of AD are *both* enormous and escalating with an aging population. Millions of aging citizens—your grandparents and your parents—will be needing someone like you to understand, respect, and enjoy the changing self.

DISCUSSION QUESTIONS

1. This case study used Alzheimer's disease as an example of a health issue for which a malignant social psychology milieu might make symptoms worse for someone. What other physical or mental diseases, disabilities, or conditions are good examples of contexts in which other people might make life more difficult for the person experiencing symptoms?

2. Mr. R. was likely unaware that he was conferring some of the malignant social psychological characteristics to his wife (see the list from Kitwood, 1997). First, identify which

two or three items on this list that you think are the most emotionally or psychologically damaging for Mrs. R., and explain why. Then, discuss the psychological reasons why Mr. R. might—on an unconscious level—do this to a wife he loves. Why would Mr. R. perceive his wife to be in more need than she really was?

3. What are three specific ways that Mr. R. and/or the staff at the adult daycare could increase the personhood Mrs. R. experiences on a daily basis?

KEY TERMS

- **Archival data**: Data originally collected for a different purpose but that can be analyzed in new ways later to test for patterns and trends (e.g., police records, medical costs)
- **Excess disability**: Loss of abilities or opportunities that occur from something besides a disability itself, such as from social discrimination or lack of resources
- **Disempowerment**: The loss of power or authority to make decisions in your own life
- **Agency**: Our capacity to make decisions, act independently, and have power over your own life

- **Self-fulfilling prophecy**: When our prediction about someone else changes how we act toward them in ways that make our prediction come true
- **Malignant social psychological environment**: One that decreases people's agency through disempowerment, stigmatization, invalidation, and other techniques, even when those techniques are done unconsciously or with good intentions
- **Personhood**: Acknowledging someone's agency and respecting them as an individual with rights

3.4 THE PREGNANT SELF: DOES MY BUMP LOOK BIG IN THIS?

The Social Situation

Many women look forward to becoming mothers.

Before it happens, the self-concept is understandably focused on the individual self. But once pregnancy occurs, the individual self may quickly become a social self that now includes the future baby. "Me" starts becoming "Mom."

Social identity theory anticipates many changes in a woman's sense of self *after* the baby has arrived. For fathers as well as mothers, what worries you, brings you joy, or monopolizes your time will probably be different after an infant comes to live with you. Changes in the body also lead to changes in the self, for all genders and across ethnic groups (see Fawkner & McMurray, 2002; Grabe & Hyde, 2006). But what happens to a woman's sense of self *during* pregnancy?

Theory and Method

This case study demonstrates the research value of conducting in-depth interviews.

Surveys and experiments are helpful research tools. They can tell us, for example, about changes in body satisfaction during pregnancy and compare the pregnancy experience between individuals and across cultures. But Johnson et al. (2004) relied on an in-depth qualitative approach of **semi-structured interviews**. Their study had a specific goal: to reconcile a strange contradiction in the scientific literature about the self-esteem of pregnant women.

When two scientific studies produce contradictory findings, there are four possible explanations: (1) Study A is correct and Study B is flawed in some way. (2) Study B is correct and Study A is flawed in some way. (3) Both studies are flawed. (4) Both studies are correct, and there is something else going on that we don't understand.

Some studies found that women's attitudes toward their bodies became progressively more negative when pregnant. However, other studies found opposite effects, including a shift to a more positive attitude toward their body among women who were overweight prior to pregnancy. Johnson et al. (2004) used qualitative interviews to test the possibility that both studies were correct, and we just didn't understand the experience of body satisfaction among pregnant women. Their interviews collected data from a sample of six women who were 33–39 weeks into their pregnancies. Then they used a process called **content analysis** to identify themes in their data.

Results and Discussion

The contradictory findings in the literature provoked new ideas.

Johnson et al. (2004) created a clever title for their article: "Does My Bump Look Big in This?" Three themes emerged from interviews about changes in body satisfaction during pregnancy:

1. Body satisfaction during pregnancy was dynamic—positive at one stage, negative at another

2. The impact of pregnancy on perceptions of the body varied

3. The physical and social boundaries surrounding women's bodies changed

Theme 1: Body Satisfaction During Pregnancy Is Dynamic

The initial excitement changed.

One interviewee (called "Bea" in their report) demonstrated how her sense of self changed during pregnancy. She was initially excited, especially as she watched early changes in her belly. However, that initial excitement changed.

> After [my] bump started to develop, things really started to change about how I felt about me, and it was quite distressing. . . . I never contemplated that . . . I was paranoid about becoming a really big, fat, pregnant person. (Johnson et al., 2004, p. 365)

But Bea's body self-image changed once again "when it became more obvious that she was pregnant" (p. 365). Bea's dynamic (changeable) body self-esteem helps explain why some previous pregnancy studies found both positive and negative body satisfaction. Her comments also demonstrate why the self is indeed a social self. Her body self-esteem was influenced by what she believed others believed about her appearance (e.g., prejudice against people with larger bodies or "fat shaming")—and that changed at different stages of her pregnancy.

Theme 2: Pregnancy Led to Varied Perceptions of the Body

Social comparisons influenced body self-esteem.

One of the mothers-to-be followed her cultural tradition of not washing her hair at the start of her pregnancy—setting up an unflattering social comparison with other women. Her perception of her own body demonstrates again that the self is social, as well as the importance of social comparisons on body satisfaction and self-esteem. Most of the women interviewed in the study spoke about being physically impaired, uncomfortable, and restricted. One mother-to-be, identified as Felice, admitted that

> I feel a bit robbed in some ways, just the fact that I've had to slow down and I can't do this and I can't do that . . . I'll do a few things and then sit down . . . so sometimes I feel frustrated because I can't do what I used to do, I can't do the sports I used to do as well. (Johnson et al., 2004, p. 366)

However, there were also positive self-perceptions of their bodies during pregnancy. For example, the baby moving created an experience that was simultaneously weird, reassuring, and a stimulus for bonding with their baby. This kind of qualitative study captures the subtle variability of the pregnancy experience in ways that a conventional quantitative, self-report scale (such as ranging from 0 to 7) would not pick up unless you had a hypothesis directing you to look in that direction.

Theme 3: The Boundaries Around Their Bodies Changed During Pregnancy.

Others assume rights to your body.

The social space around their bodies changed in two ways. First, even strangers would suddenly feel privileged to feel their tummy. One interviewee identified as Sum said, "You become public property, and anyone can touch you." More than a few strangers had far too personal approaches to their apparent "rights" to touch their bodies.

A second way that the space around their bodies was violated was through health exams. Most of the women had an understanding reaction to professional health exams. One interviewee, Denise, commented that "to some extent they burst the bubble that you are special because the care of pregnant women was a matter of routine to them." Sum, however, was not comfortable exposing her body to medical professionals:

> And you could have loads of people in the room and to them, you know, if they've seen one woman's bits they've seen everybody else's . . . but this is mine, this is me and it's private and it's between me and my husband and the baby as far as I'm concerned it's not for anyone else to see but, you kinda like feel you're open to, um, to public view. (Johnson et al., 2004, p. 367)

Some of the women enjoyed the attention, and others were offended. Some felt that the relatively impersonal health exams were reassuring because they suggested professionalism and competence; others were understanding but still found the experience deeply uncomfortable. Several women appeared to feel differently about the boundaries of their bodies at different stages of pregnancy.

It's not surprising that quantitative surveys missed these important, nuanced details of the pregnancy experience. Scales can be helpful, but it's only one of the knowledge-building tools in the social psychologist's toolbox. The contradiction in the literature about women being *both satisfied* and *dissatisfied* with their bodies was reconciled by using a qualitative approach.

Replicating Qualitative Research

We tend to trust studies that can be replicated, where the same results are found again by different researchers with different participants.

About 6 years after publication of the study with the unusual title ("Does My Bump Look Big in This?"), Chang et al. (2010) also asked 18 pregnant women about their body satisfaction. They had two goals: (1) to capture the complexity of how the self can change during pregnancy, and (2) to understand how "pregnant Taiwanese women in large cities" negotiate cultural conflicts related to pregnancy.

These women were navigating between longstanding traditions that were important to their families—and practices that they did not personally endorse. It was, in some ways, a study of the conflict within mothers-to-be between having an **independent** versus an **interdependent self-construal**.

There was a similar cultural conflict in the Johnson study when one of the six mothers reluctantly followed a cultural tradition of not washing her hair. The overlap between these two qualitative studies appears to be how pregnancy combines with cultural expectations to force changes in the self. It's not a perfect **replication**—but it may be more meaningful because it wasn't trying to be a replication.

Descriptive and Explanatory Social Psychological Theories

These qualitative studies are thick with social psychological theories about the self.

For example, the improvement in Bea's body satisfaction occurred when she knew that others could tell that she was pregnant. It demonstrates that Bea's self was social (social identity theory). Her private sense of self was influenced by what she perceived that others perceived about her (**social mirror theory**). The mechanism that triggered Bea's assessments of her body was comparing herself to other women (social comparisons).

The effect of those social comparisons depended on how she explained to herself (**attribution theory**) what she imagined other people were thinking of her when observing the size of her belly. A big belly without the attribution of pregnancy decreased her body self-image and her **self-esteem**. Bea also struggled with the balance between her ideal hopes and dreams versus the reality of what she was experiencing (**self-discrepancy theory**).

That's a lot of social psychology for recognizing that her body self-esteem improved when she knew that others could tell she was pregnant!

Folk Wisdom About Pregnancy

Some ancient beliefs and behaviors endure as folk wisdom.

Some endure because they were once useful adaptations. Their usefulness may have disappeared generations ago. However, they persist as traditions, folk wisdom, and "old wives' tales" about pregnancy:

- Carrying high? It's a girl. Carrying low? It's got to be a boy.

- If you have heartburn, then your baby will have lots of hair.

- If the baby's heartrate is over 140 beats per minute, then it's going to be girl.

- Craving ice cream means it is a girl, but a taste for salty foods means it's a boy.

- Taking a bath can drown your fetus.

- Walking or eating spicy foods induces labor.

- Cats have a natural urge to smother babies.

It's a reach, but there might be a grain of natural selection truth in some of these sayings. For example, cats are creatures of comfort so they seek out the warmest, coziest place to take a nap—and there is nothing so cozy as a new (sleeping) baby. However, it seems more likely that one mother may have feared the idea of their cat smothering their baby and told someone about it, that person passed it on, and pretty soon, an untestable rumor was racing around the network of anxious young mothers, becoming a superstition.

In the Chang et al. (2010) study, some Taiwanese practices related to pregnancy were clashing with modern medicine. But the clash between traditional ways of doing things and modern cultures forced the mothers-to-be to reimagine a new, more modern self. And that also makes sense in term of evolution. After all, there is nothing more crucial for the process of natural selection than a successful pregnancy.

DISCUSSION QUESTIONS

1. This case study discussed how a mother's sense of self changes through pregnancy and motherhood. But what about fathers or step parents? Discuss similarities and differences that each kind of parent experiences when they become a parent the first time, in terms of their sense of self.

2. Discuss how women's experience of pregnancy, in terms of body self-esteem changes, is different from one woman to the next. Identify two or three personality traits or situational variables that you think might be correlated

to either satisfaction or dissatisfaction with experiences during pregnancy. Explain your hypotheses.

3. Identify at least two stereotypes about pregnant women that your culture promotes or seems to endorse through things like media images. For each stereotype, do you agree or disagree with this stereotype? And for each, does cultural expectation for this stereotype help or hurt pregnant women in terms of both pragmatic matters (such as access to resources) and in terms of self-esteem?

KEY TERMS

- **Social identity theory**: The idea that our self-concept is made up of two parts: (1) a personal, individual identity, and (2) a social identity, made up of our group memberships such as family and culture
- **Semi-structured interviews**: A qualitative research method in which participants are interviewed with a set of questions that can be modified during the interview session as needed

- **Content analysis**: A method of finding themes and patterns in qualitative data such as interviews
- **Social comparison**: When we evaluate ourselves by thinking about those in both "better" and "worse" situations, relatively speaking
- **Replication**: When the results of a study can be found again, by different researchers with different participants

- **Independent self-construal**: When someone's self-concept is mostly based on their individual traits, preferences, and choices
- **Interdependent self-construal**: When someone's self-concept is mostly based on their relationships with others, groups, and cultural expectations
- **Social mirror theory**: The idea that our sense of self is influenced by our perceptions of how other people see us
- **Attribution theory**: How we make guesses about why people do things
- **Self-esteem**: Our evaluation of whether we like our self-concept, including an assessment of our strengths and weaknesses
- **Self-discrepancy theory**: The idea that we all maintain (1) an actual self, (2) an ideal self, and (3) an ought self, based on our perceptions of social expectations

Social Cognition

4

4.1 INTUITION IN THE NEONATAL INTENSIVE CARE UNIT

The Social Situation

"I get a feeling about something, and I know I'm right."

That's how many people experience **intuition**, a way of knowing without knowing how we know. Intuition is useful because the business of living is full of uncertainties. But then an intuition lands—kerplop!—in our thoughts and feelings. The uncertainty disappears, and we know how to move forward.

Warning! Feeling certain does not guarantee accuracy—or a good decision.

A fire chief has uncertain information when deciding whether to send firefighters into a burning building (Klein, 2003). Smoke, for example, has a color, produces a smell, appears with a particular density, and has a burning rate that together suggest what and where materials are burning. A fire on a small dairy farm is different from a fire on the 15th story of a downtown office building. Firefighters must make several intuitive decisions about how to fight a fire under conditions of profound but consequential uncertainty. Sometimes they get it wrong.

Another context in which life and death decisions are made every day is a neonatal intensive care unit (NICU). The mission of a NICU is to save the lives of very sick newborn babies. It's a place where we can see how human decision making often relies on the ideal balance between intuition and **logic**. Sometimes they get it wrong.

This particular case study has a happy ending.

Theory and Method

Consider the high stakes inside a NICU.

Many NICU babies are born prematurely. The average gestation of a human birth is 40 weeks. Classification of a "preemie" is a birth before 37 weeks of gestation or at a birth weight less than 2,000 grams (about 5.5 pounds). Less than 1,500 grams is considered a very low birth weight, and the risks of infant mortality increase dramatically. The average birth weight of one sample of at-risk Canadian preemies (gestational age 23–25 weeks) was 715 grams (Fenton et al., 2013).

The survival rates of preemies are positively correlated with birth weight: A higher birth weight predicts higher survival rates. A study in France found only a 0.7% survival-to-discharge rate for preemies born before 24 weeks of gestation but 59.1% at 25 weeks, 75.3% at 26 weeks, and 98.9% at 32–34 weeks (Ancel et al., 2015). Klein (2003, pp. 13–20) takes us inside a NICU, where intuition in a world of uncertainty has profound meanings for death, life, tragedy, and hope.

Infection Inside a NICU

The preemie enters a world that its body is not equipped to survive.

Thus, the NICU creates its own tiny environment in an isolated bassinette, sometimes called an *isolette*. The temperature is controlled, and the baby's vital signs are monitored through various leads. Nourishment is delivered through an intravenous tube or a drip tube slipped down the esophagus and into the tiny stomach.

The danger of infection, especially around these mechanical interventions, is carefully managed. But it is a constant threat, just as it is with older patients. Anyone physically contacting the infant, including anxious parents who want to hold and touch their child, must scrub thoroughly. Siblings, exposed at their schools and playgrounds to many childhood diseases, are generally not permitted to touch their new sister or brother in the NICU.

The baby's health status is constantly monitored through visual inspection and a variety of blood tests. Alarms sound whenever a monitoring device indicates that extra attention is required by a particular infant. They often indicate nothing more urgent than a lead that has become separated or a fussy baby. Klein (2003) described a frequent situation that calls for an intuitive response from observant, experienced NICU nurses:

> With infants in these fragile conditions, many things can go wrong, and practically all of them can become life threatening. One of the greatest and most common dangers is sepsis, a systemic infection that spreads throughout the infant's circulatory system. . . . Sepsis can be detected by a blood culture, but this test takes twenty-four hours and by then the baby might be overwhelmingly infected and beyond help. (p. 14)

The Case of Baby Melissa

Consider the case of two nurses, Darlene and Linda, and a preemie named Melissa.

Both Darlene and Linda were experienced nurses, but Linda was new to the NICU and being mentored by Darlene. Linda's training was progressing well, and Darlene was monitoring her work less as Linda's skills increased.

It was near the end of the night shift. Baby Melissa's parents had gone home for a few hours of sleep after an uneventful day. Linda noticed that Melissa had been a bit lethargic at her feeding but not severe enough to seem concerning. After all, tiny Melissa had been welcomed into the world with a great deal of testing, poking, and sticking.

Melissa's temperature also was in the normal range but slightly low. Blood from a heel stick from a fairly new medical technician had left slightly more bleeding than a skilled med tech would leave behind—but again, nothing terribly out of the ordinary. There were reasonable, logical explanations for what Linda was observing.

Darlene—the more experienced nurse—glanced as she passed Melissa's isolette, and her intuition sent a warning. Something was not right, or as she later expressed it, something "just looked funny . . . didn't look good." She inspected Melissa more closely. The heel stick had not stopped bleeding. Her skin appeared "off color" and "mottled." Melissa's tummy might have been a little more rounded than expected. An exam indicated that Melissa was slightly bloated, and the pattern of her temperature, while within the normal range, was trending downward.

Results and Discussion

"We've got a baby in big trouble."

Darlene reported her intuition to the on-duty physician, who immediately ordered antibiotics. They also ordered a blood test that, 24 hours later, confirmed the presence of sepsis. But those 24 hours would have been too late for Melissa if they had waited until they had the results to take action. Darlene's intuition, captured with a passing glance at an infant that she was no longer monitoring, had saved baby Melissa's life.

Why Is Experience the Best Teacher?

Intuition is not magic.

Calling intuition a gift is also misleading. Folk wisdom from the world of medicine says, "Good judgment comes from experience. And experience comes from bad judgment." Making bad judgments about others' lives is a hard way to learn that we can't always trust our intuition. "Experience is a good teacher," and it makes it easier for you to think about what you did wrong and right in the past.

Darlene's intuition, in contrast to Linda's limited intuition, was the product of deep experience. Darlene had invested many years in the NICU; she had seen many cases; she had followed the arc of the stories of many infant illnesses. She had observed their small beginnings, participated in their climatic turning points, and observed their varied resolutions. She could think in story form and anticipate endings.

Linda had noticed all the same details as Darlene, but she had not perceived the story of the struggle for life going on right in front of her. The details included Melissa's lethargy, the still-bleeding heel stick, the slightly rounded tummy, the mottled skin, and the lower temperature. But Linda's baseline observations were not as seasoned as those of Darlene.

Linda noticed the lethargy but also knew that babies sleep a lot. She noticed the bleeding heel stick but had little experience about how long she could expect an infant's heel stick to keep bleeding. Linda had observed most of the other signs, but the details did not come together in her mind with the other observations. It was, Klein (2003) reported, not so much the individual symptoms that were key, but a particular constellation of symptoms. Linda could see all the signs but she was unable to piece them together into a story that revealed the larger pattern. . . . In our research we found that Darlene was typical of highly experienced NICU nurses who can detect sepsis in premature infants, even before the blood tests pick it up. (p. 18)

Darlene's intuition was the result of deep, detailed experience in the NICU. Research in **social cognition** has helped us understand that experience nourishes intuition because it increases mental accessibility.

Intuition Requires Mental Accessibility

A medical student startled her classmates and professors.

She made what seemed like an uncanny diagnosis of a skull deformity. Her "intuition," in this case, was because someone had left a journal article about this particular condition on a lunch table. She had glanced through the article during her lunch break. The source of this intuition was **priming**; the diagnosis came easily to mind because she had just read about it. Priming, or having something come more easily to mind because we had just been exposed to it, is just one way that intuition is helped by **mental accessibility**, or the ease with which something comes to mind.

So, yes. We want to listen carefully to our intuition as it pieces together the meanings of our observations. Linda's intuition put together a weak story that baby Melissa was just a little tired and fussy—but Darlene looked for a story that was a better fit with her deeper experience inside a NICU. In this case, intuition saved a life.

DISCUSSION QUESTIONS

1. Identify two contexts from your life where you rely on using a balance of intuition and logic. Explain how both types of thinking processes are useful in that context and what the consequences would be if you had only one type of thinking instead of both.

2. Have you ever traveled to another region of the country, traveled to another country, or even attended an event that was unfamiliar to you? How did you use your intuition to learn how to act? Did your observations of how other people were acting surprise you—and did that surprise lead you to reflect on your own habits or cultural assumptions in new ways?

3. Think of two times when your intuition turned out to be wrong. Can you identify why your intuition made a mistake in these two circumstances? What was it about the environment, your frame of mind, your emotional state, and so on that caused your intuition to fail you?

- **Intuition**: The ability to know something quickly and automatically; a "gut feeling" that takes little mental effort
- **Logic**: The ability to use reason, think systematically, and carefully consider evidence when making a decision
- **Social cognition**: The study of how we process information and make decisions using a combination of intuition and logic

- **Priming**: When thinking about a concept earlier makes it easier to come to mind again later
- **Mental accessibility**: The ease at which a certain idea comes to mind

4.2 DUAL PROCESSING MEDICAL DIAGNOSES

The Social Situation

You're waiting for your turn to see a doctor.

You've been scratching your arm and neck. Some of the red bumps are turning into blisters. They seem to be moving up your left arm toward your neck. You tried household lotions in your medicine cabinet: no improvement. You tried over-the-counter medicines: no effect. It's time to go to the doctor.

Theory and Method

This case study helps you recognize how a family practice physician is thinking during a diagnosis.

They are using two types of thinking—**dual processing**—at the same time. Their thinking demonstrates cognitive load shifting as they use both (1) three kinds of intuition and (2) their highly trained logic and to keep working their way toward an accurate diagnosis.

Family practice doctors reach diagnoses by combining logic and intuition. Figure 4.1 summarizes our two thinking systems. One is fast and intuitive; the other is slow and logical. Both carry risks. You probably want a fast diagnosis because you are scratching and suffering. You don't want the doctor to tell you that the tests will take a month! Your physician is probably thinking through possible diagnoses as quickly as possible, but as slowly and rationally as needed to be accurate.

The Logic of the Differential Diagnosis

Physicians have been trained in a logical, rational process called **differential diagnosis**.

It's been an intense training. It may have started with medical volunteering in high school or even earlier. That was likely followed by 4 years of pre-med classes. If accepted

FIGURE 4.1

Humans Evolved Two Distinct Thinking Systems, One Based on Intuition, the Other on Logic

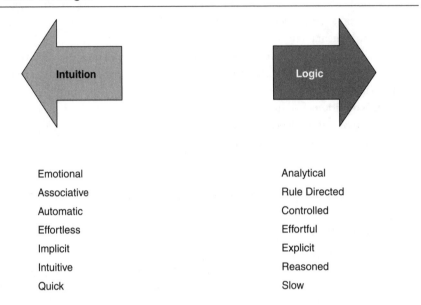

Intuition	Logic
Emotional	Analytical
Associative	Rule Directed
Automatic	Controlled
Effortless	Effortful
Implicit	Explicit
Intuitive	Reasoned
Quick	Slow

into medical school, the doctor-to-be studies 4 more years in medical school and then spends another 3–5 years in a residency, learning a medical specialty.

That often is followed by a fellowship in a particular area of medicine and research. At every stage, physicians get more practice distinguishing among different types of diseases: differential diagnoses. The application of a differential diagnosis requires a physician to systematically rule out possible explanations. For example, they will ask questions about your symptoms, how long you have experienced your symptoms, what aggravates your symptoms, and so forth. They're thinking to themselves, "Well, it's not X; it doesn't fit with Y; so it is probably Z."

The Rule of Frequency, Intensity, and Duration

The Rule of FID can quickly narrow down a diagnosis.

Listen carefully to the questions your physician asks. You may notice that they focus on frequency (F), intensity (I), and duration (D): FID. How frequently does this rash appear? (*I never had it before.*) How intense is the itching? (*Getting worse, fairly painful.*) How long have you experienced the rash and the itching? (*About 10 days*). Clinical psychologists and psychiatrists also use the logic of FID to help with differential diagnoses related to whether anxiety, for example, is due to a specific phobia or to a more generalized anxiety disorder (D'Avanzato et al., 2013). FID is just a start, of course, but sometimes it's enough.

However, there is always a risk of being wrong.

The Power of the Situation: Wait Times

Meanwhile, the ugly little blisters on your arm and neck are starting to pop.

Social psychologists recognize that there is more to getting a proper diagnosis than just the objective symptoms. For example, the situation in the waiting room can influence a physician's diagnosis. If the waiting room is empty, then your doctor might be eager for a little mental stimulation. They will want an interesting case that takes advantage of all those years of logical training.

However, if the waiting room is crammed with frantic people, crying babies, and unhappy patients, then your doctor may be tempted to use the intuitive, first response that comes to mind so they can move you along and get to their next patient. Wait times are a big issue in the world of diagnostics, perceptions of patient satisfaction, and actual care (see Jennings et al., 2015; Waters et al., 2016).

Intuition in Medical Diagnoses

Untrained friends and family seem to enjoy diagnosing medical problems.

However, they don't use differentials or the Rule of FID. If you happen to mention just one of your symptoms, then their technique is usually based on the "someone who" approach: "I knew someone who had this problem, and here's what happened." Such friendly diagnoses seem to be given confidently, especially when the speaker is also the "someone who." Differential diagnoses tend to be cautious rather than confident, looking for more data rather than getting excited about one symptom.

Amanda Woolley and Olga Kostopoulou (2013) looked more closely into the role of medical intuition. They started their case study with a specific warning: "The clinical literature advises physicians not to trust their intuition" (p. 60). But they also pointed out that the medical literature's understanding of intuition equates intuition with early impressions, the first diagnosis that comes to mind.

Woolley and Kostopoulou (2013) hypothesized that family physicians experience intuition from multiple sources, not just early impressions. Furthermore, doctors can't turn off their intuitions like a light switch. If something is nagging at them, then they can't help but listen. They may be skeptical about their intuition, but even when a nagging intuition turns out not to be helpful, it is still there for a reason. So, it pays for us to understand where intuitions come from.

Analyzing Interviews

Woolley and Kostopoulou (2013) interviewed 18 family physicians.

> A week before the scheduled interview, participants were sent a standard e-mail asking them to think of 2 occasions when they felt they knew the diagnosis or prognosis of a patient but did not know how they knew: one case for which their

feeling was correct and one for which it was incorrect. We requested 2 cases to overcome an anticipated bias to recall only positive instances. (p. 62)

Their analyses were more complicated than their procedures because they were dealing with qualitative data that could be interpreted in several ways. Fortunately, there are methods that help reduce the possibility of interpretive bias. Such methods typically involve raters who are blind to the hypothesis and rely on independent judgments made by people not allowed to speak with one another.

In this case, Woolley and Kostopoulou used an approach called the **critical decision method** to analyze data from interviews (Hoffman et al., 1998). Here, interview answers from content experts (like the physicians) are coded with multiple passes by the researchers. Answers are broken down into key phases or decision points. How exactly did the physicians decide what to do—and what helped them get it right?

Results and Discussion

Their analyses found that family physicians experienced three kinds of intuition.

Gut Feelings

"Gut feelings" was the most common way to experience intuition (50% of the reported cases).

First there was an initial impression based on the patient's medical chart or their expressed reason for being there. Early impressions are the kind of intuition that the medical literature says cannot be trusted. Gut feelings, as these physicians used the term, were different.

Their gut feeling intuitions signaled an alarm because "something didn't seem right," and it cast doubt over the first impression. The intensity of gut feelings was strong enough for these doctors to make an assessment that contradicted their rational training.

Recognitions

They termed a second type of intuition "recognitions."

They selected the term because it represented a subtle but important difference compared to gut feelings. With recognitions, "Physicians were aware of conflicting information and/or the absence of key symptoms and signs" (Woolley & Kostopoulou, 2013, p. 63). They also were aware that colleagues might disagree with them. One physician reported that his rational guidance about one patient was to interpret the symptoms as an anxiety attack—but that he kept thinking about chest pain. The patient turned out to have heart disease; the intuition had been correct.

Insights

They named a third type of intuition "insights."

In this type of intuition, there was no apparent pattern of symptoms or clues that led to a diagnosis. However, insight seemed to occur after several possibilities had been considered and then discarded through the process of a differential diagnosis. But then a clear interpretation occurred to the physician that made sense of all the symptoms and signs. One physician reported that "it suddenly flashed in my head. Something I'd read some-where . . . something about lupus connected with celiac disease. And so I got really excited" (Woolley & Kostopoulou, 2013, p. 64).

The Diagnostic Trade-Off: Speed Versus Accuracy

Meanwhile, you're still itchy and uncomfortable.

Diagnosing your now gross-looking skin rash may not require much more time, but skin diseases can be tricky. Consulting the Internet tells you that your rash is consistent with herpes simplex, herpes zoster, poison ivy, and bed bugs. Do you want your doctor to use a slow but rational differential diagnostic process that prolongs your discomfort, or take the risk that a fast, intuitive diagnosis and treatment doesn't make matters worse?

Figure 4.2 tells us about three sources of intuition identified by the science of social cognition. Priming, experience, and heuristics all have the same effect of allowing something to come more easily to mind. Priming means that thinking about something once makes it easier to think about it again later. Experience, however, may be intuition's best teacher (see Case 4.1). If you have a lot of experience with something, you are pre-primed to go to the next step. **Heuristics** have the same effect. They are mental shortcuts that make it easier to get to an answer—but not always the correct one.

Priming, experience, and heuristics all have one thing in common: mental accessibility. All three make it easier for certain ideas to come more easily to mind. Hopefully, the effect of all those years of medical training has made it easier for the right diagnosis to come more easily to your doctor's mind.

FIGURE 4.2

Three Frequent Sources of Intuition: Priming, Experience, and Heuristics

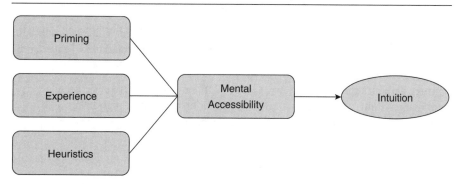

Dual Processing Diagnoses

Differential diagnoses that combine logic and intuition are like learning to tell the difference between identical twins.

If you know both twins well, then it's not much of a problem; they each have developed tells that signal their identities. Twin 1 tends to smile out of the side of her mouth, clears the hair away from her face with her left hand, and wears casual clothes. Twin 2 has a fully balanced smile, straightens up to clear the hair away from her face, and is a snappy dresser. You may not be able to articulate what it is about one twin that tells you who it is, but your brain conducts a rapid, intuitive differential diagnosis. You confidently declare, "Twin 1 is Anita."

Woolley and Kostopoulou (2013) were cautious about the implications of their study. They noted the higher prevalence of "gut feeling" intuitions and compared it to a similar sensation of slowing down reported by surgeons "who realize that they need to be more deliberative at a certain moment during an operation but cannot always explain why" (p. 64; see also Moulton et al., 2010).

Whatever called, dual processing that combines logic and intuition is your best bet as your physician tries to diagnose and then treat those annoying blisters on your arm and neck.

DISCUSSION QUESTIONS

1. This case study mentions that dual processing is useful for mental health diagnoses (such as anxiety), as well as medical diagnoses. Identify two additional mental health issues that would benefit from a doctor or therapist who uses both intuition and logic to help a client, and explain how each type of thinking could be used.

2. Identify a specific area or talent that you, personally, have, in which you feel that intuition guides your thoughts and behaviors (e.g., athletics, music, studying). Explain how the three variables that contribute to mental accessibility (priming, experience, and heuristics) each contribute to your enhanced intuition in this particular context.

3. Several of the doctors mentioned that they believed their intuition might lead to a diagnosis their colleagues would disagree with. How do you react when you have a gut feeling that your friends or family seem to disagree with? Do you

   a. doubt your intuition, thinking that they might be right after all;

   b. stick to your intuition, telling yourself that you have more information and experience than they do? Or

   c. tell them that you have a persistent intuition and ask for their help explaining it.

KEY TERMS

- **Dual processing**: The ability to make decisions using both intuition and logic
- **Differential diagnosis**: A medical strategy in which doctors systematically rule out possible explanations for someone's symptoms until left with a single answer

- **Critical decision method**: A technique when interviewing content experts designed to understand how they make decisions via key phases or decision points
- **Heuristics**: Mental shortcuts we make through intuition

4.3 GIRL OR BOY? GENDER SOCIALIZATION BEGINS AT ULTRASOUND

The Social Situation

Our culture teaches us who to be, from our very first moments.

These notes are from Kara Smith's (2005) case study titled "Prebirth gender talk."

From the moment of birth, one of the first questions a new parent is asked is, "Is it a boy or a girl?" In the hospital, girls are wrapped in pink blankets and boys in blue. Pink potted flowers arrive for mothers of daughters and blue vases and balloons for mothers of sons. Boys are described as "big," "strong," and "independent"; girls as "fine," "gentle," and "beautiful" (O'Reilly, 1988; Ricks, 1985; Thompson, 1975).

Theory and Method

U.S. culture has only recently recognized a **sexual spectrum**, in which there may be more than two sexes.

Beyond just male or female, there are actually other options—and those options are probably more common than you think. **Intersex** individuals, or those who have unusual hormone or chromosome combinations, make up about 1.7% of the general population (www.intersexequality.com), making them about as common as people with red hair.

Most people assume a new birth means a new little boy or little girl. However, Kara Smith (2005) uses a narrative case study to investigate when gender socialization begins. Smith is the first-person author of her own case study, based on notes from her second pregnancy. So this case study also uses introspection as she writes and sometime later reviews her own notes.

Smith is also an accomplished education researcher and expert scholar in Women's Studies. She was as likely as anyone to be able to recognize and resist the impulse for gender socialization. She explained why she recorded and then reported her observations as an expectant mother:

When I was pregnant with my first child, I began to address the child differently following an ultrasound identifying its sex. This bothered me, and yet I could not consciously control, nor identify, the gender socialization that was taking place. Thus, when my second child was in utero, I began to document what was said to the child and what feelings were transmitted to the child both before and after a sex-identifying ultrasound in an effort to more fully understand the gender socialization process taking place as early as pregnancy.

Results and Discussion

After delivery, Smith eventually reviewed her field notes (Smith, 2005).

She wrote these notes as comments to herself, like a journal, but also to her baby. She was not conscious, at first, of how much her feelings and behaviors changed after learning of the baby's sex. For example, here are two entries from the third month, prior to ultrasound:

> Hi you, I can feel you moving around in there. Are you going to be an active one? I have lots of upset stomach with you.

> Everyone wants to know if you'll be a girl or a boy. Because I have started to fill out to the sides, instead of out front, this time, they say you'll be a girl, but who knows.

The second comment seemed curious because the baby already had a certain sex, based on its chromosomes. "They say you'll be a girl" should be "They say you are a girl." Smith sees this kind of language as a social signal that a baby without a sexual identification seems to lack a certain amount of personhood, "it" rather than "he" or "she."

> I do not think of the baby as one sex or another. It is an androgynous being to me, the "baby" is much like a "plant." No genitals, no gender. I imagine it growing and developing, like a "plant." I "rub my belly clockwise," send it mental 'hugs of love', and talk to it, but "it" is only "it," or "little one"—a nameless, colorless being with no label.

That hint of an unwelcome attitude in herself reappeared more clearly when comparing her notes taken just before and just after learning the baby's sex. After learning that "it" was "a boy," she expressed more triumphant, stereotypically male emotions after this discovery.

> When I said, "you'll show them," you really did! Your Daddy was so surprised. Another little boy! Now your brother will have someone to play with.

Apparently, an older brother would not be able to play with a younger sister. Reviewing her own notes, Smith was surprised at her own reactions.

Prior to the ultrasound, I say to the baby, "we're going to find out who you are today." This implies that if I do not know his sex, I do not "know who s/he is." That is, "knowing the sex" somehow indicates what type of personality the baby will possess. I was surprised to read this statement in the field notes.... Without thinking, I wait to hear the sex, then, and only then, begin to use established gender stereotypes to label "who s/he is."

Her field notes indicated how her use of nonverbal language changed after the identifying ultrasound in the sixth month of pregnancy. Her first self-observation was that her tone of voice changed after learning it was a boy:

Suddenly, there was less tenderness in the way I addressed the baby. He was a boy. He was "stronger" now than the child I had known only one minute before. He did not need to be addressed with such light and fluffy language, such as, "little one."

She noticed also how her attitude changed. Knowing that "it" was a "he" meant that he "did not need to be coddled." She needed to lower her voice and reprimanded herself because,

I had been too gentle and careful with him. He must be tough and strong.... The tone in my words was more articulate and short, whereas, before, the pitch in my voice was high and feminine.

She noticed other vocal changes.

I wanted him to be "strong" and "athletic," therefore, I had to speak to him with a stereotypical "strong," "masculine" voice to encourage this "innate strength." Thus, I lowered my voice to a deeper octave. It lost its tenderness.

Her field notes revealed that she had changed in many other subtle, but to her important, gender stereotypical ways after the ultrasound announced "Boy!" Kara Smith's (2005) candid case study forced her to confront herself in unexpected ways.

Was I, someone who lectured on the ill-effects of gender socialization, inadvertently engendering my own child? As it turns out, I was, and I was doing so even while being conscious of it. How early did the gender socialization for my own children begin? Their socialization began the moment their sex was known, or, during the second trimester of the pregnancy, in utero.

DISCUSSION QUESTIONS

1. This case study highlights how an expecting mother changed how she thought about and behaved toward a fetus that was to become a boy (not a girl). What differences might have occurred if the ultrasound revealed that the fetus might be an intersex individual? How would Smith's own parents, friends, and colleagues might have responded if, when they asked her if the baby was a boy or girl, she responded, "The baby doesn't fit into that gender dichotomy?"

2. Look at baby pictures of yourself (or, if those aren't available, baby pictures posted online). Is it obvious if the baby is a boy or girl, simply based on how it is dressed or the props in the photo? Why do parents feel the need to make their baby's gender obvious?

3. Think about your favorite games or toys when you were little. Were they things typical for children of your sex? If not, did other children ever show negative reactions to your preferences? If so, why do you think you liked those games or toys—do you think it had anything to do with your culture or your parents?

KEY TERMS

- **Sexual spectrum**: The idea that sex and gender are continuous, not categorical variables, and that there are more classifications than simple male or female

- **Intersex**: Individuals who are neither traditionally male nor female, because of either atypical prenatal hormones or atypical chromosome patterns

4.4 SEXUAL SCRIPTS AND SEXUAL REGRETS

The Social Situation

Sex got your attention in two ways.

First, you noticed your own sexuality as your body matured (nature). Second, from childhood onward, you observed the sexual attitudes and behaviors of the people all around you (nurture). Social cognition is concerned with human sexuality because few behaviors have the potential to shape our lives more deeply than sex.

Sex is a social act. Even if there are only two of you in a room, each brain populates that room with social influences. They include other people's expectations, social norms, fashion statements, attitudes, self-esteem, impression management, images from romantic movies, and much more. Sometimes it can feel noisy and crowded in a room with just two people.

Theory and Method

How did you learn how to have sex?

The same way you learned how to read. Sort of. Notice that you don't have to relearn how to read every time you pick up a book. Why? You have **schemas** that organize your ability to read. Your memory structures contain information about how marks on a piece of paper represent letters that represent sounds that can be combined into words and then into sentences that have purpose and meaning. Your schemas are so firmly built that you would have difficulty looking at a book and *not* reading the words.

Sexual Scripts

You also have acquired schemas that tell you how to have sex.

Schemas are mental structures that organize information (Bartlett, 1932; Poldrack & Yarkoni, 2016). **Scripts** are one type of schema that tells you the expected sequences of events in particular locations or at particular events. You may experience only one or two marriage proposals in your entire life, but you still know how they usually go.

For example, your marriage script probably looks something like this: one person buys a ring, kneels as they present ring, requests marriage. In a heterosexual couple, it's probably the man paying for the ring and initiating the proposal. You don't have to follow this script in your own life. But every culture has some shared knowledge about the "proper" way to make a marriage proposal.

Sexual scripts theory explains how we acquire the mental habits we use to think about and guide our sexual behavior (see Gagnon & Simon, 1987; Laumann et al., 1994; Weiderman, 2005). For example, a widely shared script about consensual sex begins with kissing and then proceeds in a predictable sequence to other parts of the body (see Gagnon & Simon, 1987; Laumann et al., 1994; Weiderman, 2005). It may feel spontaneous when it is happening to you, but you are probably following some culturally acquired sexual script.

The Biological Imperative

Why do you have sex?

Because you want to. Most people have sex, eventually, and for most people it feels great (or at least could be great). But from an **evolutionary psychology** perspective, sex is a "biological imperative." We need to keep doing it to perpetuate the species. Sex also organizes societies into laws and informal rules (Marshall, 2020). And evolutionary psychology assumes that (1) people are heterosexual and (2) they want to have and nurture children.

Obviously, these two big assumptions are simply not true for thousands, if not millions, of people on the planet. But the idea of evolutionary psychology is to think about how human instincts have evolved over countless generations. Genes that led people to survive longer and have more sexual opportunities are more likely to be passed on—and genes that led people to die early and have fewer sexual opportunities will get washed out of the gene pool.

So, for the majority of humans (heterosexuals who want kids), sexual instincts really matter. And it appears that it also matters if you are a man or a woman, in terms of your sexual strategies. Step 1 to having children is making a pregnancy happen.

Sexual strategies theory helps explain sex differences in the rules of sexual behavior. **Sexual strategies theory** (see Buss & Schmitt, 1993) recognizes that a woman confronts a much greater obligatory **parental investment** (at least 9 months) in producing children. A pregnancy is serious business for her—important decisions have to be made, and relatively quickly.

On the other hand, a man who has contributed to a pregnancy faces a much lower obligation to parental investment. He doesn't have to carry the fetus, and if a baby is born, he's not expected to breastfeed it. So from an evolutionary point of view, having sex is potentially far more consequential for women than for men.

Results and Discussion

Sexual regrets expose the different social rules of sexual conduct for women and men.

Sexual regrets develop when we sense that we have broken one of the informal rules or social norms of sexual conduct. High parental investment accurately predicts that women are more likely than men to regret having sex with low-quality partners. That is seldom a problem for men. Perhaps women have an instinct to have higher standards for sexual partners than men, because of the risk of pregnancy they have with each sexual encounter. Note that one way around this is to engage in other kinds of sexual contact, such as oral sex (see Eshbaugh & Gute, 2008).

Men's comparatively low parental investment leads men to seek out sex with lower standards. They are more likely to regret missed sexual opportunities (see Fisher et al., 2012). These double-standard gender differences in regrets over sexual behavior appear to apply even in relatively permissive cultures (e.g., Norwegian society; see Kennair et al., 2016).

Anatomy and Culture Lead to Different Sexual Scripts

Weiderman (2005, p. 497) suggests that sexual scripts begin with anatomy.

Boys' genitals are easily viewed, and boys are taught to handle their penis for urination—it's nothing to be afraid of and, if you pee in the snow, it's sort of interesting and fun. Girls' genitals are hidden from their own view, and girls are taught to clean themselves carefully after urination. It's difficult to pee in the snow, and probably not considered (much less associated with) fun.

> The end result? Boys and girls are given two subtly different sets of messages regarding their own genitals. Boys readily discover that their genitals feel good when handled and are not necessarily any "dirtier" than other parts of their body that they can see. Girls readily learn that their genitals are difficult, if not impossible, for them to see and that there are "dirty" aspects that require appropriate precautionary measures. (Weiderman, 2005, p. 497)

Culture (and parents) also reinforce different sexual scripts for women and for men. For example, boys are encouraged to be independent and assertive; daughters to exercise restraint and self-control. Parents tend to provide their daughters with more information about sex, information that is often accompanied by warnings (Fisher, 1986). Men are encouraged to get out into society and explore.

The result of these differing anatomical and cultural messages is that women and men develop different sexual scripts. Women are instructed to play the scripted role of **sexual gatekeeper**, angling for a man who understands long-term parental investment. The idea is to only make sex available to a partner after he has made some show of commitment, like saying "I love you" or offering monogamy. Men, on the other hand, are instructed to play the scripted role of independent explorer, free to "play the field" before eventually settling down.

Perplexing Differences

The differences in women's and men's sexual scripts can create relationship problems.

"Young adult men," Weiderman (2005) observed, "who have not realized that their female peers hold a different set of sexual scripts are often perplexed" (p. 499). Table 4.1 summarizes several of the insights that emerge when we apply sexual scripts theory to heterosexual relationships.

TABLE 4.1

Gendered Sexual Scripts

The Female Sexual Script	The Male Sexual Script
Women with a strong interest in sex may be labeled as deviant or desperate.	Men with a strong interest in sex may be labeled as an adventurous go-getter.
The woman's role is often to limit and manage sex.	The man's role is often to outwit her defenses.
There may be high costs for having sex.	There may be few costs for having sex.
The woman plays the role of the sexual gatekeeper.	The man plays the role of the sexual adventurer.
Women tend to count the number of sexual partners carefully.	Men tend to "round up" when making numerical estimates of sexual partners.
Desire for a relationship increases after a sexual conquest.	Desire for a relationship declines after a sexual conquest.

Source: Based on Wiederman (2005).

Weiderman (2005, p. 500) approaches sexual script theory from a therapist's perspective. The goal is to help clients recognize that men and women often follow different sexual scripts learned from their cultures. That insight alone can help normalize some difficulties couples typically encounter in the bedroom. Rather than validate one partners' script over the other's, therapists can challenge the couple to construct their own shared sexual scripts.

A Unifying Purpose

The fact that women and men having different sexual scripts is not a deal breaker.

People persist in finding ways to have sex, to discover and apply their culture's sexual scripts. Our species is not stopped from having sex by forbidding religious dogmas, immigration laws, cultural differences, sexual regrets, or social norms. And certainly, lots of people have sex outside of heterosexual relationships and/or for purposes other than having children.

Easy access to birth control has also changed the culture in terms of sexual expectations. But evolutionary psychology argues that our biological instincts are the legacy of generations past, when condoms weren't even invented. Couples have consistently looked for alternative methods of birth control such as withdrawal (see Fisher & Szreter, 2003) and rhythm (see Weibe et al., 2004)—with limited success. It will be interesting to see how sexual scripts change as each generation sees sex and relationships in new ways.

DISCUSSION QUESTIONS

1. Some couples who have sex with the hope of creating a pregnancy experience a negative side effect of feeling that the sex is no longer as romantic or pleasurable—it might start feeling like a chore or a means to an end. How might these couples reframe their sexual activities to increase enjoyment again?

2. Many people criticize evolutionary psychology's hypotheses as inherently sexist and heterosexist. Critically analyze this argument—do you agree with it? Why, or why not? How might evolutionary theory explain homosexual, pansexual, and asexual individuals?

3. The discussion of this case study notes that sexual scripts may change quickly as culture changes, which is an idea contrary to evolutionary psychology. Which explanation (evolution or culture) do you find more persuasive in explaining most people's scripts and expectations for sexual encounters?

KEY TERMS

- **Schemas**: Mental structures or frameworks that help us organize the world and remember events

- **Scripts**: A schema for the expected order of events at a specific event or location, such as a wedding or funeral

- **Sexual scripts theory**: The idea that our sexual behaviors are guided by habits or expectations created by culture
- **Evolutionary psychology**: A subfield that examines human thought and behavior in terms of Darwinian principles such as natural selection and sexual selection
- **Sexual strategies theory**: The idea that heterosexual men and women make choices in mate selection based on evolutionary instincts
- **Parental investment**: The amount of time, effort, and resources required for someone to successfully reproduce a child
- **Sexual gatekeeper**: The idea that women will be more hesitant to engage in sexual activities because of potential pregnancy and the responsibilities that go with pregnancy

Person Perception

5.1 "TELL ME THE TRUTH—AM I TOO PRETTY?"
MARILYN MONROE AND THE HALO EFFECT

The Social Situation

Marilyn Monroe was that kind of beautiful.

Movie star Marilyn Monroe (1926–1962) started life as plain Norma Jeane Mortenson. The identity of her biological father was unclear, and her mother, Gladys, spent most of her adult life in-and-out of a state mental hospital, diagnosed with paranoid schizophrenia. One of her grandfathers died of syphilis, which invaded his brain.

Marilyn Monroe had a hard childhood.

What the Family Believed

Marilyn Monroe may have believed that she was destined to become mentally ill.

The result of knowing her family's history, according to Monroe's biographer (Spoto, 1993), was that the entire family believed that most of them were afflicted with serious mental disorders. Marilyn Monroe seemed to confirm that belief when she died from a barbiturates overdose, and many consider that she committed suicide.

Spoto (1993), however, dug deeper into the Monroe family's medical records than any family member ever had. The grandfather's syphilis was probably "not of the type contracted through sexual activity but through the dangerously unsanitary, virus-infested conditions in which he had worked in Mexico." And her mother never displayed any of the classic symptoms of paranoid schizophrenia. Depression, possibly, but not schizophrenia. Spoto suggests that the family story of severe mental illness may have been a fiction, or at least a misunderstanding.

Norma Jeane was working in a defense plant factory when an army photographer took her picture. She soon signed a contract with a modeling agency, dyed her dark, curly hair, and started calling herself Marilyn Monroe. She became the iconic-looking "blonde bombshell" that decorated soldiers' barracks. She soon started appearing in movies.

Becoming Marilyn Monroe

She usually played the stereotypical dumb blonde.

However, she also recognized that her beauty gave her social power. She skillfully leveraged that power. In business, she defeated the entrenched studio system in Hollywood. She reached even higher and developed a controversial personal relationship with the president of the United States. But her physical attractiveness was a two-edged sword.

Monroe had to fight within herself, with others, with the movie system, and with the general public to be taken seriously. However, scriptwriters slowly began to recognize the intelligence lurking within the blonde bombshell with a gift for comedic timing. In the film *Gentlemen Prefer Blondes* (1953), she is accused by a wealthy father of dating his son for his money.

Son: I love her. I've never had a feeling like this.

Father: Oh, shut up! [To MM] Young lady, you don't fool me one bit.

MM: I'm not trying to. But I bet I could, though.

Father: No, you might convince this jackass that you love him but you'll never convince me.

MM: [To the son] That's too bad, because I do love you.

Father: Certainly. For his money.

MM: No. Honestly.

Father: Have you got the nerve to stand there and expect me to believe that you don't want to marry my son for his money?

MM: It's true.

Father: Then what do you want to marry him for?

MM: I want to marry him for *your* money. [pause] Don't you know that a man being rich is like a girl being pretty? You wouldn't marry a girl just because she's pretty, but my goodness, doesn't it help?

Theory and Method

This case study relies on multiple theories and recent archival data to help explain Marilyn Monroe's unusual life and tragic death. The "experts" in any age have perceived people with mental illness according to the dominant theory of their time (see Appignanesi, 2008). The "raving lunatic" in one era or culture might be locked away but credited as a genius in another time and place. Monroe's death spawned numerous conspiracy theories (suggesting murder), as well as clinical-psychological (suicide) and narcotic (accidental overdose) explanations for her death.

This teaching case study adds data-driven social psychological insights to the explanations.

Psychoanalytic Explanations

There's no doubt about it: **psychoanalytic theory** is interesting.

Sometimes weird, to be sure. But that and the breadth of Sigmund Freud's vision are probably what has contributed to his enduring influence. However the bigger problem with psychoanalysis is that it is so difficult—and often impossible—to test its explanations.

Still, those psychoanalytic explanations influenced Marilyn Monroe. She lived from 1926 to 1962, a time when Freudian theory was the dominant perspective in the world of counseling and mental health. That view of the human condition was combined with the emergence of new and powerful drug therapies. While she was alive, Monroe communicated with psychologist Anna Freud, Sigmund Freud's famous daughter. The Freudian view of life must have influenced how Marilyn Monroe perceived herself.

One postmortem psychological diagnosis of Monroe described her as a "psychoanalytic pathography of a preoedipal" (Chessick, 1983)—a Freudian approach that focuses on a lost parental attachment. It sounds as dramatic as Marilyn Monroe's difficult childhood and multiple marriages. Whether or not Freudian explanations fit, those early life experiences probably did have some effect on how Marilyn Monroe/Norma Jeane understood herself.

Archival Data

Social psychology tries to ground its theories in testable observations.

A recent approach to understanding Marilyn Monroe relies on archival data she supplied through personal notes, letters, and poems she wrote (see Fernández-Cabana

TABLE 5.1

When Monroe's Writing Is Analyzed, Four Distinct Periods of Her Life Seem to Emerge

Time Period	Words / # Entries = # Words per Entry	Life Events
1943–1951	2,341 / 8 = 292	From her first marriage to her first film success
1952–1955	2,838 / 15 = 189	Marriage to and divorce from baseball player Joe DiMaggio, founding her production company, classes at Actors Studio, first contact with psychoanalysis
1956–1959	2,786 / 21 = 133	Marriage to playwright Arthur Miller
1960–1962	3,806 / 6 = 634	Psychoanalysis with Dr. Greenson, divorce from Arthur Miller, difficulties in meeting her work commitments, brief psychiatric admissions, and relationships with J. F. and R. F. Kennedy

Source: Fernández-Cabana et al. (2013).

FIGURE 5.1

Mean Number of Words in Marilyn Monroe's Writing Across Four
Time Periods

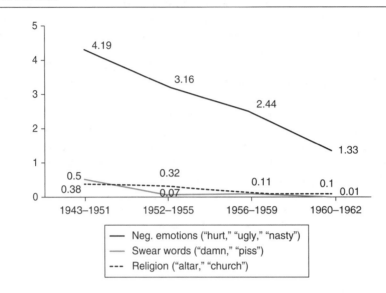

Source: Fernández-Cabana et al. (2013).

et al., 2013). The technique relies on a computerized text analysis that language researchers call Linguistic Inquiry and Word Count (LIWC).

These researchers identified four distinct periods in Monroe's adult life. A collection of the materials containing those words was published (many for the first time)
in the book *Fragments* (Buchthal & Comment, 2010). This archival data approach to
understanding her life allowed them to apply LIWC to conduct a **content analysis** of
Monroe's writings across the four life stages shown in Table 5.1 and Figure 5.1.

The researchers counted the number of words, entries, and words per entry for each
period. The research team also analyzed Monroe's writing according to the use of words
with more than six letters, personal pronouns, third-person plural pronouns, swear words,
words related to negative emotions, and words related to religion.

Results and Discussion

One of the chief goals of any theory is to explain observations.

Social psychologists are always looking for **parsimony,** an interpretation of data that
explains patterns as simply as possible, but no simpler. Social psychological theories are
grounded in data. These social psychological explanations for Marilyn Monroe's life
may provide simple and accurate, but still incomplete, explanations for her unusual life
and mysterious death.

What Is Beautiful Is Good

We're biased when it comes to perceiving physically attractive people.

Social psychology has established that physically attractive people enjoy a bright **halo effect,** which is when a single trait in a person affects our entire impression of them (in this case, their attractiveness). Their attractive "glow" shines in a way that we perceive them (often unfairly) to have other positive traits as well. This includes crediting them with being not only smarter (Clifford & Walster, 1973) but also deserving of higher salaries and more raises (Frieze et al., 1991).

That's unfair, of course. But the beauty bias doesn't end there. Beautiful people also are given lighter prison sentences if they should get caught committing a crime (Gunnell & Ceci, 2010). But why should they?

Why commit crimes when physically attractive people are more likely to be given scholarships (Agthe et al., 2010), get more friend requests on Facebook from strangers (Wang et al., 2010), and get more opportunities to practice their social skills (Feingold, 1992). Being physically attractive also leads to a vague assumption of moral goodness called the **what-is-beautiful-is-good effect**.

Physically attractive people have a few problems that don't plague the rest of us. First, they sometimes have difficulty diagnosing the sincerity of compliments (Carrington & Carnevale, 1984). Second, highly attractive women do not always report having higher self-esteem (Fleming & Courtney, 1984; Marsh & Richards, 1988). Third, being "too pretty" might lead to jealousy and discrimination against the beautiful by others competing for scarce resources such as jobs (e.g., Agthe et al., 2010).

Marilyn Monroe may have grown weary of the beauty bias and its constant attention. Yet she demonstrated remarkable **self-insight,** the ability to understand one's own motivations and behavior. And that self-insight gave her insight into how others perceived her and her fame. She wrote

> I've never fooled anyone. I've let people fool themselves. They didn't bother to find out who and what I was. Instead they would invent a character for me. I wouldn't argue with them. They were obviously loving somebody I wasn't.

Age Discrimination and Self-Fulfilling Prophecies

Physical beauty fades.

Hollywood has a long history of **age discrimination,** working against women in particular. Nancy Etcoff (1999) writes in the book, *Survival of the Prettiest,* that "physical beauty is like athletic skill: It peaks young" (p. 63). Marilyn Monroe was only 36 when she took her own life. Fashion model Lauren Hutton explained why so many starlets tend to age out of entertainment in their mid-thirties: "As soon as they were out of eggs, women were out of business" (see Etcoff, 1999, p. 73; Gross, 2011, p. 222). Aging in an industry that doesn't like older women was only one of her problems.

When Spoto (1993) looked into Marilyn Monroe's family (on her mother's side), he found more than physical beauty. He found a self-perception that did not match the medical record—the belief that serious mental health problems ran deep in the family's history. And perhaps they did. But the subtle work of a self-fulfilling prophecy also may have influenced the tragic course of Marilyn Monroe's life. She believed in her own propensity for mental illness, and her beliefs became her reality.

We will never know whether these social psychological explanations provide a simpler, more realistic explanation of the life and death of Norma Jeane Mortenson. But there is one more way to try to understand her.

We could just ask her.

Content Analysis of Archival Data

We're not talking about communicating with the dead.

We are asserting a place for content analysis of archival data. The content analysis of Marilyn Monroe's own written words doesn't answer all our questions. But it helps. The most prominent pattern is that her use of negative emotion words (not shown in Figure 5.1) steadily declined across the four life periods identified in the study.

At the same time, the number of her words increased dramatically in the last, shorter period of her life (shown in Figure 5.1). Her use of singular first-person pronouns ("I") increased, while the plural version ("we") decreased. The research team noted that several of these trends were consistent with some theories of suicide, but that is hardly definitive.

Untestable theories can appear to explain anything. The psychodynamic theorists tried to understand Norma Jeane Mortenson through a particular theoretical lens. They voiced confident declarations based on a grand psychodynamic theory of hidden (and therefore untestable) motivations and fears. By contrast, the language researchers reached limited, evidence-driven conclusions based on what they acknowledge is helpful but thin, archival data. Social psychology often offers simpler, less comprehensive explanations. But those explanations are usually grounded in more established scientific findings such as halo effects, age discrimination, and self-fulfilling prophecies.

There is a critical question for all of us as we try to understand the life and death of Norma Jeane Mortenson. Do we prefer to believe grand, comprehensive explanations that cannot be tested or limited explanations based on observable patterns?

DISCUSSION QUESTIONS

1. Which way of knowing about Marilyn Monroe do you think is more effective: the psychodynamic approach or the linguistic analysis using archival data such as poems and journals? What are the strengths and weaknesses of each?

2. What are the advantages of using a case study approach to understanding Marilyn Monroe, the life she lived, and the decisions that she made? How useful is the social history of that time period, for example?

3. Is the what-is-beautiful-is-good effect real? List some ways that you see beauty bias operating in the people and events you are familiar with (in other words, think of real examples you've seen in your own life). Try to identify at least two specific ways that being physically attractive seems to be beneficial for people, as well as at least two specific ways that being attractive may be a *dis*advantage.

KEY TERMS

- **Psychoanalytic theory**: Explanations for behavior based on a traditional Freudian perspective, such as unconscious sexual desires
- **Content analysis**: An approach to archival data that looks for patterns and trends in the words someone used
- **Parsimony**: An interpretation of data that explains patterns as simply as possible, but no simpler
- **Halo effect**: When a single trait in a person affects our overall impression of them

- **What-is-beautiful-is-good effect**: The tendency to perceive physically attractive people as having moral goodness and other positive qualities
- **Self-insight**: The ability to understand one's own motivations and behavior
- **Age discrimination**: Negative behaviors or policies toward people simply because of their age

5.2 FROM STREET KID TO MAGICIAN: SELF-FULFILLING PROPHECIES

The Social Situation

Robert Merton had a knack for naming things.

He even re-named himself—more than once. He was born Meyer R. Schkolnick, the child of immigrant parents from Eastern Europe. He was just one of thousands of street kids living in South Philadelphia.

But the adult Merton, with the sociologist's insistence on precise language, was not comfortable with calling his neighborhood a slum. South Philadelphia was full of **social capital** that could be spent by taking advantage of nearby cultural and educational opportunities.

The family home was in rooms "above my father's newly acquired milk-butter-and-egg shop." It was uninsured, however, and after it was destroyed in a fire, they moved to a smaller, red-brick row house. That small house had everything a young boy with lots of curiosity could want.

His new home had a dining room where he built a crystal radio. There was a kitchen with a coal-burning stove, even an outhouse in the back yard. More important, his mother made sure their home was "fueled with the unquestioned premise that things would somehow get better, surely so for the children" (Merton, 1994, pp. 3–4). Robert Merton would live up to his mother's belief in him.

Theory and Method

This case study follows the life course of Robert Merton.

The **life course perspective** is a general theory used by many disciplines to understand how time and social structures affect people's lives. Its formal beginnings are associated with Karl Mannheim's (1923/1952) essay about how social problems are sustained across generations (see Pilcher, 1994). Developmental psychologists also have focused on the timing and social context of life events (see Elder et al., 2003; Elder & Rockwell, 1979).

Most of the personal information about Robert Merton's life comes from a speech in 1994 to the American Council of Learned Societies, the Charles Homer Haskins Lecture. Merton was the first sociologist to be honored by this group. The event took place at the Benjamin Franklin Hall of the American Philosophical Society in Philadelphia. It was within walking distance from the home in which Merton was born 84 years earlier.

Geography: An Opportunity Structure

Many called South Philadelphia a slum.

But in retrospect, Merton realized that South Philadelphia's geographical advantages taught him something important about education: "much consequential education takes place outside the walls of classrooms" (p. 4). He told his lecture audience that

> I had a private library of some 10,000 volumes, located just a few blocks from our house, a library thoughtfully bestowed upon me by that ultimately beneficent robber baron, Andrew Carnegie. The neighborhood was secure enough for me to make my way alone to that library of mine from the tender age of five or six. (p. 4)

That local public library exposed the growing boy to alternative lives. It allowed him to travel with the help of friendly librarians. He could also listen to the famed Philadelphia orchestra from the 25-cent cheap seats in the concert hall a few blocks away. He described the urban village of South Philadelphia as an "opportunity structure" because so many cultural resources were within walking distance. South Philadelphia had everything except financial capital. Merton observed that the

> seemingly deprived South Philadelphia slum was providing a youngster with every sort of capital—social capital, cultural capital, human capital, and above all, what we may call public capital. (p. 7)

From Street Kid to Magician

Geography conspired with chance after Merton's father lost his job at the Navy yard. They moved, and their new young neighbor, Charles Hopkins or "Hop," stopped by with a strange question: Had they seen his pet mice and rabbits? It was not the most elegant introduction. Hop was courting Merton's older sister (and later became her husband).

Whatever his motivation, Hop's animals were related to his real work as a magician. He soon took Merton on as his apprentice. He was a quick learner and "became fairly adept by the time I was 14." The street kid was becoming a magician. It soon would be time for a new name.

Role Models

Merton is credited with coining the phrase **role model.**

Merton personally benefitted, several times, from people whose lives he wanted to imitate. As the life course perspective anticipates, different role models were critical at different stages of his life. For example, "Hop" was an early role model. As his entertainment skills increased, Merton adopted a more famous role model: the internationally known magician and escape artist Harry Houdini.

Houdini's original name was Ehrich Weisz, and he had grown up in Appleton, Wisconsin. But when he became interested in magic, Ehrich Weisz renamed himself after the celebrated French magician Robert Houdin. So, the 14-year-old magician Meyer R. Schkolnick did the same thing. He re-named himself Robert K. Merlin (after the wizard from the King Arthur legends).

Self-Fulfilling Prophecies

Merton's skills as a prestidigitator supported him when he started college.

He went to nearby Temple College but continued to perform "at children's parties, at Sunday schools and, for part of one summer, in a small and quite unsuccessful traveling circus" (p. 8). And he changed his name. Again. This time from "Robert K. Merlin" to "Robert K. Merton"—"Bob Merton" to his college friends. By the time he finished college, Merton had renamed, relabeled, and re-created himself for a third time:

> With the warm consent of my devoted Americanizing mother—she attended night school far more religiously than the synagogue—and the bland agreement of my rather uninterested father, this was followed by the legal transformation of my name some 65 years ago. (p. 9)

Merton's mother was the energy behind a now familiar social psychological concept that Merton named: a self-fulfilling prophecy, a belief that makes itself come true. She believed, and her belief helped make it come true. Merton was learning that he could rename and relabel himself whatever he liked. He also named several social psychological effects in language that penetrated into general public use: "unanticipated consequences," "dysfunction," "the Matthew effect," and the "focused interview" (what we now call focus groups).

From Magician to Scholar

Merton found his next role model at nearby Temple College.

The college represented another form of neighborhood social capital. On one life-changing day, Merton "ventured into a class in sociology given by a young instructor, George E. Simpson, and there I found my subject" (p. 10). Simpson was working on his doctoral dissertation titled *The Negro in the Philadelphia Press*. George Simpson recognized a promising student and became Robert Merton's next role model.

Networking Opportunities

When Simpson recruited Merton, Merton said yes.

Simpson needed help in a simple but labor intensive archival research project. He was to summarize "all the references to Negroes over a span of decades in Philadelphia newspapers." In those pre-computerized days, tracking down that information represented a great deal of work. But the stories of the people embedded in that topic fascinated Merton.

Simpson used that project to create more networking opportunities by bringing him into contact with Ralph Bunche and Franklin Frazier and, some time later, with Kenneth Clark who became president of the American Psychological Association. Those connections allowed him to participate on the social science brief that influenced the famous *Brown v. Board of Education of Topeka* (1954) legal case decided by the Supreme Court.

Merton, of course, could not know the life-changing networking opportunities that were waiting for him. He had just followed his own curiosity into Simpson's classroom. But when those opportunities became available, Merton knew how to say yes.

Mentoring Opportunities

Simpson did more than plug Merton into his research topic.

Simpson took the young magician-scholar to a professional meeting of sociologists and made sure he attended particular presentations. That was where he met a remarkable scholar, Pitirim Alexandrovice Sorokin, the founding chairman of the Department of Sociology being established at Harvard. He would become another role model. Merton reported that

> I would surely not have dared apply for graduate study at Harvard had not Sorokin encouraged me to do so . . . he was the teacher I was looking for. Moreover, it was evident that Sorokin was not your ordinary academic sociologist. Imprisoned three times by czarists and then three times by the Bolsheviks, he had . . . a death sentence commuted into exile by the normally unsparing Lenin. . . . I did nervously apply to Harvard, did receive a scholarship there, and soon found myself on a new phase in a life of learning. (p. 11)

The Importance of Saying Yes

Merton now had a mentor for graduate school.

That meant, as many graduate students have learned, that he became Sorokin's research assistant, teaching assistant, "man-of-all-work," and an occasional stand-in for other responsibilities.

> Summoning me to his office one day, he announced that he had stupidly agreed to do a paper on recent French sociology for a learned society and asked if I

would be good enough to take it on in his stead. Clearly, this was less a question than an unforgiving expectation. . . . This turned out to be the first of several such unpredictable and fruitful occasions provided by the expanding opportunity structure at Harvard. (p. 11)

That project led to another, and to another, and suddenly this second-year graduate student had become a published scholar. He also developed some peculiar academic habits, based on yet another role model, named Talcott Parsons. As an instructor, Parsons had developed the habit of what Merton called "oral publication"—the working out of new ideas in lecture, seminars, and workshops.

The young magician was becoming a scholar.

Results and Discussion

Merton began to see that self-fulfilling prophecies were influencing others' lives, too.

For example, despite his impressive networking skills, Merton described himself in graduate school as an "inveterate loner working chiefly in libraries and in my study at home." He was especially reluctant to approach the well-known historian of science, George Sarton. Sarton was rumored to be such "a remote and awesome presence, so dedicated to his scholarship as to be wholly inaccessible." But looking back, Merton commented

Thus do plausible but ill-founded beliefs develop into social realities through the mechanism of the self-fulfilling prophecy. Since this forbidding scholar was unapproachable, there was no point in trying to approach him. And his subsequently having very few students only went to show how inaccessible he actually was. But when in the fall of 1933 I knocked on the door of Sarton's office in Widener Library, he did not merely invite me in; he positively ushered me in. (p. 13)

Merton had named the assumptions and subsequent behaviors leading most people to stay away from Sarton to be a self-fulfilling prophecy. However, he recognized that it was not a new idea. Merton pointed first to W. I. Thomas (see Thomas & Thomas, 1928), who asserted that "if men define situations as real, they are real in their consequences" (see also Merton, 1994). He also credited the concept to "observant and disciplined minds" in previous centuries: in the 17th century to Bishop Bossuet, in the 18th century to Mandeville in *The Fable of the Bees*, in the 19th century to Karl Marx, and in the 20th century to Freud.

Sociological Social Psychology

Merton did not grow up knowing people with social power.

His South Philadelphia upbringing did produce social connections that would ease his way through life. Nevertheless, Merton's life was rich and diverse, and the elements of his successful life were not complicated: recognizing opportunity structures, role models, self-fulfilling prophecies, and saying yes. They all were paying dividends to Merton personally. Merton reinvested those benefits back into **sociology**, an approach that, compared to social psychology, is more concerned with society than individuals and favors sociologists' methods over experimental social psychology.

Integrative Thinking and Clear Communicating

Part of Merton's success was due to his reading and communication habits.

Those wide interests were nourished at the Carnegie Library in South Philadelphia. The hours spent thinking and reading began paying intellectual dividends. For example, when Merton introduced the concept of self-fulfilling prophecies, he didn't use the customary empirical formulas familiar to sociologists and social psychologists. Instead, Merton used what he called a "sociological parable."

Merton described how

> in 1932, bank manager Cartwright Millingville was feeling justly proud that his bank was flourishing in the midst of the Great Depression. One Wednesday morning, the men from the local steel plants were coming in too soon—payday wasn't until Saturday. But a nasty rumor had gotten started that the bank was insolvent. More and more customers starting withdrawing their money—and by the end of the day the bank *was* insolvent.

Rumor had become reality: a self-fulfilling prophecy. The bankruptcy would not have happened unless the workers at the steel plants believed it was true. A self-fulfilling prophecy had caused a bankruptcy. And Merton's brief story made the concept of a self-fulfilling prophecy easy to understand.

Merton's Life Course

Merton's life was rich and complicated.

A child of immigrant parents was raised on the rough streets of South Philadelphia, and he was first named Meyer R. Schkolnick. He renamed himself Robert Merlin after being inspired by magician Harry Houdini. He renamed himself again as Robert Merton as he became a world-renowned scholar. Robert Merton used the social capital in South Philadelphia to live the self-fulfilling prophecy that his mother had predicted.

DISCUSSION QUESTIONS

1. Merton described the tough streets of South Philadelphia and the refined atmosphere of Harvard as "opportunity structures." What are opportunity structures, and can you identify any opportunity structures in your own life? Have you been blessed by privilege and opportunity—or have you had to overcome challenges that were the lack of opportunity for most people in those environments?

2. Did Merton's ability to name social phenomena contribute to his fame and the many honors that he received? Do you find that the name for a phenomenon—such as self-fulfilling

prophecy, halo effect, or mere exposure—can help or hurt understanding of the concept and whether it becomes popular?

3. What might Merton have learned as a magician that contributed to his life as a scholar?

KEY TERMS

- **Social capital**: An effective social group that provides a sense of identity and shared resources
- **Life course perspective:** A theoretical approach to analyzing how time and social structures affect people's lives
- **Role model**: Providing a positive example of how to live to someone younger or less experienced than yourself

- **Sociology**: The academic study of society, groups, and cultures, which favors research based on archival data and naturalistic observation more than on experiments

---

5.3 INTELLECTUAL BLOOMERS: THE SLOW CREATION OF A CLASSIC STUDY

The Social Situation

Perhaps there is some faster way to gain scientific knowledge.

The long story arc of the most famous study of self-fulfilling prophecies is made up of many smaller research stories. The formal beginnings began with Robert Merton's anecdote about how the perception of a bank failure led to a real bank failure (see Case 5.2). Merton (1948, 1987) stayed with this idea, blended it with many others, and passed it along to the next generation.

Theory and Method

This collection of studies is about the power of perceptions and their associated expectations.

About 20 years after Merton got things started, Robert Rosenthal began to use controlled experiments to systematically test the idea that perceptions can create their own reality. However, he was working under a different conceptual banner. Merton was the sociologist; Rosenthal was the experimental social psychologist. The classic experiment would be conducted in a San Francisco elementary school.

Replications Mean Slow Science

There are still debates over the relative influence of self-fulfilling prophecies.

After the San Francisco study (described below), skeptical researchers spent another 20 years questioning, qualifying, and refining. The research community slowly started to gain confidence that a self-fulfilling prophecy was a trustworthy, fairly accurate description of one social force that helped describe how life unfolded for many people (see Crum & Phillips, 2015). It would have been nice to get to that level of understanding more quickly.

But science is a slow process, usually because it requires so many replications that retest the same basic idea with slightly different methods and theoretical justifications. But the end of the story—as it stands now—is that self-fulfilling prophecies are one of the many ways that person perceptions can turn into everyday realities.

The concept of self-fulfilling prophecies has spread to clinical psychology. What if successes in psychotherapy only work when people believe that the therapy will work? The type of therapy would be less important than believing in the therapy (Seligman, 2002). The debate is unsettling the foundations of both pharmaceutical and talk therapies for depression. Expectations create self-fulfilling prophecies that are reinforced by confirmation biases that lead us to pay attention only to evidence that supports what we already believe.

Manipulating Person Perceptions: Expectancy Effects

Expectations are the beliefs that allow self-fulfilling prophecies to come true.

Medical and pharmaceutical researchers have to control for **expectancy effects** (also called placebo effects) that occur when a bogus drug produces positive medical outcomes. This may be a bigger deal than you imagine. A meta-analysis by Kirsch and Sapirstein (1998) of depression-prescribed medications found that "the placebo response was constant across different types of medication (75%), and the correlation between placebo effect and drug effect was .90" (p. 1).

The take-home message from that meta-analysis is that placebos work as well as anti-depressants. The expectation effect that Prozac will reduce depression has become part of what Wampold and Imel (2015) refer to as "the great psychotherapy debate."

Lie 1: "Maze Bright" Vs. "Maze Dull" Lab Rats

Rosenthal's initial experiments started with a lie, or what researchers call **deception.**

He was working with students who thought they were doing an experiment on how rats learn mazes. He told half of his student-experimenters that their particular rats had been bred to be either "maze bright" (faster) or "maze dull" (slower). That was an experimental deception so that the students would not know the hypothesis ahead of time. It was a lie because the only real difference was in the students' expectations. There were not systematic differences in the rats assigned to each group of students.

Creating different expectations in the students was the **independent variable** being manipulated by the experimenter (Rosenthal). Running speed of the rats was the measurable outcome or **dependent variable** that was responding to changes in the independent variable. The results: The rats' maze-running abilities fulfilled whatever their student-experimenters had been led to believe (Rosenthal, 1994; Rosenthal & Fode, 1963). Why? Maybe the students with so-called maze bright rats worked a little harder, fed their lab rats more often, or exercised them more frequently. Whatever the specific mechanism, just believing that you had a smart rat meant the rat became better at running mazes—a self-fulfilling prophecy.

Lie 2: "Intellectual Bloomers" Among Elementary Students

Our understanding of expectations and self-fulfilling prophecies accelerated.

Robert Rosenthal began corresponding with Lenore Jacobsen, a school principal in San Francisco. Their correspondence set the stage for *Pygmalion in the Classroom,* one of psychology's most famous—and still debated—experiments. Rosenthal and Jacobsen (1968) gave students in 18 different classrooms across six different grade levels a test with a fancy (but bogus) name: the "Harvard Test of Inflected Acquisition." The name had to convince elementary school teachers that it really meant something.

What's in a Name?

Let's reflect with Shakespeare about the name of this test.

In *Romeo and Juliet,* Juliet tried to cross the bridge between two families by asking, "What's in a name? That which we call a rose by any other name would smell as sweet." Juliet's point was that if Romeo had a different last name, their problems would be solved. But names matter.

The Harvard Test of Inflected Acquisition sounded authoritative: It had "Harvard" in its name. Each of the remaining words sounded important: "Test of Inflected Acquisition." Every elementary school teacher knew what each of the words probably meant. But when they were strung together, they left an impression that, "Well, this is beyond me. But it has 'Harvard' in its name, so it must be okay" (see Lilienfeld, 2010; Sagan, 1995).

This word combination seems designed to intimidate teachers and encourage them to turn off their critical thinking skills. The test was made up, but it sounded good and was coming from their school administrator. They didn't question it. As part of a lie, it was an excellent lie. Teachers in the school administered the test to their students and believed it would tell them something important about their students.

Previously, Rosenthal had lied to his students.

That lie created an expectation that their lab rats were maze dull or maze bright. This time, Rosenthal and Principal Jacobsen lied to the teachers about a randomly selected 20% of the students. They created an expectation that, according to the Harvard Test of Inflected Acquisition, 20% of students across six grade levels would be "intellectual bloomers."

The students identified as intellectual bloomers by the (Bogus) Harvard Test of Inflected Acquisition would "show surprising gains in intellectual competence during the next eight months of school." What a welcome message: Expect to be surprised at how wonderful these students would grow, academically. Remember that the students identified as bloomers were really chosen randomly. But would their teachers' expectations lead to them really doing better in school, just like those bogus maze-bright rats?

Results and Discussion

After 8 months, did teacher expectations matter?

Yes and no. Differences in the students' abilities were tracked using an IQ test. Each student's IQ at the beginning of the year could be compared to their score on the same test at the end of the year. For students in third, fourth, fifth, and sixth grade, their IQ scores didn't change much at all. That was true for students in both the control group and the experimental group—the group that had been labeled as "bloomers."

On the other hand, for students in first and second grade, teacher expectations had a huge influence. For these younger students, IQ scores improved for everyone over the year of school—but the improvements were much higher in students whom the teachers expected to do well. Being labeled a bloomer by their teacher helped these students gain significant advantages, compared to the students who did not benefit from their teacher's confidence (see Figure 5.2).

Halo Effects and Shadow Effects

The positive label of intellectual bloomer glowed with powerful halo effects.

For example, teachers described the children in the experimental group (the "intellectual bloomers") as more likely to succeed, more interesting, and more curious. But that wasn't the end of it. They also described these positively labeled students as more appealing, better adjusted, less in need of social approval, and even happier.

That's one bright halo for students chosen at random. But it still wasn't the end of the self-fulfilling prophecy. The glow from this positive halo was so bright that it cast a shadow in teachers' expectation about the other kids—the ones who *weren't* expected to do well.

This next observation may sadden you (or disturb you). Some students who were not identified as intellectual bloomers also showed significant gains in IQ. What effect did their *un*expected success have on their teachers? "The more children in the control group gained in IQ, the more *un*favorably they were judged by their teachers" (Rosenthal, 1994, p. 179). Expectancies demanded that these non-bloomers remain in the shadows, and it apparently annoyed teachers when they did better than expected.

FIGURE 5.2

Process of Self-Fulfilling Prophecies From Teachers to Students

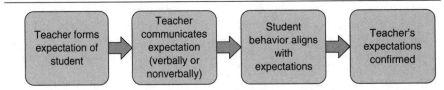

Source: Rosenthal and Jacobson (1968).

It makes you wonder what in the world a kid with a negative label has to do to shake off a bad reputation.

The Science Continues

Skeptical researchers are never satisfied.

Later scientists scrutinized how the research was conducted and tried to replicate the findings—always a scientifically sound endeavor. Hundreds of studies testing the reality of self-fulfilling prophecies have been conducted since that first dramatic experiment. In 2005, Jussim and Harber published a review of what we have learned about self-fulfilling prophecies since 1968:

1. Self-fulfilling prophecies do occur in the classroom, but they are only one of many influences on student achievement.

2. The effect of a self-fulfilling prophecy declines over time (as we saw in the first study, where expectations affected younger students more than older students).

3. Self-fulfilling prophecies can be especially influential on students who belong to groups that are already stigmatized (prelabeled in a negative way).

4. It is unclear whether self-fulfilling prophecies tend to do more harm than good. More research is needed.

5. Sometimes, what looks like a self-fulfilling prophecy is an accurate assessment made by a teacher.

In 2002, Rosenthal himself also reviewed the now-sophisticated scientific literature that he had helped create almost 40 years earlier. By looking at the meta-analyses, Rosenthal identified four ways in which teachers unknowingly communicate their expectations to particular students:

1. *Emotional climate,* through nonverbal cues that create a warmer social-emotional environment

2. *Expectations of effort,* by teaching more material and more difficult material

3. *Increased opportunities,* by giving students more opportunities to respond, including more time to respond

4. *Differential feedback,* by giving certain students more individualized feedback that allows them to assess their own progress

Wouldn't it be nice to have a faster way to understanding? It has taken decades of research, professional experience, and reflection to arrive at our present understanding of how self-fulfilling prophecies work in the classroom (and beyond), and more research always reveals even more nuance and information. Self-fulfilling prophecies are only one of several powerful social psychological dynamics that skilled teachers are called upon to harness for the welfare of their students.

DISCUSSION QUESTIONS

1. Identify one teacher from your own life who had a positive prophecy about you and one who had a negative prophecy about you. Did each become a self-fulfilling prophecy? In other words, did you live up to those expectations or defy them? Explain your answer.

2. The research reviewed here provides evidence that teacher expectations can have at least some influence on student outcomes. However, the pattern in Figure 5.2 showed that the results were only significant for students in first and second grades. What might explain why the pattern wasn't significant for older children? How could you design a study that tests your hypothesis?

3. Imagine that you are the parent of a 6-year-old child. Identify three specific expectations that you would try to have for your child that might become a positive self-fulfilling prophecy. Is this type of optimism setting your child up for success—or will it put too much pressure on them? Defend your answer, either way.

KEY TERMS

- **Expectancy effects**: When our expectations make something happen (see *placebo effect*)
- **Deception**: When participants in a study aren't told the true nature of the study because it would affect the results

- **Independent variable**: The variable an experimenter manipulates to create different comparison groups within a study
- **Dependent variable**: The variable an experimenter measures at the end of a study as the outcome

5.4 THE ROCK IN THE COFFIN: TERROR MANAGEMENT THEORY

The Social Situation

Diamonds are useless and expensive.

"All you can do is grind them up and put them on drill bits. Unlike gold or silver, carbon allotropes aren't malleable or electrically conductive; diamonds just sit there and sparkle" (Twitchell, 2000, pp. 90–91). How did we come to perceive a diamond as a symbol of a life-long romantic commitment—and people who exchange them as deeply in love?

In 1447, the Archduke Maximilian of Austria honored an ancient Egyptian belief that a vein of love ran from the heart to the tip of that finger. So he placed a diamond ring on the finger of Mary of Burgundy. The idea did not catch on with the common people, however, and the diamond trade remained an indulgence for royalty.

In 1866, a 15-year-old boy named Erasmus Jacobs found a transparent rock on his father's farm in South Africa. The De Beers Consolidated Mining Company soon flooded the world with diamonds. Once reserved for royalty, diamonds now became common and relatively cheap.

The oversupply of diamonds persisted after World War I and was met with low demand. De Beers needed to transform perceptions of a pretty but useless rock into something everyone was eager to buy and never to sell. De Beers knew they had to apply social influence to somehow change people's attitudes and behavior toward diamonds. De Beers didn't turn to social psychology; they turned to advertising.

In 1938, the N. W. Ayers advertising agency had developed a reputation for in-depth research. The agency quickly recognized a critical gender divide about diamonds: Women did the romantic wanting, while men did the reluctant buying. Twitchell (2000) summarized the advertising agency's challenge to influence men and diamonds.

> A practical system had to be concocted that would calm them down and get them safely through the buy-hole. Hence the scientific-sounding voodoo about carat weight, color, cutting, clarity of the stones, *and* prices that invariably appeared in the bottom margin of the early ads. Women looked at the picture and read the body copy of the ad. Men were shown the small print over in the corner of the page. (p. 95)

What could ad copy say to such men? One early ad simply read, "Is two months' salary too much for a diamond engagement ring?" But their most effective slogan was even simpler: "Diamonds are forever." With that slogan, the De Beers company had stopped selling diamonds.

De Beers was now selling immortality.

If their advertising campaign worked, then some grieving spouse might even place their diamond wedding ring in the coffin when a husband or wife passed away. Any keepsake gathering dust in a jewelry box would be just as effective as a rock in a coffin: They both reduced the problem of oversupply. Now they had to work on the demand side of their marketing equation.

Theory and Method

This case study describes interviews, experiments, and gender stereotypes to present a disturbing idea.

The interviews include young lovers in China, especially from their rapidly rising middle class. The experiments measure people's reactions when they are confronted with their own inevitable death. The gender stereotypes are used for mass marketing.

The disturbing idea is **terror management theory (TMT)**, a theory that can be used to explain the success of the De Beers marketing strategy.

Warning: This case study may change your personal perceptions of someone, maybe even yourself, who hopes to buy or receive a diamond wedding or engagement ring.

Terror Management Theory

What if, after life, there is . . . nothing?

To people raised in some religious faiths, doubt itself is wrong and therefore terror inducing. Many people without a religious orientation also want to believe that there is something we can experience after this life. Maybe we'll be reincarnated, survive as ghosts until we get used to eternity, enjoy a blissful existence with our relatives . . . something.

Believers can only believe. None of us *knows* what will happen after death. But we also can't avoid thinking about our own mortality. Every time we pass a funeral home, hear a siren, cry over a departed pet, or notice someone's graying hair, we are nudged by another reminder of our own eventual death.

The TMT defines the human condition as an anxiety-producing conflict: We are desperate to live yet know we must die (Pyszcznski, 2019). And when we're reminded of our mortality, we respond in various ways, such as clinging to beliefs or relationships that seem meaningful. Keep in mind that a theory is not a fact. TMT has stirred many thoughtful debates and strenuous disagreements within psychology (see Greenberg et al., 1990). But fear of death is also a familiar topic in the history of psychology (Becker, 1973; Freud, 1927/1961; Malinowski, 1948). Two questions with simple answers summarize TMT:

Q1:   What can we do about our inevitable demise?

Answer: Nothing. That's the problem.

Q2:   What can we do to lower our anxiety about death?

Answer: Lots of things.

And that's where the fun begins, at least for those who look at the world through the lens of TMT (Becker, 1973; Solomon et al., 1991). TMT suggests that we can buffer our existential fear of death in obvious ways, such as by embracing a comforting religion (see Lifshin et al., 2018) or strengthening our attachment to our existing **worldview**. For people already high in religious fundamentalism, awareness of death increases their apocalyptic beliefs (Routledge et al., 2018). Others reduce anxiety about death by burying themselves in work, going to Disney World, debating politics, disappearing into a video games, or dedicating our lives to a cause we decide is vital.

De Beers and their advertising agencies understood the consequences of TMT—and how to use it to make money—long before it was named terror management theory.

Secular Immortality

The N. W. Ayers advertising agency understood the desire for immortality.

But they couldn't really do anything about it. The best they could offer was **secular immortality** (see Hirschman, 1990; Rindfleisch & Burroughs, 2004): consumer products indicating our worth as a substitute for an uncertain immortality. Book writing, for example, holds out the vague promise of possibly making some enduring contribution (at least, the authors hope this is true!). Working for a charity that brings clean water or safe living conditions to people in need is also reassuring. The social norm is to believe; being around others who believe makes it easier for you also to believe.

Elizabeth Hirschman (1990) pointed out that some religions merge secular and spiritual immortality. They promote the idea "that material wealth reflects one's true worth or value as a person" (p. 31). That would be appealing if you wanted to take credit for inheriting a great deal of money, sometimes described as "being born on third base and thinking you'd hit a triple."

De Beers promises only secular immortality, but that seems to be enough to sell lots of diamonds.

Operationalizing Mortality Salience

To test a concept, we need to measure it.

Measuring requires **operationalizing** the concept so everyone knows the procedures used to measure it. "Operationalizing" is the kind of talk that gets social psychologists excited because it means we can test the concept with controlled experiments. For TMT, reminding people of death is called **mortality salience**. You can probably think of other ways to create the experience of mortality salience. One common approach (see Jong et al., 2012) uses two randomly assigned groups that receive different instructions such as

- Mortality Salience Condition: " . . . what you think will happen to you physically as you die and once you are physically dead. Describe the feelings that arise from these thoughts."
- Control Group Condition: " . . . what happens to you as you watch TV and the feelings that arise from these thoughts."

All sorts of things pop out of humans who have to write their reaction to the mortality salience condition (see Kasser & Sheldon, 2000). For example, Fransen et al. (2008) observed that people experiencing mortality salience expected to "spend more money on luxury items in the next fifteen years." Across many experiments, the dominant reactions to mortality salience appear to be responses designed to enhance social self-esteem in the present life: secular immortality.

Results and Discussion

De Beers discovered they could sell their brand of secular immortality in China.

It's not surprising that De Beers noticed the huge, emerging market in China. A team of Chinese researchers interviewed young urban professionals accustomed to city life, as well as relative newcomers from more rural areas. Those of marriageable age all faced similar daunting financial prospects, including the high cost of getting married.

Gender Stereotypes

De Beers entered the Chinese market in the early 2000s.

They had an immediate impact by using some familiar gender stereotypes (see Sun, 2017). In their first decade, Chinese spending on diamond rings went from 0% to 10% of all jewelry sales. China has since become the largest consumer of diamonds in the world, and it has more room to grow. About 30% of all brides have received a diamond engagement ring.

De Beers exploited the same gender stereotypes in China that helped them succeed in previous markets. In one ad, a young couple is watching the moon's reflection in the water. He says, "I'll get that for you" and dives into the water. He resurfaces with a diamond ring while the voiceover declares, "A diamond is forever, just like your love."

In another ad, a young couple enters a garden maze. He blindfolds her and ties a red thread connecting their two fingers. He puts a ring on his end so that it slides through the maze to her finger. Once again: "A diamond is forever, just like your love."

Like before, De Beers is negotiating with some reluctant men. But their exploitation has hit a raw nerve, at least among some men. One interviewee said,

> Romantic? Give me a break! If I could, I'd block the TV so my girlfriend can't see it. It's bad enough already for us men, because we're expected to buy a flat and pay for the cost of the wedding. Now they've come up with yet another thing my girlfriend will pressure me to buy.

Blood Diamonds: The Price of Secular Immortality

There is another, more urgent humanitarian problem: blood diamonds.

De Beers has thrived despite bitter revelations about blood diamonds mined from the earth at the cost of amputated limbs—and murder of the most defiant workers. De Beers has tried to use its market dominance to limit the sale of these blood diamonds (or "conflict diamonds"). But it still is widely criticized for its role in an industry they have dominated for 150 years. Consumers in distant jewelry stores have no way of knowing whether a particular stone was mined from the earth through the blood of powerless people (Global Witness, 2017).

The De Beers advertising campaign to sell diamonds promised an immortality that the company knew they could not deliver. When Moore (2011) studied the De Beers advertising campaign, he recognized how expertly the campaign constructed a mental bridge that allowed consumers to psychologically cross back and forth between secular and spiritual immortality. If you had one, then you felt connected to the other.

A few select people and families, by their extreme wealth and generosity, have achieved secular immortality. Those great "cathedrals of learning" (your local library) in many towns across the United States were the product of a brutal Andrew

Carnegie's immense wealth and generosity. Those libraries have survived many generations.

The Carnegie Foundation continues to support several social causes. The Rockefeller Foundations, the Morgan Library, the Whitney Museum, Nobel Prizes, and the Gates Foundation all have been designed to use their founders' immense wealth to extend individual influence well beyond the lives of their founders. Some of the super wealthy have achieved secular immortality.

But where does that leave the rest of us who have not achieved fabulous wealth, fame, influence—or even infamy? Most of us will not be remembered with a national monument, a local statue, or even a plaque on a bench. We may be lucky to get a one-time mention in the local newspaper. How do the rest of us achieve immortality? The De Beers diamond advertising campaign gave the rest of us a way to buy immortality. And TMT explains why we are so eager to buy it.

DISCUSSION QUESTIONS

1. Terror management theory suggests that we distract ourselves from fears of death by becoming interested in relatively meaningless trifles, such as television shows or sports rivalries. Try to identify three things in your own life that might serve as evidence for their hypothesis. Does thinking about your interests from this perspective dampen or increase your enthusiasm?

2. Watch a few short clips from the movie *Blood Diamond* and discuss whether it has changed your attitude toward buying diamonds for someone you love. On a broader level, do you support companies that have politics or policies in place with which you agree or disagree? Do you boycott some companies and support others based on whether you agree with the way they do business?

3. Diamonds and other expensive, luxury items are one way for wealthy or privileged people to secure secular immortality or to feel that they have brought meaning to their lives. What can poor, struggling people with fewer consumer opportunities do instead? Which option seems like it might lead to greater, lasting happiness or a sense of satisfaction?

KEY TERMS

- **Terror management theory (TMT)**: The idea that when confronted with our own inevitable death, we cling to worldviews and relationships that help bring meaning to life
- **Worldview**: Systems of belief or perception that help us see life as meaningful and orderly
- **Secular immortality**: Consumer products that bring us a feeling of worth or lasting life, despite our actual mortality
- **Operationalizing**: Describing how an abstract variable will be defined and measured in a research study
- **Mortality salience**: Reminding people of death in an experimental study

Attitudes and Persuasion

6

6.1 COGNITIVE DISSONANCE, PART I: PRELUDE TO A THEORY

The Social Situation

This much seems clear: Jesus did not return in 1843 or in 1844.

William Miller was raised in a devout Christian home. But his visits to the local library transformed him into the kind of deist that F. D. Nichol (1944, see pp. 17–42) described as "a halfway station . . . to atheism." Miller would even lampoon the preaching peculiarities of his uncle and grandfather, both Baptist preachers (Bliss, 1853). When William Miller converted to something, he went all the way.

Miller's Private Conversion

Miller's scorn for religion was challenged during the War of 1812.

The grim realities of battle and the unexpected American military victory at Plattsburgh convinced him that "The Supreme Being must have watched over the interests of this country" (Nichol, 1944, p. 8). At war's end, Miller returned to the life of a farmer while raising 10 children. But now he was praying for answers to life's big questions—and frustrated by the lack of answers (Nichol, 1944):

> The heavens were as brass over my head, and the earth as iron under my feet. ETERNITY! *What was it? And death, why was it?*. . . The more I thought, the more scattered were my conclusions. (p. 40)

Miller began a systematic self-directed study of the Bible. When he reached the Book of Daniel, he noticed a prophecy specifying that it would be 2300 years until Jesus would return to earth to "cleanse the Temple." The Bible could not be wrong, so Miller started doing the math. Differences between the Jewish and the Christian calendar complicated the calculations. But William Miller knew, almost to the month, when Jesus would return.

Learning From History

Jesus, however, did not return in the mid-1840s.

The Millerite movement was born during a period known as the Second Great Awakening. This strange period generated so many new religious and reform movements in the same region in upstate and western New York that it became known as the "burned over district." A partial list includes the Shakers (~1826), Mormons (~1828), Millerites–Adventists (~1834), Spiritualism and the Fox sisters' seances (~1848), the Oneida Society (~1848), and the Jehovah's Witnesses (~1878).

Failed predictions that Jesus would return have been common. Jesus did not return in the second half of the second century, as predicted by a prophet named Montanus. Jesus failed to return again in 1533, as predicted by the Anabaptists. In each case, some believers left and some changed allegiances. But a significant number somehow kept on believing. More recently, Harold Camping used the Family Radio Network of 66 stations to warn listeners that the end of the world as we know it would happen on May 21, 2011, at 6 p.m. It was possibly his 12th prediction of the end of the world, but he was still on the air preaching to some receptive audience.

Confirmation Bias: Believing is Seeing

William Miller estimated that the prophecy in the Book of Daniel was made in 457 B.C.E.

That put the return of Jesus sometime in 1843, only 25 years away. The discovery was a thrilling moment for the soldier-farmer-theologian in upstate New York (Nichol, 1944):

> Joy that filled my heart in view of the delightful prospect, nor of the ardent longings of my soul, for a participation in the joys of the redeemed. The Bible was to me a new book. It was indeed a feast of reason. (p. 12)

Miller studied his Bible for another 5 years, carefully looking for flaws in his theory. Previously, he had not been able to find reasons to believe. Now he could not find reasons to doubt. Today, we call this confirmation bias, perceiving only evidence that supports what we already believe, while ignoring evidence that contradicts our beliefs. Everything Miller read in his Bible confirmed what he wanted to believe.

However, Miller discovered that few people were interested in what seemed so obvious to him. So, he kept studying for another 6 years until he finally decided to bargain with God. He would not preach this good news unless, out of the blue, he received an invitation to preach. And that afternoon, there was a knock on his door asking him to deliver a sermon! That first sermon became a revival that lasted for a week. The revival became a movement.

Theory and Method

This case study uses historical archives to document one case study of cognitive dissonance.

Leon Festinger was a foundational experimental social psychologist. But he did not start with experiments when he developed the theory of **cognitive dissonance**, the motivating mental turmoil produced when a person holds two incompatible beliefs. Festinger developed the theory over three stages; he

1. observed a barely-noticed pattern in historical archives;

2. documented a case study of that pattern, using participant-observation; and

3. designed experiments to test the validity of theory.

Festinger's theory of cognitive dissonance was partially inspired by his study of the Millerites.

Incompatible Beliefs

Miller calculated the date window for the return of Jesus was between March 21, 1843, and March 21, 1844.

But Miller also had calculated a few high-probability dates, one of which was April 23, 1843. When that day came—and went—the Millerites were of course disappointed. But they were not discouraged. There were major Millerite conferences in New York, Philadelphia, and Washington, DC. At its peak, there may have been as many as 200 "radiantly happy" ministers and another 500 lecturers. The end really was near—and that holy event demanded that people get ready!

For Millerites, the situation unexpectedly evolved into a public test of their private beliefs. How do you "go forward nonchalantly to all their routine labors" when you know and have publicly declared that Jesus will be splitting the clouds in April? They could anticipate the even greater mental turmoil if they declared belief in Miller—and then Jesus did not show up.

The mental turmoil of cognitive dissonance is the product of **dual attitudes**, trying to maintain contradictory beliefs. It was hypocritical to place their bet on Miller, but also hedge their bet by planting next year's crops. To resolve their cognitive dissonance, many believers did not plant their crops. They had to commit fully—to use a poker metaphor, they had to put all their chips on the table.

Doubt had to be banished.

Religious Excitement on a Variable Reinforcement Schedule

The uncertain dates of Jesus' arrival increased the Millerites' religious excitement.

Like the uncertainty created by casino games with variable reinforcement, the uncertainty from imagining this greatest of all possible rewards created religious excitement and anticipation that made it difficult to continue normal functioning. Four states (Maine, New Hampshire, Vermont, and Massachusetts) began tracking the number of admissions to mental health asylums due to Religious Excitement (coded as RE in their reports) during the years 1842, 1843, and 1844. Across all four states, 6.5% of all admissions were coded exclusively as RE, and more than 22% involved RE (see Nichol, 1944, Appendix G, p. 513).

Jesus, however, did not return on any of the high-probability dates in 1843, or in the early months of 1844. There was, at last, only one last possible date remaining: October 22, 1844. One shop window posted a sign declaring, "This shop is closed in honor of the King of kings, who will appear about the 20th of October. Get ready, friends, to crown Him Lord of all" (Nichol, 1944, p. 91).

The editor of the Millerite newspaper *The Midnight Cry* wrote, "I intend, by the help of the Lord, to act as if there was no possibility of mistake . . . in less than one month the opening heavens would reveal my Saviour." The Millerites who gathered in their homes and churches on October 22 "were no longer believers in the 'advent near' but in the advent here."

Results and Discussion

To Leon Festinger, October 23, 1844 was the most interesting day in Millerite history.

That was the first day *after* prophecy failed and the *beginning* of intense cognitive dissonance. Festinger et al. (1956/2008, p. 4) stated four "conditions under which we would expect to observe increased fervor following the disconfirmation of a belief":

1. A belief must be held with deep conviction.

2. The person holding the belief must have committed to it.

3. The belief must be sufficiently specific and sufficiently concerned with the real world so that events may unequivocally refute the belief.

4. Such undeniable disconfirmatory belief must occur and must be recognized by the person holding the belief.

These conditions articulated in 1956 anticipated the refinements to cognitive dissonance theory that emerged from decades of subsequent experimental research. Cooper (2019) referred to them as "But onlys" that summarized that cognitive dissonance would only occur under conditions of choice, commitment, an unwanted consequence, and a foreseeable outcome. To the Millerites, the initial impact of cognitive dissonance was so powerful that it came to be called "The Great Disappointment."

The Great Disappointment

Francis Nichol (1944) recorded Millerites' emotional reactions the day after the prophecy failed (see pp. 94–99):

- Joseph Bates (preacher, and sea captain): "The effect of this disappointment can be realized only by those who experienced it."

- Hiram Edson (preacher): "Our fondest hopes and expectations were blasted and such a spirit of weeping came over us as I never experienced before . . . We wept and wept, till the day dawn.... Is there no God? Is all this but a cunningly devised fable?"

- Luther Boutelle (a Millerite lecturer): "Everyone felt lonely...I found about 70 believers in a large house, living there and having meetings daily. They had put all their money in a milk pan, and when they paid for anything they took the money from the pan. All was common stock."

- N. N. Whiting: "We were in some danger from the mob last Sabbath [October 20] at Franklin Hall [New York City]. The mayor, however, offered to put down the mob with strong hand if...."

- And from William Miller himself: "And the next day, it seemed as though all the demons from the bottomless pit were let loose upon us."

Nichol observed that

to suffer so keen a disappointment was exquisite pain in itself, but to that were added the jeers and ridicule of scoffers....They know not how to answer the taunting question, "why didn't you go up [to heaven]?"

Those are painful consequences: disappointment, despair, loneliness, weeping, jeers and ridicule, spiritual and physical threat...and even doubt. But there were comforting reactions too: mutual support, regular gathering of believers, and a spontaneous sharing of resources for the common good.

The leaders of the Millerite movement had to figure out how to financially support the believers who had sold all their possessions. They also had to respond to a long series of juicy rumors against the treasurer of the Millerite movement. Many left the faith. But many others still believed—they just didn't know exactly *what* they now believed.

Self-Justification: A Theological Shift

But gradually, convenient theologies evolved that explained everything.

To the social psychologist, the Millerites' slightly altered theologies beginning on October 23 appear to be **self-justifications** that provided acceptable explanations for an undesirable outcome. (The shorter definition of self-justifications is "making excuses.") The Millerites fit all four of Festinger's necessary conditions for cognitive dissonance.

Here's the Millerites' critical theological shift: The Great Disappointment had been "a test to discover those who really loved the Lord and His appearing...God overruled to make this disappointing experience serve a divine purpose" (Nichol, 1944, p. 277). After-the-fact explanations are often the result of the **hindsight bias**, or motivated interpretations of the past that comfort us by making it easy to think we could have predicted what happened. It happens when people think, "I knew it all along."

Now that they had a face-saving explanation, familiar scriptures came alive. The confirmation bias helped Millerites find examples of similar tests in the Bible:

- Jonah preaching to Nineveh

- Job suffering family deaths and misfortunes

- Abraham offering his son on an altar.

Instead of despair and doubt, the Millerites soon began to see the wisdom of God in other ways. Hiram Edson had a vision while walking through a field. The vision informed him that the verse in the Book of Daniel referred to a heavenly sanctuary rather than to an earthly sanctuary.

The cognitive dissonance created by Jesus not appearing led to attitude change. For some, the change meant giving up on their beliefs entirely. For others, like Edson, the change required only a slight, relatively painless adjustment in their theology.

These theological shifts were persuasive for about 2 years. Nichol (1944) concluded that there was a point beyond which even the strongest faith could not struggle against reality. "The scorching sun of disappointment beat down, and the burning winds of ridicule swept in from every side" (p. 290). Festinger et al. (1956/2008, pp. 13–25) reached a similar conclusion in their book *When Prophecy Fails:*

> Although there is a limit beyond which belief will not withstand disconfirmation, it is clear that the introduction of contrary evidence can serve to increase the conviction and enthusiasm of a believer.

However, it's difficult to guess where those limits might be. The Millerites' theological shifts eventually became a branch of Protestantism called Seventh Day Adventists (Knight, 2010). In the 21st century, the Adventists may have as many as 20 million baptized believers. They were Millerites who only needed a minor adjustment in their theology.

For his part, William Miller acknowledged that he had made a mistake. But his admissions were not about a misplaced faith; they were about his mathematical calculations. Right before Miller died in 1849, he was still not discouraged. Despite poor eyesight, his last unfinished letter was in large and shaky handwriting: "We shall soon see Him for whom we have looked and waited."

DISCUSSION QUESTIONS

1. What current, modern-day examples can you identify of times when people cling to their beliefs, even when they are presented with evidence that they are wrong? Do these examples also seem to fit the theory of cognitive dissonance?

2. Can you identify any times when you have chosen to ignore evidence that was uncomfortable or went against what you preferred to believe? What eventually led you to see things from a more objective perspective?

3. Identify a time when you've used hindsight bias—a time when you said, "I knew that was going to happen." Do you think you *really* knew it was going to happen, or did you just tell yourself that afterward, to feel better?

KEY TERMS

- **Cognitive dissonance**: The idea that incompatible cognitions, feelings, and behaviors create mental turmoil that motivates attitude change
- **Dual attitudes**: Simultaneous but incompatible judgments or evaluations

- **Self-justification**: Rationalizing or coming up with socially acceptable explanations for bad behavior or undesirable outcomes
- **Hindsight bias**: Motivated interpretation of the past that makes it easy to think we could have predicted outcomes

6.2 COGNITIVE DISSONANCE, PART II: THE FLYING SAUCER THAT NEVER CAME

The Social Setting

It was a small cult, as religious cults go.

The names of the major participants are known, but we will use the false names researchers assigned to each person in this case study, to protect the privacy of their ancestors. Their attraction to the group is relatively easy to explain: They were "searching for something more" but unsure what "it" was. This case study isn't focused on why they joined, but it does help us understand why they didn't leave, even after prophecy failed.

Post-War Anxieties

It depends how you count, and when you start or stop counting.

But the total number of people killed in WW II may have been about 60 million people. Our 21st century view obscures what it was like to live in post-war America in the 1950s. The established meanings of life had been thoroughly shaken by a global war. The barriers to space exploration were being penetrated. The atomic bomb made it plausible to believe in the end of all human existence.

There was relative openness to the idea of flying saucers from outer space and other mysterious phenomena. Mrs. Marian Keech's communications from the spirit world were full of authoritative but meaningless terms. They were outlandish, but they were slightly more plausible in the 1950s than they are today. The "sciency" language of Mrs. Keech's communications might have added some **self-affirmation** that she needed to convince herself that the words she was writing really came from another source:

> the waves of ether have become tactable by the bombs your scientists have been exploding. This works like an accordion. . . . We have been trying to get through for many of your years, with alcetopes and the earling timer. (p. 37)

In Mrs. Keech's strange messages from another world, there were also spirit beings, new planets, "sunspots," "magnetism," and "vibratory impulses." There were lots of made-up words and vaguely familiar concepts. "Avagada" meant spaceship. Something called "the thermin" supposedly "records our thoughts, action," in the "Losolo," a type of school. The authors of *When Prophecy Fails* encouraged readers not to conclude that "Mrs. Keech's pencil is merely the unique raving of an isolated madwoman"; instead, her ideas were well adapted to "our contemporary, anxious age" (p. 54).

Searching For a Meaningful Life

"I have always wanted to be of service to mankind."

For 15 years, Mrs. Keech had explored various psychic phenomena and searched her own consciousness for signs of a deeper life (Festinger et al., 1956/2008, pp. 33–35). And then early one morning,

> I had the feeling that someone was trying to get my attention. . . . My hand began to write in another handwriting . . . somebody else was using my hand, and I said: "Will you identify yourself?" And they did. (p. 33)

Her first "automatic writings" were messages from her dead father. They weren't especially interesting—he was concerned mostly with his garden. But communication from other worlds had been established! The most thrilling communications came from a spirit being named Sananda. It was an implied promise to Mrs. Keech and a select few of her followers that sounded strangely like a dinner reservation:

> We are trying to make arrangements for a party of six from Westinghouse to visit our territory. Is that a surprise to you? There is one in Syracuse, New York, one in Schenectady, New York, one in Rockford, Illinois, one in California. (p. 45)

Judgment was coming, and the messages started coming faster. Perhaps the most important message of all was that the Earth would soon be devastated by a massive flood. Mr. Keech, Mrs. Keech's husband, "simply went about his ordinary duties . . . and did not allow the unusual events in his home to disturb in the slightest his daily routine" (p. 38). On the morning of July 23, Mrs. Keech's busy pencil wrote,

> The cast of light you see in the southern sky is . . . a turning, spinning motion of the craft of the tola [spaceship] which is to land upon the planet . . . at Lyons field. (p. 47)

A Prophecy Unfulfilled

"They" were coming to the local airfield, and believers would be saved from the flood!

But on the great day, they were expected to land, the flying saucer did not arrive. Keech reported her own tortured self-assessment, "I am more or less responsible if I have misled anyone today." Nevertheless, the messages from the spirit world now moving through outer space kept coming at a furious pace. Keech sometimes wrote for 14 hours per day.

Her most devoted follower, Dr. Armstrong, worked at the campus health services. He produced 50 copies of a seven-page "Open Letter to American Editors and Publishers" that warned of the coming catastrophe the aliens had described. A copy released in October added in handwriting, "Date of evacuation Dec. 20." Armstrong had made a testable prediction—the kind of thing that gets social psychologists excited.

Theory and Method

This case study relies on **participant observation**.

The researcher-observers included students and paid research assistants, guided by three social psychologists. The account of this case is outlined in the same book that references the Millerite movement (Case 6.1): *When Prophecy Fails* by Festinger et al. (1956/2008). The case study was a critical step in the development of Leon Festinger's new theory of cognitive dissonance that proposed that incompatible cognitions, feelings, and behaviors created mental turmoil that motivated attitude change.

The social psychologists first sent a male sociology student who presented himself to Dr. Armstrong as a lost soul ripe for recruiting. But Dr. Armstrong never tried to convert him and never mentioned Mrs. Keech. However, a second attempt by a female sociology student was more successful. She contacted Armstrong, who responded enthusiastically, interpreted a (fictitious) dream the student had prepared, and "showered her with information about flying saucers" (p. 72). The social psychologists had found their way into a small cult of believers.

Profiles of Members

The people Mrs. Keech attracted came from various backgrounds.

For example, the most important followers were Thomas and Daisy Armstrong. They and their three children had been medical missionaries in Egypt but returned to the United States at the end of World War II. Their idealistic hopes for a life of service were shattered, in part by Daisy Armstrong's nervous breakdowns.

The Armstrong's college-aged daughter, Cleo, had endured teasing at school and was worried about the new problems she would face if the prophesied flood did not come: Her father would be humiliated and lose his job, and she would have to quit college. Yet she also began buying lots of expensive clothes "because she wanted to enjoy wearing pretty things while she could, before the flood came" (p. 76). Cleo was right to be worried. Dr. Armstrong was asked to resign from the college health service because he had upset so many students.

Another believer, Bob, was an Army veteran and an older college student. He sold off some valuable property to settle his personal debts and then spent Thanksgiving saying goodbye to family and friends. Kitty O'Donnell, a single mother and a friend of Bob's, was far more skeptical, apparently more interested in Bob than in flying saucers.

Kitty O'Donnell's initial commitment was minor, but she would become one of the most committed members. She explained that, "I have to believe that the flood is coming on the 21st because I've spent nearly all my money. I quit my job, I quit computer school, and my apartment costs me $100 a month. I have to believe" (p. 80). She was so worried that she might be separated from her 3-year-old son when the flying saucer arrived that she gave him his Christmas presents 3 weeks early.

Don't stereotype the believers in Keech as weak-minded, poorly educated people. At various points in time, the group included a physician, a PhD in the natural sciences, and others with varying degrees of education. Many were in college while attending meetings with Keech and Dr. Armstrong. Neither education nor mental capability helps us understand the appeal of groups with such extreme beliefs.

Results and Discussion

This case study triggered decades of experimental research.

Most of the research has explored why incompatible cognitions create a motivating mental turmoil. For example, continuing to smoke while believing that cigarettes are harmful are incompatible cognitions. And those conflicted beliefs and behavior will generally create mental turmoil, as many people struggling to quit smoking have discovered.

You can reduce the mental turmoil by (a) changing your behavior (quit smoking), or (b) changing your beliefs (smoking won't really harm me). The first strategy of quitting smoking is difficult but real and effective. The second strategy is much easier but unreal and ineffective. Furthermore, some situations also can reduce mental turmoil.

Your mental turmoil also disappears if you are smoking a last cigarette as you stand before a firing squad. You're still smoking and still believing that smoking is harmful. But now your responsibility for creating negative consequences for yourself has become irrelevant (see Cooper, 2019). The experimenters studying Keech and her followers wanted to figure out why mental turmoil was so motivating.

Layers of Mental Turmoil

There were several kinds of mental turmoil brewing in Mrs. Keech's living room.

Dr. Armstrong was surprised that none of the 50 media outlets had responded to his lengthy news release about the end of the world. Armstrong tried again with a single-page dramatic summary that led to some light publicity. But the news of the impending destruction of the world was mostly ignored.

However, the press did start paying attention when they heard about Armstrong's dismissal. A television truck was parked outside, and it was starting to get crowded in Mrs. Keech's home. A number of pranksters started ringing the Keechs' doorbell, calling them, and generally harassing them.

Cleo Armstrong suffered more mental turmoil when reporters besieged her with questions about why her father had been dismissed and what she believed. Cleo quickly discovered the politician's trick of "no comment," hoping to survive an ordeal that was sure to make her social life more difficult. She would be fine as long as the world ended from a flood within the next few days. But if it didn't, then she had a lot of explaining to do even as she tried to defend her father's honor.

Mrs. Keech faced an unexpected spiritual power struggle with a new member. Bertha Blatsky, a former beautician and scientologist, began to speak authoritatively from the spirit world as well! But she claimed to be the voice of "the Creator." This effectively reduced Mrs. Keech and her automatic writing to a position of minor authority. There were some tense power skirmishes.

For example, Blatsky belittled the "thee" and "thou" pseudo-biblical speech used in Keech's writings. Blatsky determined what lights would be turned on, where Keech could sit, who could reject someone wanting to join them, and who could call for such meetings in the first place. For the faithful, their experience of life became more petty as they approached the end of the world.

The faithful endured. But in many ways, their lives became more exhausting, confusing, and small as the end of the world drew near. Some of the believers in Mrs. Keech had abandoned their faith after the first prophecy went unfulfilled. Other believers hung on longer "just in case." Eventually, only the true believers remained.

The Still, Small Voice of Doubt

Mrs. Keech received new information and instructions.

First, Sananda was an incarnation of Jesus (good to know). It also reestablished her spiritual position relative to Berth Blatsky's voice of the creator. Second, the flying saucer was again on its way. Very exciting! Third, they were to remove all metal from their clothing. One of the participant observers reported back to social psychologists Festinger et al. (1956/2008) that

> Edna took me aside and said, "How about your brassiere? It has metal clasps, doesn't it?" I went back in the house and took my brassiere off. The only metal on me was the fillings in my teeth and I was afraid someone would mention those. (p. 145)

That would have been quite a test of her faith. If she really believed, then she would have consented to last-minute dental surgery!

The reports from the participant-observers made the 14 hours leading up to that hectic moment almost peaceful. It felt like a harassed family that had finally arrived at the airport for a long-postponed vacation. There were 15 people gathered in the Keechs' living room as the final hour approached. Calm, happy, excited people: believing people.

However, the voice of doubt crept in accidentally. Keech was writing down last minute instructions on behalf of Sananda/Jesus, while Blatsky was speaking on behalf of the Creator. But they felt the doubt-inspired need to carefully check one another's messages for independent verification and interpretation. The social psychological participant-observers summarized the resulting instructions:

> Precisely at midnight a spaceman would come to the door and escort them to the place where the saucer [tola] was parked. Everyone was instructed to be perfectly silent while en route to the saucer. When their escort knocked on the door at midnight, Thomas Armstrong was to act as the sentry and ask the caller: "What is your question?" (p. 160)

The group carefully rehearsed an elaborate series of questions and answers, like coded communications and passwords in a cold war spy novel. They were to leave all identifying information behind. The secret books of Keech's messages were carefully packed in a large shopping bag for transportation. It was important to preserve, for the future, the history of this momentous event.

At 11:15 p.m., Mrs. Keech received a message ordering everyone to put on their coats. One believer remembered at the last moment that his shoes had metal toecaps; they agreed that he should step out of them at the last moment before entering the spaceship. Then there was another problem.

At about 11:35, one of the authors reported that he had not removed the zipper from his trousers. This produced a near panic reaction. He was rushed into the bedroom where Dr. Armstrong, his hands trembling and his eyes darting to the clock every few seconds, slashed out the zipper with a razor blade and wrenched its clasp free with wire-cutters. By the time the operation was complete it was 11:50, too late to do more than sew up the rent with a few rough stitches. (p. 161)

And Nothing Continued to Happen

And then they suddenly had nothing to do for 10 long minutes.

Midnight approached, came, and went. It was 12:05, and there had been no knock on the door, no spaceman, and no flying saucer. But then someone noticed that there were two clocks in Keech's living room—and they did not tell the same time. The slower clock on the mantel must tell the right time. That clock began to chime midnight . . . and once again, nothing happened.

And nothing continued to happen.

After 5 more minutes, the voice of the Creator (Blatsky) assured them that there had been a slight delay. The phone rang from time to time with reporters inquiring whether they were still there. "No comment," was the standard reply.

They remained sitting, and then, at 12:30, they were startled by a knock on the door. Armstrong rushed to the door as everyone reminded him of the proper questions and answers. But he returned disappointed. The visitors were just some boys, he reported, just some ordinary boys playing a prank, not the space visitor they all were waiting for.

They all had some explaining to do . . . to one another, but most of all to themselves.

DISCUSSION QUESTIONS

1. What do you think the members of the group did next—over the next hour, week, and years? What does cognitive dissonance theory predict about how they will react to the continued disconfirmation of their previous beliefs? What specific explanations would keep the group together and energize them to become even more committed to their beliefs? Later, after the case study timeline described here, Keech did receive another message from

Sananda, and it brought them tremendous joy. What do you think it was?

2. Were the social psychologists behaving ethically when they became participant-observers without telling Keech and the others why they were there?

3. This case study claims that "neither education nor mental capability helps us understand the appeal of groups with such extreme beliefs." If this is true, what variable could be used to predict interest and commitment to groups such as the one described here? What kinds of people will be most likely to join cult-like fellowships?

KEY TERMS

- **Self-affirmation:** Comforting beliefs that increase our positive self-esteem and self-concept; they support our value or worth
- **Participant observation:** A technique used in naturalistic observation studies in which

experimenters go "under cover," so the people they are observing continue to act naturally

6.3 UNDERSTANDING DRUG USE: THE THEORY OF PLANNED BEHAVIOR

The Social Situation

By 1969, the U.S. Army had finally become concerned about soldiers' drug use.

It was about time. It was an open secret that many U.S. soldiers in Vietnam were using "recreational" drugs. But that is a polite term for what was happening among these men and women overseas. This was a serious, widespread drug problem. So many returning veterans from the war in Vietnam had become heavy drug users that their adjustment back into civilian society was bound to be difficult.

Many soldiers' readjustment was aggravated with a confusing psychological disorder often viewed as a personal weakness: posttraumatic stress disorder (PTSD). Along with barely-acknowledged PTSD, the soldiers were returning home to a public that was often unsympathetic, crudely accusing soldiers of being murderers rather than patriotic warriors. So it is not a surprise that drug use was heavy both overseas and when soldiers returned home.

Theory and Method

This case study is based on a national assessment survey that changed public policy.

Social psychologists can make contributions to society by separating data-driven reality from wishful thinking and myths—and then communicating that reality to the appropriate audience. Surveys based on interviews and previously collected archival data are one common way to collect such data, and often used by public agencies. The data in this report were commissioned by the Department of Defense (DoD).

Social Norms

Recreational drug use had become a social norm in the army.

There was an informal expectation, quickly perceived by arriving soldiers, that they were expected to use recreational drugs. There was little effort to stop them, and it seemed as if everyone was doing it. As people looked deeper into the results of this now classic study (see Blomqvist, 2007), they were surprised in three more ways.

First, the DoD was surprised that so many soldiers were addicted in the first place. It was surprised, perhaps, at the proportion of soldiers using narcotics, but not at the general reality of drug use. Drug use was not hidden.

Second, the DoD was surprised to discover that the so-called **gateway drugs** (alcohol and marijuana) were *not* steppingstones into harder drugs (opium and heroin). Many soldiers didn't need to be seduced into addiction. They went directly to the hard stuff.

Third, given those high numbers, type of narcotics, and the level of use, the DoD was surprised that relatively few returning veterans relapsed into narcotic use when they got home: 5% after 1 year and 12% after 3 years. Robins (1993) reported that their post-Vietnam "addiction had usually been very brief."

Let's not minimize the problem. A 12% addiction rate represents a big problem. That translates to about 168 of the 1,400 addicted soldiers returning home *every month* (or about 20,000 soldiers per year). They also were still using hard narcotics 3 years after their planes touched down on American soil. That's definitely a serious problem. But the problem of addicted soldiers was far less severe than the DoD had feared.

"It was not treatment that explained this remarkable rate of recovery. Only a third of the men addicted in Vietnam received even simple detoxification . . . and only a tiny percentage . . . went into drug abuse treatment after return—less than 2%" (Robins, 1993, p. 1045). So it was good news, sort of, to learn that the problem of veteran addiction was not even worse than they had feared. Had some of the soldiers' favorable attitudes toward narcotics magically changed when they boarded the airplane coming home?

Attitudes

Social psychologists once pinned almost all their hopes on the concept of attitudes.

Attitudes were thought to predict behavior—and it made intuitive sense. **Attitudes** are the product of beliefs and emotions. People are expected to behave in ways that were consistent with their beliefs and emotions. If you had a positive attitude toward religion, then it was expected that you would attend religious services. That was the theory; the reality was something different.

The **attitude–behavior discrepancy** is the gap between what people believe and what they do. For example, people may believe in democracy but seldom bother to vote. Many addicted veterans returned to the United States with the same positive attitude toward narcotics they had in Vietnam.

They then came home to a society in which recreational drug use was widely celebrated and openly practiced by their age peers. Yet many more veterans than the DoD anticipated were able to shrug off their addiction. The Army was able to breathe a small, partial sigh of relief. But from a psychology point of view, it was a surprising discrepancy. What happened?

Results and Discussion

The Army understood what kind of soldiers they were sending back home.

One in 10 of the soldiers returning to the United States were "so addicted they could not stop their use when warned that they would be screened" (Robins, 1993, p. 1044). When you know that you are going to be caught and still can't stop using . . . well, that's a serious problem.

How Many Soldiers?

The DoD released a formal study.

It is now regarded as a classic assessment (see Robins, 1993), but the news wasn't good. About 45% of the Army's enlisted soldiers had tried narcotics, 34% had tried heroin, and 38% had tried opium (and some had tried both). Over 90% had used alcohol and almost 80% had used marijuana. One out of every five soldiers had felt strung out or addicted to narcotics. They had "used narcotics heavily for a considerable time and suffered the classic symptoms of withdrawal for at least several days" (p. 1044).

You can see why the polite term of recreational drug use doesn't fit the experience of these young returning soldiers who had been risking their lives fighting an unpopular war. Not every member of the Army was stoned at the same time. However, a significant proportion of the American Army in Vietnam was stoned much of the time.

The Theory of Planned Behavior

That is why the DoD was surprised that the addiction problem wasn't even worse.

It took many experiments for social psychologists to figure out why, but eventually a better explanation for the attitude–behavior discrepancy emerged from the data. The **theory of planned behavior** (see Ajzen & Fishbein, 1977; Fishbein & Ajzen, 2010) clarified that there are three roughly equal predictors of how people intend to behave—and those intentions predict how people actually behave. Figure 6.1 portrays that attitudes are just one of three factors or major influences on our **behavioral intentions** and subsequent behavior.

Perceived Control

About $6.00 per day.

In Vietnam, the cost of addiction to a pure version of opium or heroin was only about $6.00. For the American soldiers serving there, getting stoned was easy, cheap, and convenient. They hardly had to do anything to access narcotics, and it was always within their budget; they had a strong sense of **perceived control** of their access to narcotics.

FIGURE 6.1

Three Factors That Predict Our Intentions and Our Behaviors

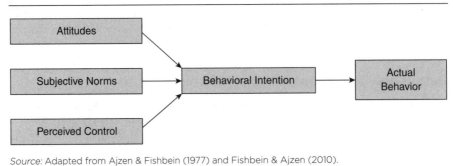

Source: Adapted from Ajzen & Fishbein (1977) and Fishbein & Ajzen (2010).

After soldiers returned home, they could still find ways to buy their drugs—but now it was less convenient. Yes, it was a period of widespread drug use in the United States, but it still required more effort to get their drugs than it had in Vietnam. Perceived control went way down. The addicted veterans would have to work harder to find a ready supplier of what were now generally less pure and more expensive drugs.

Subjective Norms

The subjective norms in Vietnam during the war encouraged use of narcotics.

Subjective norms are the informal version of social norms. In some parts of the United States, the subjective norm for exceeding the speed limit is about 10–15 miles per hour. It's what everyone else is doing, so you simply match their speed and don't think much of it. But when you cross a state or county line, you may discover that their subjective norm matches the social norm stated on the road signs.

The subjective norm experience of American soldiers in Vietnam was that "everyone was doing it." It is difficult to say no to any behavior when it has become a common, everyday practice. Moreover, it wasn't just the lower-ranking soldiers. A significant proportion of the Army leadership, from sergeants through captains, were also using narcotics.

Getting high with opium had become a pervasive subjective norm among U.S. soldiers. But that all changed when the soldiers got home—even during the infamous 1960s and early 1970s. The returning veterans were no longer surrounded by people using narcotics every day. Subjective norms made it easier for them to stop using.

Attitudes Again

The soldiers' attitudes toward narcotic use probably didn't change very much.

When they came home, opium still provided a welcome escape; heroin still felt good; the soldiers' bodies were accustomed to having the drugs. They still believed that opium could help them escape their PTSD and related troubles, at least for a while. Attitudes probably played a minor role in the relatively low rate of drug abuse among returning Vietnam veterans.

However, narcotics were no longer as cheap, convenient, or popular as they were in the army. There was no more rolling out of bed and reaching for some opium to get the day started. Convenience—or perceived control—and subjective norms appeared to be far more powerful than attitudes when it came to predicting drug use. So, many addicted soldiers stopped using.

The case study about the DoD's classic report of drug use demonstrated one of those hard-to-learn insights from psychology: What is obvious is not necessarily true—and what is true is not necessarily obvious (see LeDoux, 1998). It had seemed obvious that attitudes would predict behavior—but it wasn't true. What was true was that attitudes were just one of three predictors—and that wasn't obvious.

The combination of attitudes, perceived control, and subjective norms was a much more precise predictor of what people intended to do—and those intentions were an even better predictor of how people actually behaved. Attitudes about race prejudice, politics, drug use, and everything else were only part of the answer to why people behaved in a particular way during the years after the Vietnam War. Attitudes are still important. But they aren't quite as important to social psychology—or to human behavior—as was once believed.

DISCUSSION QUESTIONS

1. In this case study, there was some evidence that subjective norms and perceived control became more important behavioral predictors than attitudes were. Can you think of examples when attitudes would be the most important predictor? Why are attitudes more important in those cases?

2. One attitude that mattered in this case was soldiers' attitudes toward drug use. However, other attitudes might have been at play, such as the attitude of being a good family member once home, an attitude about being an "addict," and so on. Describe three additional attitudes not already identified that may have been involved in the soldiers' drug usage after returning home.

3. Identify a behavior in your own life that is particularly influenced by each of the three variables in the theory of planned behavior: perceived control, subjective norms, and attitudes. Has your behavior changed over time, as these three variables fluctuate?

KEY TERMS

- **Gateway drugs**: Drugs like alcohol and marijuana that are more commonly used and often believed to be steppingstones into harder drugs (although this claim is often not supported)
- **Attitudes**: Evaluative judgments of people, objects, or ideas

- **Attitude–behavior discrepancy**: When there's a gap or mismatch between someone's beliefs and their behaviors
- **Theory of planned behavior**: The idea that our behaviors are predicted by not just our attitudes, but also by perceived control and subjective norms

- **Behavioral intentions**: What we plan to do
- **Perceived control**: Our assessment of whether we are in control of our environment and can make independent decisions (e.g., if we can afford to do something)

- **Subjective norms**: Our assessment of what other people are doing and what our culture expects of us

Social Influence

7.1 OBEDIENCE PLUS: MORE DATA FROM THE SHOCK EXPERIMENTS

The Social Situation

You can count on nervous giggles.

That's the sound that many students make watching Stanley Milgram's (1962) documentary film *Obedience*. The sound echoes the nervous giggles the study's participants experienced themselves. Normal citizens accepted a small amount of money to be part of a memory experiment. But they ended up participating in a study in which they thought they were delivering lethal levels of electric shock to an innocent gentleman. The shocks were not real but some 70 years later, the original film footage still prompts a disturbing question: What would I have done?

Stanley Milgram joined other social psychologists trying to explain the **compliance** and **obedience** that produced the Holocaust of World War II. Just "being German" is not a "good enough" explanation. A backward glance into history tells you that just being German, Russian, Nigerian, Turkish, American, or any nationality is an inadequate explanation for large-scale atrocities such as genocide (see Assembly, 2019).

Individual and political explanations also fall short. Adolf Hitler and Joseph Stalin did not have time to point and pull the trigger on each of the millions of murders committed in their names between 1939 and 1945. It was more efficient to let people starve than to kill them one by one.

Social psychologists recognized that mass murder in the 20th century also needed architects and bricklayers, accountants and plumbers, transportation experts and typists. Mass murder required many people turning valves just the right amount and flipping switches at just the right times.

Stanley Milgram wanted to use the tools of social psychology to explain what happened.

Theory and Method

This case study describes archival data from Stanley Milgram's shock experiments.

The qualitative data in the Yale archives come from interviews that Milgram collected during and after the experiment. Quantitative analyses provided fascinating insights (see Haslam et al., 2015). These new data expand Milgram's original explanations and offer new ideas regarding the psychology of compliance and obedience. The title of their article tells their unhappy conclusions about why humans harm one another: *Happy to Have Been of Service.*

The Experimental Paradigm

Stanley Milgram was willing to take scientific risks.

He was asking urgent questions and wanted empirically grounded answers. He invented an **experimental paradigm** that created repeatable procedures that could be varied systematically. To test his hypothesis, Milgram needed to induce (critics would say "trick") ordinary people to behave in extraordinarily harmful ways, yet still not *really* harm anybody.

Repeatable Procedures

Milgram had participated in and written for theater (see Blass, 2004).

His theatrical training may have helped him create the experimental paradigm of ordering someone to deliver (phony) electric shocks for failures on a memory test. He knew how to stage a scene by using procedures that could be replicated across many performances. A constant in (almost) all variations was the presence of a lab-coated, authoritative male scientist who prodded reluctant participants to keep delivering higher levels of electric shock.

Milgram started by placing an announcement in the New Haven, Connecticut, newspaper: "Persons Needed for a Study of Memory." It was a **cover story** that camouflaged the true nature of the experiment. When they arrived, the participants were assigned (through a rigged lottery) to play the role of a "Teacher" in the so-called memory study. Hence, there were two experimental deceptions before the experiment even got started.

The job of the Teacher was to read word pairs out loud (such as *fast/car* or *white/bird*) to the Learner. The Learner's job was to memorize the word pairs and take a memory test. The Teacher was to respond to any memory failures by delivering gradually increasing levels of electric shock—15 volts more with each failure, to a maximum of 450 volts.

Testable Variables

The electric shocks were not real.

They were another deception that made it possible to simulate the psychology of ordinary people behaving in extraordinarily harmful ways. The dependent variable was simple: How far up the electric shock scale would they go? It was an easy-to-measure, testable outcome.

Milgram conducted 18 variations using his basic experimental paradigm. The different conditions represented Milgram's independent variable. He could manipulate small differences to compare their effects on the dependent variable.

For example, in one set of experiments, he examined the effect of physical proximity on the numerically assessed willingness to deliver electric shocks. Would being physically closer to the person you were harming influence how far up the shock scale you were willing to go?

Theory 1: Obedience to Authority

Stanley Milgram looked to evolution and culture to explain obedience to authorities.

Milgram recognized that because organizations have "enormous survival value for any species. . . . [W]e are born with a potential for obedience" (Milgram, 1974, pp. 3 and 126). The shock experiments needed a lot of explaining. His opening experiments established that approximately 65% of participants delivered the *highest possible* levels of electric shock: 450 volts.

This baseline became the **control condition** that Milgram used to make comparisons under different conditions. He reasoned that people are trained from early childhood to obey authority figures, and this is why so many people participated in both his own study and in situations like the Holocaust. The power of the situation made them go unwillingly along with unethical behaviors, simply because they were told to do so.

Milgram died in 1984, so we do not know how he would have reacted to new interpretations of the data. We must join the many others who have surmised how he might have reacted to criticisms of how he conducted his experiments, followed up with participants, or reported his results (see Baumrind, 1964; Chernew, 2018; Kaposi, 2016). But modern social psychologists are excited about fresh ideas emerging from old data buried in Yale University's archives of the Milgram experiments.

The data seem to be saying, "Listen carefully. There's more to this story than obedience to authority."

Theory 2: A Noble Cause

The new qualitative data suggest a possibly more frightening motivation.

The noble cause explanation rises from the observations that many people involved in the Nazi atrocities were eager participants, "glad to be of service" to a higher cause. The noble aspiration in the Holocaust was the reign of a "righteous" Germany. How could this motivation to participate in the German cause compare to Milgram's study? Some people are suggesting that the "noble aspiration" in the shock experiments was the cause of science (see Reichert et al., 2012). Evaluate the evidence for yourself as you compare old and new details emerging from this famous set of experiments.

Results and Discussion

Milgram's experimental variations in the shock experiments were, well, shocking.

The combination of quantitative and qualitative data help us understand the path to disobedience by adding richness and nuance, but also contradictions.

Quantitative Observations

In Milgram's first experiment, 26 of 40 Yale students (65%) applied the maximum voltage available.

The Learner was behind a wall and said nothing. Milgram himself was surprised by this high rate of obedience, so he started changing the situation to see what might change the responses. What would stop participants from these high levels of obedience? What would help them disobey?

Physical Proximity

The compliance rate of 65% was only slightly lower in Experiment 2 (62.5%).

That was another surprise, because Milgram added a scripted voice in Experiment 2 so that the Teacher heard the Learner screaming in pain and complaining of a heart condition. The compliance rate was much lower in Experiment 3, when the Teacher and Learner were in the same room: 40%. They continued to decline in Experiment 4, when the Teacher forced the Learner's hand onto the electric plate to receive the shock: 30%.

The pattern in the data suggests that physical proximity reduces the willingness to harm someone. The hesitation to harm others based on physical proximity between the Teacher and the Learner seemed to be important and is something to consider in a world of remote, drone warfare. Yet it's pretty disturbing that even when the Teacher had to physically grab the Learner's hand and force it onto a shock plate, 30% of the participants were still willing to obey an authority directing them to hurt an innocent person.

Female "Teachers"

Milgram conducted only one experiment with women in the role of "Teacher."

The women behaved like the men: 65% of women shocked to the maximum voltage. However, based on post-experiment interviews, Milgram believed that women's experience was different. He suspected that women were caught between competing social norms. Their traditional social role was to be warm, caring nurturers ("do not shock").

But a competing social role for women was to be obedient and submissive to a male authority ("do shock"). In this case, social role expectations may have sent conflicting messages of what to do. The social role closest to their experience at that moment (obeying the male experimenter) appeared to exert more control over their behavior than the more distant social role of being warm and nurturing.

A Role Reversal

In Experiment 12, the experimenter paused the experiment.

The experimenter told the Teacher that he was concerned about the Learner's heart condition. But surprisingly, the voice of the Learner then came over the microphone and stated that he *wanted* to go on with the experiment. So, the roles were reversed: The experimenter said to stop the experiment, and the Learner wanted to continue.

In this condition, every person playing the role of Teacher followed the experimenter's orders and stopped delivering shocks. Only the scientist's views mattered; the victim's opinion didn't seem to count. This is an important detail in light of the new interpretations of Milgram's data. Why did the authority figure of the scientist wield such extraordinary power?

Qualitative Observations

Milgram made several curious qualitative observations.

In the initial pilot study, the Learner (whom Milgram sometimes refers to as the "Victim") could be seen vaguely through silvered glass. Milgram noticed that the Teachers often averted their eyes when shocking the Learner. This observation suggested that the Yale students were willing to harm the Learner, but they did not want to see him as they were hurting him. It reminded Milgram of some odd social conventions, such as blindfolding a person about to be shot. Who benefits from that? Certainly not the person being shot.

Nervous Laughter

Milgram (1963) also reported nervous laughter.

Similar to what students often display, nervous laughter was a "regular occurrence" that sometimes "developed into uncontrollable seizures" (p. 371). M. B. was a 39-year-old social worker whose laughter began as a "light snicker." But the snickers gradually became more disruptive, breaking into wheezing laughter triggered by the Learner's screams. The experimenter's notes report that M. B. was "rubbing his face to hide laughter," and later that he "cannot control laughter at this point no matter what he does." M. B. later described his own behavior as "peculiar" and tried to explain.

"There was I. I'm a nice person, I think, hurting somebody and caught up in what seemed a mad situation . . . and in the interest of science, one goes through with it." He emphasized, "This isn't the way that I usually am." His laughter was "a sheer reaction to a totally impossible situation. . . . I just couldn't deviate and I couldn't try to help. This is what got to me."

Family Reactions

M. B. described his wife's blunt reaction.

"You can call yourself Eichmann"—referring, of course, to the infamous Nazi bureaucrat who conscientiously helped murder millions of innocent people. Eichmann's dramatic trial began in August 1961, the same month that Milgram started the shock experiments (Benjamin & Simpson, 2009). M. B. said, "I hope I can deal more effectively with any future conflicts of values I encounter." M. B. (and his wife) believed that his participation had provided important insights into his own behavior.

Politeness

The people playing the role of Teacher tended to be courteous.

Some participants called the experimenter "sir" or used other expressions of institutional respect for the scientist. A few participants described the person they were shocking as a "gentleman," even when they were privately convinced that they were killing him. Their language may partly reflect the social norms of mid-20th-century America.

Milgram interpreted this consistent courtesy as a sign of excessive deference to authority. It also might indicate their high regard for a Yale scientist and the privilege of participating in an important experiment.

Taking Responsibility

F. B. was a 50-year-old man who asked an important question.

"Who's going to take responsibility if anything happens to that gentleman?" Assured that the experimenter would take responsibility, he reluctantly continued. At 195 volts, he once again tried to rebel. "Aw, no. I'm not going to kill that man. You mean I've got to keep going up with the scale? No sir."

But he continued to 450 volts even though he asked, "What if he's dead in there? I mean, he told me that he can't stand the shock, sir. I don't mean to be rude, but I think you should look in on him." Perhaps by saying these things, F. B. felt like he was no longer responsible for what happened—even though he was the one flipping the switch.

Secretly Trying to Help

E. R. was a college-educated homemaker.

She was a good citizen who volunteered for the Girl Scouts and the local parent–teachers association. As shock levels increased, she began muttering to herself, yet administered the memory test with a show of officiousness and outward strength. When she noticed the many remaining shock levels, she hesitated.

"Are we going all the way up there? Can't we stop? I'm shaking." At 270 volts, E. R. began giving the Learner hints by emphasizing the correct answer. At the post-experiment interview, she learned that she really had not harmed the Learner. She added, "I tried to push the switch down lightly."

Disgust for the Victim

B. B. was a 37-year-old welder.

He voiced respect for the scientist-experimenter but disgust for the Learner. At 330 volts, B. B. brutally informed the now-silent Learner, "You better answer and get it over with. We can't stay here all night." After 450 volts, he respectfully asked the experimenter, "Where do we go from here, Professor?"

He was always deferential to authority. But he reported that he felt disgusted when the victim—presumably now dead or at least unconscious—would no longer cooperate.

Growing Up in Germany

By chance, one participant (G. B.) came of age in Germany during Hitler's rise to power.

She had been repeatedly exposed to Nazi propaganda during her childhood. G. B. was a 31-year-old medical technician when she participated in Milgram's so-called study of memory. When the Learner began to complain about his heart condition, G. B. calmly asked the experimenter, "Shall I continue?" After administering 210 volts, she stated, "Well, I'm sorry, I don't think we should continue."

Experimenter: It is absolutely essential that we continue....

G. B.:   I like you to ask him. We came here of our own free will. If he wants to continue, I'll go ahead....

Experimenter: You have no other choice.

G. B.:   I think we are here on our own free will. I don't want to be responsible if he has a heart condition if anything happens to him. Please understand that.

G. B. refused to continue, and the experiment ended. Milgram observed that her "straightforward, courteous behavior in the experiment, lack of tension, and total control of her own action seems to make disobedience a simple and rational deed ... what I had initially envisioned would be true for almost all subjects" (Milgram, 1974, p. 88).

G. B. had followed the path to *dis*obedience by having inner doubts, expressing them, dissenting, threatening to end her participation, and then refusing to continue. When asked about how her experience as a youth might have influenced her, G. B. slowly replied, "Perhaps we have seen too much pain."

DISCUSSION QUESTIONS

1. Have you ever obeyed an authority figure or gone along with a crowd, even though you didn't agree with what they were doing? What motivated you to go against your own inner nature or better judgment? How do you reconcile your actions now, upon reflection?

2. Milgram's series of studies have been used as examples of highly unethical procedures, even though he claimed that his participants suffered from no long-term negative effects. Do you think these procedures were unethical, even if the participants reported being fine? When studies from the past are unethical, should we continue to highlight them in books such as this—or does that only glorify them?

3. If they could be done in an ethical way (or if ethics weren't a concern), what other interesting variations would be possible with the basic Milgram paradigm? For example, the Learner (or false-shock victim) could be kind versus derogatory to the Teacher before the shocks begin, or the Learner could be a child, an older person, or a woman. Think of three variations that you think would be interesting, and explain what your hypotheses would be in each condition.

KEY TERMS

- **Compliance**: When we behave in response to someone else's direct or indirect request
- **Obedience**: When we behave in response to direct orders from someone with more power or status than ourselves
- **Experimental paradigm**: A structure or framework for the methodology used in a study or series of studies

- **Cover story**: A false purpose of a study told to participants when knowing the true nature of the study might affect their responses and behaviors
- **Control condition**: In an experiment, this is the group of participants who are under neutral circumstances or serve as a comparison to other groups in the study

7.2 MODS AND ROCKERS: A MORAL PANIC

The Social Situation

The Clacton, England, shopkeepers were annoyed.

The coldest day in 80 years had discouraged people from shopping on what should have been one of the busiest days in their beautiful seaside town. The shopkeepers were also annoyed at the bored youths roaring up and down the street on their scooters (the Mods) and motorcycles (the Rockers). The two groups were then only loosely identified to the British public by their clothing and motorbike preferences.

"An Orgy of Destruction"

The merchants weren't the only frustrated people in Clacton.

A rock-throwing incident between the Mods and the Rockers broke a few windows and overwhelmed a modest police force. There were 97 arrests, but the event was far less dramatic than was portrayed by the media. For example, property damage was estimated at only 513 British pounds, a modest amount even after inflation.

But the *Daily Mirror* (Hughes, 1964) printed a large, bold print, provocative headline: "'WILD ONES' INVADE SEASIDE—97 ARRESTS." The first two sentences suggested that "wild ones" was the name of an identifiable group that posed a serious social threat: "The Wild Ones invaded a seaside town yesterday—1000 fighting, drinking, roaring, rampaging teenagers on scooters and motor-cycles." (p. 1).

Their "orgy of destruction" included stealing a drink from a vending machine and fraudulently obtaining credit—to buy an ice cream. The media reported that, "all the dance halls near the seafront were smashed." That was technically true because Clacton had only one dance hall, and some of its windows were broken (see Thompson, 1998, pp. 32–34).

Media Exaggerations

There were many other fear-promoting exaggerations.

The publicity encouraged three similar incidents at resorts over the next holiday. But each successive conflict between the Mods and the Rockers produced fewer arrests and lower estimates of property damage. The actual problem was declining at the same time that the public panic was increasing, fed by a media frenzy.

The rising public panic produced a resolution in the House of Commons that led to specific legislation. The resolution began with, "In light of the deplorable and continual increase in juvenile delinquency" and ended with pleas that young hooligans be subject to "such financial and physical punishment as will provide an effective deterrent" (Cohen, 1973/2002, p. 151).

The British minister sponsoring the legislation later acknowledged that "some of the reports of what happened at Clacton over the Easter weekend were greatly exaggerated" (Cohen, 1973/2002, p. 153). But by then, it was too late. The belief in what Cohen calls "folk devils" had settled in the public's imagination.

Theory and Method

This case study describes the development of a social psychological construct: moral panic.

A construct is an idea that cannot be directly observed. It represents the central idea related to similar concepts. Anxiety, for example, is a construct related to worry, fear, and concern for the future.

Psychologists have referred to the construct of moral panic with slightly different terms: *mass hysteria, mass psychosis, mass panic,* and *social contagion.* The term *moral panic* comes from sociology; *mass hysteria* and *mass psychosis* come from psychodynamic psychology; *mass panic* and *social contagion* are closer to social psychology. The most precise term depends on which theoretical lens you are using.

A student offered a useful definition of a moral panic: "It's when people go crazy over something that never happened." A **moral panic** is an exaggerated concern over a perceived threat that identifies specific groups (such as the Mods and the Rockers) as dangerous social deviants (see Krinsky, 2013; Goode & Ben-Yehuda, 2009).

Social Contagion

Moral panics are a form of **social contagion**.

Social contagions are fairly common. Like a social meme, social contagions happen when an idea, emotion, or symbol spreads (like a physical virus) rapidly through a group of people. When an online meme about cute kittens "goes viral," a social contagion is behind its wide distribution. When entire communities start hoarding toilet paper, it's probably because of social contagion.

A literally laughable social contagion was the **Tanganyika Laughter Epidemic** of 1962. It started with just a few teenage girls in a boarding school who got the giggles. They eventually "infected" about 1,000 other children so severely that 14 schools had to be closed (see Hempelmann, 2007; Provine, 1996). People laughed hysterically for hours at a time. It lasted 18 months, and no physical or medical reason was ever found for the strange phenomenon.

A moral panic is another form of social contagion, but it promotes fear rather than fun. Moral panics are common across cultures. They probably express some ancient tribal impulse to protect our own, but from imagined others rather than real enemies. It is sometimes called a **herd mentality** when humans behave like conforming sheep following a mindless flock.

A Brief History of Moral Panics

Philosopher Friedrich Nietzsche (1887/1996) proposed a similar idea: *ressentiment*.

It's the French translation of the English word *resentment*. Nietzsche was referring to a profound hostility displaced onto a **scapegoat**. Selecting someone or some group to blame is a key characteristic of a moral panic, and common in human affairs. But moral panics also include elements of Le Bon's (1896) general description of contagious crowd behavior that can influence otherwise-normal individuals to behave in an abnormal and often violent way. Le Bon (1896) observed that

> In crowds the foolish, ignorant, and envious persons are freed from the sense of their own insignificance and powerlessness, and are possessed instead by the notion of brutal and temporary but immense strength. (p. 34)

The term *moral panic* first entered the sociology community in 1971. Young described how a moral panic over drug use produced a harmful self-fulfilling prophecy. The process required only three stages:

1. The public's fear of addictive drug use led to the creation of police drug squads.

2. Those drug squads searched for and found drug use and made more arrests than before.

3. Those arrests became evidence that the original source of fear and arrests were justified.

Very little had changed in terms of overall drug use, but the moral panic helped produce a self-fulfilling prophecy. A self-fulfilling prophecy is easy to understand intellectually and after the fact. But it seems to be difficult to recognize when it is happening to you.

The term *moral panic* originated with British sociologists (Best, 2013). The phrase and concept were slow to catch on until the second edition of Cohen's (1973/2002) case study, titled *Folk Devils and Moral Panics: The Creation of the Mods and Rockers*.

Results and Discussion

At the beginning of the 1960s, Mods and Rockers were barely identifiable groups.

Five years later, their actions were described in the press as without parallel in English history. Another 5 years later, the cultural panic over the Mods and the Rockers were a

FIGURE 7.1

Numbers Reflect the Amount of Entries in PsycINFO That Include Keywords and Terms Associated With the Construct of Moral Panic, Such as Mass Hysteria or Social Contagion

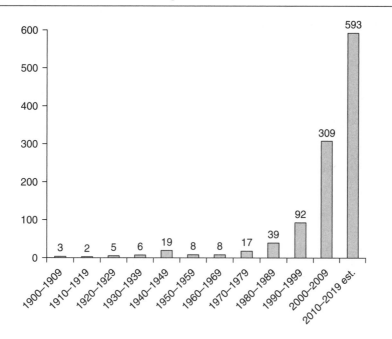

mostly forgotten footnote to England's long history. They had been convenient scapegoats during Clacton's cold weather holiday.

Their most enduring contribution may be from Cohen's recognition that this passing panic was an opportunity for a case study that captured a much deeper pattern of social behavior. Figure 7.1 demonstrates how thoroughly the construct of moral panic has entered the world of research regarding social psychological behavior.

Other Examples

Unfortunately, there are many examples of moral panics.

One long-enduring, demonstrably false moral panic was based on a terrifying belief: Poor people were killing their own children to collect life insurance money. Grey (2013) traced the course of this moral panic in England from 1875 through 1914. The publicly available data never supported it. But with the help of 19th century newspapers and medical journals, the belief was widely circulated.

This particular moral panic also produced a new society called the Prevention of Cruelty to Children. It was made up of people who apparently saw themselves playing a heroic role on behalf of innocent children. The society reported, contrary to the available data, that cases of lethal child abuse were endemic in the United Kingdom. The panic peaked in the 1880s but endured for almost 40 years. It was in decline by 1914 when World War I suddenly gave the British public something far bigger—and more real—to worry about.

The articles represented in Figure 7.1 focus on a wide variety of moral panics. A partial list of concerns addressed in these articles includes (in alphabetical order):

AIDS

ageism

asylum seekers

clergy sexual abuse

drugs in the workplace

enthusiasm for war

fetal alcohol syndrome

football hooliganism

gangs

horse maiming

Internet cyberporn

Muslim converts in prison

obesity

paint sniffing

plagiarism

police corruption

Ritalin use

runaway youth

Satanic rituals

"wilding" (random youth violence)

The Elements of a Moral Panic

Cohen's (1973/2002, pp. 16–25) case study identified four elements of a moral panic:

1. The *mass media* prime the public for panic by defining social deviance and identifying specific individuals as "folk devils";

2. *moral entrepreneurs* are individuals and groups that conduct an exaggerated but effective fear campaign to eradicate the moral threat;

3. the *control culture* calls on the institutions of government, such as the police and the court systems, to sensitize and, if necessary, prosecute the social deviants; and

4. *public opinion* shaped by vivid media imagery reduces the public's capacity for skepticism and critical thinking. A frequent outcome of a moral panic is a change in the law or how the law is enforced.

Critcher (2008; see Table 7.1) reviewed and summarized the many modifications to Cohen's initial description of a moral panic. That review makes it easier for both citizens and political leaders to ask critical questions *before* we start sending people to jail. For example, looking at events through the lens of moral panic directs us to ask

a. Are stories being exaggerated or distorted?

b. Is the media promoting panic?

c. Is the panic justified?

TABLE 7.1

Common Features of a Moral Panic

The mass media focus attention on a scapegoat.
Moral entrepreneurs posture as heroes resisting evil to protect the innocent.
A control culture creates ways to violate others' rights.
Public opinion turns against a particular group.
Those accused of evil can receive less punishment by "naming names."
People express unjustified certainty and overconfidence in their opinions.
Self-righteous statements exalt one group over another.
Panic leads to an official change in law or status.
A vulnerable group is targeted.
Exaggerated fears are publicized; contradicting evidence is ignored.
Actions are taken with a general disregard for evidence.
There is only superficial contact between the dominant and minority groups.
Legitimate anxieties are exaggerated.
A wide variety of social problems are blamed on a specific group (scapegoating).

(Continued)

TABLE 7.1 (Continued)

Public opinion supports suppressing a targeted group to make problems go away.
The rule of law is weakened, changed, or reinterpreted to justify injustice.
Stereotyping of particular groups is accepted as fact.
Prejudice turns into overt discrimination against the targeted group.

Source: Adapted from Critcher (2008).

Moral panics are academically interesting when we consider the social psychology of blame and hysteria over a group of people seen as "deviants" or "dangerous." But they are even more important as a lesson on empathy and respect for people different from ourselves. One way to remember not to condemn people just because they're different is the famous post-war confession by the German pastor Martin Niemöller, who, looking back on the Holocaust, wrote:

First they came for the socialists, and I did not speak out—

Because I was not a socialist.

Then they came for the trade unionists, and I did not speak out—

Because I was not a trade unionist.

Then they came for the Jews, and I did not speak out—

Because I was not a Jew.

Then they came for me—and there was no one left to speak for me.

DISCUSSION QUESTIONS

1. Journalists are supposed to report facts. However, newspapers and magazines are for-profit businesses, and more copies sell when facts are exaggerated. How do journalists and reporters deal with this conflict of interest, from a psychological perspective? What is behind the accusation that someone else is delivering "fake news?"

2. According to Cohen (1973/2002), one element of a moral panic is the public's loss of a capacity for skepticism and critical thinking. What psychological terms or theories you've learned about in earlier chapters of this book are relevant to this process? Explain your answers.

3. What are two examples of moral panics (in your opinion) in current events? What makes these examples of a moral panic? Why are moral panics easier to recognize after they're done, by later generations?

4. Consider Critcher's (2008) list of common elements in moral panics. Which three elements do you think are most central to this phenomenon, and why?

KEY TERMS

- **Moral panic**: Exaggerated concern about a perceived threat from some specific "deviant" group (e.g., bikers, witches, Communists)
- **Social contagion**: When an idea, emotion, or symbol spreads rapidly through a group of people
- **Tanganyika Laughter Epidemic**: A strange phenomenon in 1962 when children in what is now Tanzania started laughing and "infected" other children with laughter for no physical or medical reason
- **Herd mentality**: When many people in a group conform to what others are doing without thought
- **Scapegoat**: Singling someone out as the cause or person to blame for a problem

7.3 BIG FISH EAT SMALL FISH: SOCIAL COORDINATION IN A VIOLENT WORLD

The Social Setting

Nancy and Rod sailed their 22-foot catamaran from rural Wisconsin to Florida.

Their route took them across the Great Lakes, around (not over) Niagara Falls using the Welland Canal, through the Erie canal system to the Hudson River, down to New York City, and then through the intercoastal waterway to Florida. It was Rod's first trip to New York City. From the lowest possible elevation on the Hudson River, he looked up at New York's many skyscrapers. The Twin Towers were still there making 50-story buildings look small. After tying up at a dock on the New Jersey side, Rod asked, "How does everyone get enough water every day?"

Social Coordination of a Water Supply

It was an excellent question with an even better answer.

Social coordination is the organization of mutually productive behaviors across individuals and groups (see Claidière & Whiten, 2012; Finkel et al., 2006; Oullier et al., 2008). The canal systems that made Nancy and Rod's trip possible required social coordination, both to build and to maintain. And so does delivering water to New York City.

Every day, a network of aqueducts and tunnels delivers approximately 1 billion gallons of the world's finest water from the Catskill Mountain rivers and reservoirs to homes and businesses throughout New York City. It's wonderful drinking water, but delivering it requires regional sacrifices of land, uniform public policies across different levels of government, cooperation between different governing agencies, negotiating with real estate developers, ongoing maintenance, and much more.

Generational Social Coordination

Water is necessary for individual and group survival.

That's why most towns and villages around the world were settled near convenient supplies of water. In New York City and elsewhere, the social coordination of the water supply is a generational phenomenon. The social coordination that delivers water to millions of people is passed like a baton across generations of citizens and politicians.

It demonstrates **generational social coordination** that requires cooperation with unknown people living in an unknown future. And New York City is only one of many cities around the world that routinely accomplishes this impressive feat. The canal system and New York City's water supply demonstrate that humans have an extraordinary ability to cooperate with one another.

But it's not a given. If you have ever been in a large city or region with poor social coordination, especially around the water supply and sewage, then you understand why social coordination is necessary for individual and group survival. When social coordination fails, it fails big and can cost lives (see Case 2.3, "The Missing Pump Handle").

Theory and Method

This case study uses comparative psychology to demonstrate the rewards and risks of social coordination.

Comparative psychology explores the psychological similarities and differences between species. The theoretical framework for making such comparisons is evolutionary psychology that explores how behavioral adaptations influence generational survival. Social coordination may be found both within and between animal and plant species. This case study references social animals and one plant that demonstrate social coordination: ants, wolves, elephants, honeybees, hawkmoths, stickleback fish, sardines, herring, humpback whales, and Darwin's Star orchid. And humans.

They all demonstrate the necessary rewards and large risks associated with social coordination.

Coevolution

Ants sacrifice for other ants; wolves cooperate when hunting; elephants grieve together.

All are social animals that interact frequently with their own species. Ants, wolves, and elephants rely on social coordination to preserve both the group and individuals within the group. Social animals are influenced by external forces that can compel individual personality differences and innovations in the fight for survival (see Arbilly & Laland, 2017; Oro, 2020).

Coevolution occurs when plants and animals develop innovative traits that make reciprocal contributions to the survival of each species, in symbiotic relationships (see Guimarães et al., 2017). Dogs may depend on humans for their survival, but not entirely and not in every culture. Honeybees around the world, however, collect nectar and distribute pollen in ways that benefit both plants and other bees, and many other animals. The plants need the bees, and the bees need the plants.

Charles Darwin helped develop our understanding of coevolution after he received a mail package from Robert Bateman. It contained an orchid from Madagascar, and it came with a surprise: a 12-inch nectary. Darwin predicted that there must be a moth with a 12-inch tongue (a proboscis). The Star orchid and the hawkmoth, discovered 40 years after Darwin's death, evolved together (see Houlihan et al., 2019; Kritsky, 1991). Like the supply of water to New York City, complex social coordination was necessary for the survival of each species.

Social Coordination Among Sticklebacks

Sticklebacks are small fish (about 6 centimeters long; slightly more than 2 inches).

The two main ambitions of sticklebacks are to (a) reproduce, and (b) not be eaten by bigger fish. They are very good at reproducing, but it requires some strategic maneuvering for sticklebacks to survive in an environment in which they represent a tasty meal to bigger fish. However, they must be doing something right because the world supply of sticklebacks is not likely to disappear unless threatened by pollution.

When swimming in shallow waters, sticklebacks can assess the pros and cons of threatening situations. Their strategy is to explore their dangerous world with another stickleback to increase the chances of at least one of them surviving. Two sticklebacks then employ a "tit-for-tat" strategy, a kind of test to find another stickleback willing to partner with them when checking their environment for potential predators (Dugatkin & Wilson, 1993; Milinski et al., 1990; Neill & Cullen, 1974). There appear to be personality differences between sticklebacks related to "boldness" and "swim speed" (see Ward & Webster, 2016).

When two fish carefully swim together in a dangerous environment, the odds of being eaten by a bigger fish are cut approximately in half. Three fish lower the odds even more, and so forth. In other words, evolution has created strategies of social coordination that are good for the group even though it won't always be good for some individuals.

Social Coordination Among Sardines and Herring

You may recognize sardines from the small cans in the grocery store.

Sardines rely on a similar kind of social coordination to increase their odds of surviving. They swim in large schools that move in an astonishing, coordinated, flashing pattern to confuse big fish predators and minimize individual risk. Sardines are even selective about which of their own species they will school with. Sardines prefer "the company of individuals matching in body size" and age (Muiño et al., 2003, p. 1369; see Pitcher, 1993).

When sardines grow up, they get to change their names. Humans, of course, are the ones changing their names from "sardines" to "herring." Herring are about 45 centimeters, or 18 inches, long. They continue to use social coordination for protection from larger predators by forming enormous balls of fish.

The fascinating-to-watch (on YouTube) "ball of herring" is maintained, not by some elected leader herring, but by their senses that calculate their proximity to neighboring fish. On the one hand, they are attracted to one another. On the other hand, herring maintain a **zone of repulsion** from their neighbor (Romenskyy et al., 2017). Humans sometimes refer to social coordination as a "group mind" (Cooley et al., 2017). Herring seem to accomplish the same thing by balancing attraction and repulsion with one another in a way that produces social coordination.

You've seen this when flocks of birds gather in enormous numbers and twist and turn in beautiful displays of social coordination. Herring are so committed to the principle of social coordination that even when attacked, most herring "continue feeding while retaining the risk-dilution advantages of schooling" (Pitcher et al., 1996, p. 449).

Social Coordination Among Humpback Whales

For herring, the safety advantages of social coordination come with a corresponding risk.

Think of it as a large predator problem that occurs when the fish-like mammals we call whales take advantage of herrings' social coordination. Overall, the strategy of social coordination works extremely well for sardines and herring—and it has for many generations. However, large predators require large food supplies; they also have learned the trick of social coordination to satisfy their needs (Connell, 2000).

Humpback whales demonstrate social coordination that places entire schools of herring at risk for mass destruction. The whales' social coordination is impressive. When they have discovered a large ball of herring, one submerged humpback circles the ball while releasing a circular stream of bubbles that slowly rises to the surface.

Then, another humpback emits a long, distinctive feeding call that appears to help drive their prey—hundreds of herring—upward into the corral of bubbles. The herring display a deadly compliance, like cattle being herded into a pen on their way to the slaughterhouse. That's when several humpback whales, parked below the ball of herring, open their gigantic mouths and rise to the surface in unison, swallowing great mouthfuls of herring. Search YouTube for "cooperative whale feeding" to see how social coordination—for herring—invites mass destruction.

Results and Discussion

Sometimes humans hunt humans.

The large predator problem makes the human herd mentality useful but sometimes dangerous. It develops when we are willing to believe almost anything to be a part of the group. This normative social influence encourages unlikely beliefs simply because so many others also believe. Swimming in a dangerous ball of agreement makes for a good defense against individual attacks, but we can be blind to the whales gathering below.

It sounds ridiculous now, of course, but many Nazis talked themselves into believing that they were destined to reign for 1,000 years; 12 dark years later, that herd mentality was bombed back to its origins in its vile fantasyland. But that once popular belief helped justify murdering millions of innocent people.

We can also see the large predator problem when modern terrorists choose their targets. They aim for large gatherings of people at concert venues, in large cities, and crowded streets. However, they ignore small barns in unpopulated areas. We may *feel* safer by conforming and clustering with everyone else. But sometimes we look more like a big juicy bull's eye to human predators with big ambitions and bad ideas.

DISCUSSION QUESTIONS

1. New York City's water supply requires a vast amount of social coordination. Identify two examples of processes in your own town or campus community that require social coordination, and explain how their different elements cooperate. What added features might be necessary for generational social coordination.

2. This case study identified several examples of social coordination in nonhuman animals, especially fish and sea-based mammals. What other animals display social coordination to their evolutionary or group advantage?

3. This case study seemed to argue first that social coordination was an evolutionary advantage—but then it seemed to argue that social coordination can put a group at risk, which would certainly not be an advantage. Which side of the argument is correct? Can both be correct, under different circumstances?

KEY TERMS

- **Social coordination**: The organization of mutually productive behaviors across individuals and groups (e.g., a given community)
- **Generational social coordination**: Cooperation and organization of a community knowing they must pass this on to future people who will live there
- **Comparative psychology**: The study of psychological similarities and differences between species
- **Coevolution**: When plants and animals develop reciprocal traits and contributions to the survival of each species in symbiotic relationships
- **Zone of repulsion**: A "personal bubble" of space an animal maintains around itself to avoid collision with other animals

Group Processes

8.1 MORE THAN A GAME: THE PRISONER'S DILEMMA

The Social Situation

Trust is a social glue.

Trust holds people together, and betrayal of trust drives groups—even groups of two—apart. The decision about whether to trust someone else is a constant question, but we typically trust first and ask questions later. For example, you have to decide whether you can trust other people:

When you . . .	. . . can you trust that? (usual answer)
drive a car	. . . other drivers will stay in their lanes? (Yes)
order food	. . . the restaurant follows health codes? (Yes)
let a child walk to school alone	. . . others will not harm your child? (Yes)
go to work	. . . the organization will pay you as promised? (Yes)
sign up for a class	. . . the professor will be fair and the class have value? (Yes)
vote	. . . the voting system is not rigged? (Yes)

By default, in a social world, we trust others. If you decide *never* to trust anyone, then you will live a shriveled, fearful life because you never leave your home. And you will still have to trust that the person delivering your food hasn't poisoned you or ripped you off.

On the other hand, there is a penalty for trusting every telemarketer or chance acquaintance. Automatically trusting everyone invites people to take advantage of you. Intelligent trust is essential for business transactions, for intimate relationships, and for almost any type of interaction between two or more people.

Trust decisions cause a set of rules to descend over your life. Those same rules govern a game called the **Prisoner's Dilemma** because they both embrace a fundamental reality about our relationships with others: uncertainty. In every situation, you never know for sure how the other person will behave. The Prisoner's Dilemma summarizes

Kurt Lewin's elegant insight into social psychological behavior: Behavior is a function of both the individual person and their environment (see Marrow, 1977).

Theory and Method

It was an epic contest between computer programmers.

Each programmer privately developed a strategy for playing The Prisoner's Dilemma. Table 8.1 displays a basic Prisoner's Dilemma, discussed in depth by Axelrod (1984) in *The Evolution of Cooperation*. The Prisoner's Dilemma has been used to predict situational uncertainties related to a wide range of social issues, including

- climate change (Bisaro & Hinkel, 2016),

- immigration policies (Fourati & Hayek, 2019),

- decision making related to cocaine use (Viola et al., 2019),

- administering chemotherapy (Yeung & Hebert, 2018), and

- using seatbelts (Mendoza, 2019).

To Trust or Not to Trust . . . That Is Always the Question

To snitch or not to snitch.

The challenge of the Prisoner's Dilemma game is to predict how two guilty criminals will behave when they have to decide whether to trust one another. The police have picked them up, separated them, and now ask each to snitch on the other. Table 8.1 summarizes the rules of the game.

If both snitch by confessing to their crimes, then they both go to jail for 5 years. If they both keep quiet, then they both go to jail for 1 year. But if one snitches and the other remains quiet, then the quiet prisoner goes to prison for 10 years, while their former partner in crime goes free.

TABLE 8.1

The Prisoner's Dilemma

Each prisoner in the Prisoner's Dilemma is faced with a critical decision under conditions of uncertainty: Should they trust each other, or confess?

		Prisoner B	
		Confess	Keep Quiet
Prisoner A	Confess	Both go to jail for 5 years.	Prisoner B goes to jail for 10 years, and Prisoner A goes free.
	Keep Quiet	Prisoner A goes to jail for 10 years, and Prisoner B goes free.	Both go to jail for 1 year.

The best possible overall outcome for both individuals is that they trust each other. Keep quiet and don't snitch on your partner: 1 year in prison for each of them. You can live with that. But trust opens you up to be played for the fool if your partner sells you out: 10 years for you, while your partner goes free. The temptation to snitch on your partner is strong.

The Norm of Reciprocity: Driving, Tax Policy, and Dinner Invitations

The central dynamic in the Prisoner's Dilemma is relationship uncertainty.

The **norm of reciprocity** reduces uncertainty by expecting that we will exchange benefits. If I do something good for you, then you will find some way to return the favor. It's the old saying: You scratch my back, I'll scratch yours. Life without a norm of reciprocity can be chaotic.

For example, what if all rules of the road, traffic lights, lane lines, and directional signs suddenly disappeared? Without the rule of law, trust and cooperation can't get a toehold in society. We would look instead to some tyrant to end traffic snarls and avoid accidental traffic deaths. We would happily give up our personal freedom to drive any way we wished in order to gain some measure of social cohesion.

Nations often interact as trading partners based on trust. A trade war, for example, is a violation of that trust: If you put a tax on our goods going into your country, then fairness demands that we put a tax on your goods coming into our country. What you do to me, I must do to you.

Axelrod (1984) noted that if you invite someone to dinner multiple times, and they never reciprocate by having you over, eventually you'll stop asking. An expectation of returned favors is common in many business and political contexts. We practice it in our own personal lives when we exchange small courtesies such as thank you e-mails, taking turns to get through traffic jams, and reciprocating dinner invitations. This norm of reciprocity encourages **group cohesiveness**.

The Rules of the Game

Axelrod (1984) invited specialists in game theory to write computer programs for the Prisoner's Dilemma.

Keep in mind that this was not a contest between computers. These were *people* writing the rules competing against other *people* who also thought that their views of human behavior were most likely to win. Axelrod also measured the complexity of each program by counting how many lines of code were needed to write it.

The job of each specialist in game theory was to write a program that instructed the computer when to trust the decisions made by other programmers. Each program would play against every other program and accumulate points over multiple rounds. Some example program names and strategies included

- RANDOM was programmed to randomly decide when to trust or not to trust.

- TIT FOR TAT always started with trust but then imitated the opposing program. In effect, "do unto others as they do unto you."

- TIT FOR TWO TATS allowed its opponent to not trust twice in a row before imitating its opponent's "good" or "bad" behavior.

- TESTER started out by not trusting but responded in kind thereafter.

- DOWNING was programmed to estimate statistical probabilities "to understand the other player" and then make the optimal choice (Axelrod, 1984, p. 34).

- JOSS was described as a "sneaky" computer program. It played tit for tat for several rounds before it betrayed its implied trust.

- TRANQUILIZER began with trust but ended by trying to get away with whatever it could. It "tries to avoid pressing its luck too far" (Axelrod, 1984, p. 46).

In addition to multiple rounds of play between each program, there were also multiple rounds of the tournament. That meant that people could rewrite their programs with the knowledge of which strategy had won the previous round.

Results and Discussion

TIT FOR TAT won the first round.

TIT FOR TAT also won the second tournament, and then won five out of six variations on the tournament, coming in second place only once. TIT FOR TAT required only 4 lines of code. RANDOM required 5 lines of code. DOWNING required 33 lines of code but finished in 10th place in a field of 15 entries. The most elaborate decision-making strategy required 77 lines of code, but ended up not doing very well. These results suggest that simple strategies aren't always good (e.g., random didn't work out well, despite its simplicity), but complex strategies weren't necessarily better. TIT FOR TAT probably succeeded because it reflected reality and human nature.

The "Nice" Strategy

In the first round of competition, several computer programs were "nice."

They were not the first to decide not to trust the other computer program. "Niceness" in one computer program reinforced "niceness" in the other program. Consequently, whenever the nice programs played each other, they each accumulated many points.

Other programs had been set up to be "forgiving" of an occasional lack of trust. They all performed well—but not as well as TIT FOR TAT. The TIT FOR TAT program outperformed the JOSS program because it always imitated whatever JOSS did. When JOSS started trusting again, so did TIT FOR TAT—but the moment JOSS stopped trusting, TIT FOR TAT imitated that strategy as well.

TIT FOR TAT was nice, but it wasn't a fool.

What Makes TIT FOR TAT a Winning Strategy?

TIT FOR TAT wasn't without problems.

For example, a central criticism of TIT FOR TAT is that it does not recognize human error based, for example, on misperceptions (Nowak, 2006). When one spouse misperceives a comment made by the other as mean-spirited, they may respond in kind, and they go down the negative path of TIT FOR TAT together, based on a misunderstanding.

A possible correction to that shortcoming is a strategy called a "generous" TIT FOR TAT (Nowak & Sigmund, 1992), similar to TIT FOR TWO TATS. However, computers don't make the same kinds of mistakes as humans. So, they would not easily be factored into a computer contest. Nevertheless, there appear to be several useful insights:

1. TIT FOR TAT is a "nice" strategy because it does not hold a grudge against those who fail to trust it, and it starts from a place of trust.

2. "Niceness" reinforces niceness; the nicer the players are, the easier it is for everyone to perform well.

3. For the same reasons, TIT FOR TAT is also a "forgiving" strategy; the moment it sees trust reemerging, it trusts in return.

4. The strategy of TIT FOR TWO TATS is even more forgiving and will occasionally be more effective, but it also makes you more vulnerable to other kinds of stratagems.

5. TIT FOR TAT has a memory, but it is a very short memory. It is aware of what its opposition has done on the prior move but is unconcerned about anything other than its most recent past.

6. TIT FOR TAT is most effective under conditions of long-term uncertainty; its value declines when the future is known.

7. TIT FOR TAT is assertive. It has no hesitation about returning lack of trust with lack of trust but also trust for trust.

The Shadow of the Future

Axelrod's computer tournament highlighted strategies already working in the real world.

The general guidance is to "enlarge the shadow of the future" (Axelrod, 1984, p. 126). For example, you may have heard of a particular principle of international diplomacy called Mutually Assured Destruction (MAD). This may be the primary reason that nations armed to the teeth with nuclear weapons do not go to war with one another. MAD is a very long, dark shadow of a future that potentially ends the human race and much of life on Earth.

But that's too grim a way to end a case study. So, another example of the shadow of the future was reported by baseball umpire Ron Luciano (see Luciano & Fisher, 1982). Luciano would sometimes drink heavily the night before a baseball game and be in poor shape to call balls and strikes at home plate.

But Luciano learned that he could trust some catchers to call balls and strikes for him. The catcher would seem to be the worst possible person to turn the game over to. Luciano's explanation was about a trust that evolved out of the shadow of the future (see Axelrod, 1984):

> Over a period of time I learned to trust certain catchers so much that I actually let them umpire for me on the bad days. . . . If someone I trusted was catching . . . I'd

tell them, "Look, it's a bad day. You'd better take it for me. If it's a strike, hold your glove in place for an extra second. If it's a ball, throw it right back. And please, don't yell." (p. 178)

According to Luciano, the catchers never started making bad calls. Why? Because they knew that Luciano would be umpiring again in the near future. Luciano could take his revenge later on. Consequently, Luciano reported that

no one I worked with ever took advantage of the situation, and no hitter ever figured out what I was doing. And only once, when Ed Herrman was calling the pitches, did a pitcher ever complain about a call. I smiled; I laughed; but I didn't say a word. I was tempted, though, I was really tempted. (p. 178)

DISCUSSION QUESTIONS

1. The program TIT FOR TAT always started with trust as a first move. As a general rule, when it comes to other people, do you (1) assume you can trust them until they prove you wrong, or (2) assume you can't trust them until they prove you wrong? Which is your default assumption, and why?

2. Are there particular circumstances when you think it's ethically, morally, and/or socially acceptable to "betray" the trust of someone else? Describe these situations and justify your answer.

3. It could be argued that the American legal and criminal justice system uses a "tit for tat" strategy. Explain how the system seems to trust people initially, punishes or sets up restrictions for bad behavior, but then rewards people for acting well again. Do you think this is the best system for preventing and/or responding to criminal behavior? Why, or why not?

4. The program TIT FOR TAT had a "memory" or response for what an opposing program did in the immediately previous round—but it didn't matter what had happened before that, long term. The program "forgave" past betrayals if trust was established a single time. What are the advantages and disadvantages for applying this strategy to human interactions with friends, relationship partners, or business associates?

KEY TERMS

- **Prisoner's Dilemma**: A theoretical game in which two people who committed a crime must decide whether to trust each other; their decisions affect their own and the other person's outcome

- **Norm of reciprocity**: The social expectation that people will exchange fair benefits; if I do you a favor, you "owe" me one

- **Group cohesiveness**: Social bonds and understandings that allow several people to effectively work together over time

8.2 INTERPERSONAL REJECTION: A CASE STUDY OF 14 SCHOOL SHOOTINGS

The Social Situation

School shootings in the United States are absolute tragedies.

Discussing them, trying to explain them, is hard. But social psychology needs to be involved in trying to understand how and why they happen, so they can be prevented. We cannot guarantee that social psychology will help us do either—but we can try. Social psychology's story is linked to the changing social needs of each generation.

There was an unexpected cluster of school shootings between 1996 and 2001 that sparked researchers into action. We have unfortunately learned as a society to live with that repeating pattern of school shootings. At the time, Leary et al. (2003) named several widely publicized possible causes, including

> lax gun control laws, society-wide moral decline, the influence of aspects of popular culture that glamorize death (such as aggressive song lyrics and the so-called "Goth" movement), violent video games, and even the failure to display the ten commandments in school buildings.

Leary's research team initially focused on a situational variable: Chronic or acute **interpersonal rejection**, sometimes called **ostracism**, isolates individuals from groups they would like to belong to. In the subsequent decades, there has been added research on a personality variable: An individual difference called **rejection sensitivity** is an excessive awareness of the possibility and imagined consequences of not being included by a group they would like to be part of.

The form of interpersonal rejection has changed mainly through **cyberbullying** that uses the Internet to taunt and ostracize vulnerable peers. But the message-sending threat of being ostracized from the group is as ancient as the threat of religious excommunication, national banishment, or visual stigmas like a hand getting cut off for stealing.

In high schools, interpersonal rejection is usually experienced as (a) public teasing (ostracism), (b) bullying, and (c) romantic rejection. Sometimes, recipients of these rejections turn to deadly responses.

Theory and Method

This case study uses news reports to examine 14 school shootings between 1996 and 2001.

Straightforward experiments are ethically out-of-bounds as a way to study school shootings. So, researchers interested in school shootings developed alternative research techniques, many of them framed under the general heading of a case study. For example, Barbara Paris (2019) in her PhD dissertation for Texas State University developed an "in-depth, single case study" that interviewed one school principal who guided a school through the aftermath of a school shooting. The goal of the interview was to "explore leadership and organizational factors" related to the entire incident.

The hypothesis being tested in the Leary study (Leary et al., 2003) was whether the media reports at the time were reporting a particular explanation for school shootings: interpersonal rejection or ostracism. The idea is that peer rejection is so painful that it triggers vulnerable individuals to take the next drastic step: They start shooting their tormentors. School shootings involving interpersonal rejection typically co-occur with three other features within an individual:

1. Psychological problems, such as lack of empathy and low impulse control

2. An interest in guns or explosives

3. Fascination with death or other "dark" topics

It's likely that a combination of many factors is needed to predict and understand school shootings.

Archival Analysis

News reports offer an archival research approach to school shootings.

Leary et al. (2003, p. 204) recognized that there had to be more to explaining school shootings than interpersonal rejection. After all, "most students who experience rejection, even those who are bullied and ostracized, do not resort to lethal violence." For school shootings, archival data was simply "the method of choice for a low-frequency phenomenon such as school violence for which experimental research is impossible" (p. 204).

The researchers used three reviewers to examine the archived descriptions of the school shootings represented in numerous media sources. They included several news magazines, newspapers, news services, and respected Internet sources. Using three reviewers lightened the work load.

But the real purpose of multiple reviewers is to establish **inter-rater reliability** that typically uses a mixture of independent judgments by each reviewer, followed by discussion to reach a consensus about what story the data are telling. The goal is to reduce or eliminate any systematic bias among the people rating the news reports. The difficulties in this particular study suggest two pieces of practical advice that can help new researchers:

1. You are never going to conduct a perfect study; there always will be flaws.

2. Recognize and acknowledge those flaws, make reasonable judgment calls, and then honestly report your judgment calls and why you made them.

The Theory of Social-Physical Pain Overlap

"A metal spike being driven through a gaping hole in her chest."

That is how visual artist Frida Kahlo expressed (in a painting) the theory of **social-physical pain overlap**. Her painting represented the anguish she associated with "her husband's infidelity with her sister." That visual representation of how emotions are experienced as physical pain is supported by a cross-cultural observation by Kristina

Tchalova and Naomi Eisenberg (2016, p. 71): People in different cultures and speaking different languages use metaphors of physical pain to describe emotional pain. In other words, people from all over the world understand what it means to feel emotions so strongly that it affects us physically.

Experimentally, **Cyberball** experiments suggest the same story. A Cyberball game compares the effects of social inclusion (a ball thrown to the participant) and social exclusion (a ball thrown to another player; see Sleegers et al., 2017). In each of these (and many other examples), the data suggest that the emotional pain of interpersonal rejection can be experienced like physical pain (Macdonald & Leary, 2005).

Curiously, opiates deliver the same kind of relief from social rejection as they do from physiological pain (Panksepp et al., 1978). However, painkillers may reduce empathy as well as pain (see Mischkowski et al., 2016). More importantly, many teenagers deliver and receive both real and imagined interpersonal rejection as a form of indirect aggression (Owens et al, 2000). But if every real or imagined adolescent rejection led to a school shooting, then we might not have *any* functioning schools.

Rejection Sensitivity

"Hurt people hurt people."

That is how Ren et al. (2018) summed up support for the **ostracism–aggression hypothesis** based on correlational and experimental research (see Ren et al., 2018). Boyce and Park (1989) think of rejection sensitivity as a personality variable that features excessive awareness of the behavior and feelings of others. A meta-analysis of 72 studies (Gao et al., 2017) found that rejection sensitivity is moderately but reliably associated with a network of psychological problems: depression, anxiety, loneliness, borderline personality disorder, and body dysmorphic disorder. That's a heavy, daily emotional lift for a struggling teenager.

Kathryn Farr (2019) connected recently experienced romantic rejections to school shootings among 15 of 29 adolescent male school shooters. Farr explained her findings by asserting that

> these young shooters understand such rejections as one of many undeserved humiliations that have damaged their gender credibility and thus their school social status. . . . the norms of a traditional masculinity insist on the repudiation of feminine emotionality [and] constrain them from expressing sadness or vulnerability over the rejection. (p. 147)

These young men find themselves squeezed between **gender role expectations** and chronic interpersonal rejections. They feel as if they have nowhere to turn to relieve their suffering. But if guns are available, and they allow themselves to think about such dark possibilities, it can occur to people like then 16-year-old Luke Woodham from Pearl, Mississippi, that an attention-getting act could get back at people because, "people like me are mistreated every day." For many young men struggling with toxic masculinity and social rejection, expressing their feelings and vulnerability doesn't seem to be an option—but aggression does.

Results and Discussion

The school shootings since 2001 make the list of 14 school shootings shown further in text look like a short list.

This is a real, immediate, and terrible problem in our country. The research team for this study examined multiple media accounts looking for signals that interpersonal rejections helped motivate the shooter(s). They found that 12 out of the 14 media accounts referenced at least one of the three forms of interpersonal rejection:

1. public teasing (ostracism),

2. bullying, and

3. romantic rejection.

We have quoted media inferences related to interpersonal rejection.

Interpersonal Rejections Help Explain School Shootings

1. Moses Lake, Washington (February 2, 1996). Barry Lockaitis, 14, used a .30-caliber rifle to kill a teacher and two boys, as well as injure one girl: "severely depressed," "inferiority complex," "teased" by victim.

2. Bethel, Alaska (February 19, 1997). Evan Ramsey, 16, killed his principal and a student, as well as injured two other people: "teased by victim."

3. Pearl, Mississippi (October 1, 1997). Luke Woodham, 16, killed two students and his mother with a hunting rifle, as well as injured seven others: "often teased." Woodham reportedly said, "I killed because people like me are mistreated every day."

4. West Paducah, Kentucky (December 1, 1997). Michael Carneal, 14, killed three classmates with a semiautomatic pistol and injured five others at a prayer meeting before school: "teased as a 'dweeb' or 'faggot,'" "called 'gay' (in the school paper), and bullied," "unrequited love," and "infatuated with the first person he shot." Carneal said that he had grown tired of being teased and was quoted as saying "people respect me now."

5. Stamps, Arkansas (December 15, 1997). Jason "Colt" Todd, 14, wounded two students with a sniper's rifle: "tired of being picked on" and that "some of his schoolmates had extorted money from him."

6. Jonesboro, Arkansas (April 24, 1998). Andrew Golden, 11, and Mitchell Johnson, 13, opened fire with handguns and rifles on Westside Middle School, killing 5 people and injuring 11 others: "angry about being rejected by a girl," "repeatedly teased for being fat."

7. Fayetteville, Tennessee (May 19, 1998). Honor student Jacob Davis, 18, killed a male classmate who was dating his ex-girlfriend, who had recently broken up with Davis. The perpetrator and victim had recently had an argument about the girl.

8. Springfield, Oregon (May 21, 1998). Kipland Kinkel, 15, used a semiautomatic rifle and a pistol to kill two classmates and injure 22 others, in addition to killing his parents: "rejected by a girl," "embarrassed his parents," and "teasing from other students."

9. Littleton, Colorado (April 20, 1999). Eric Harris, 18, and Dylan Klebold, 17, used semiautomatic weapons, shotguns, and rifles, then committed suicide. At least 21 people were injured, and 13 people (12 students, 1 teacher) were killed: "taunted," "bullied, particularly by athletes," "rejected from the Marines," "turned down by a girl whom he asked to the prom," "episodes of teasing and ostracism," "I'm going to kill you all," Klebold said. "You've been giving us shit for years."

10. Conyers, Georgia (May 20, 1999). T. J. Solomon, 15, used a handgun and .22-caliber rifle stolen from his parents to injure six people: "depressed after a break-up," "picked on by a football player," and "feared becoming the school wuss."

11. Ft. Gibson, Oklahoma (December 6, 1999). Seth Trickey, 13, walked up to students at his middle school and started firing with a 9-mm handgun. He didn't seem to know the children he shot and said he did not know why he did it. Trickey was described as an honor student whom others regarded as funny, nice, and good-natured. He was popular and well liked and clearly not a loner. Trickey never explained his own actions.

12. Mount Morris Township, Michigan (February 29, 2000). A 6-year-old boy pointed a gun at a fellow first grader, said "I don't like you," and killed her. The victim had purportedly slapped the perpetrator, who wanted to get revenge by scaring her with the gun. The boy had been left in the care of an uncle, who lived in a suspected crack house, so that his mother could work two jobs.

13. Santee, California (March 5, 2001). Having boasted that he was going to cause trouble at his school, Andy Williams, 15, shot 2 students to death and wounded 13 others: "maliciously bullied" and "desired simply to 'fit in.'"

14. Williamsport, Pennsylvania (March 7, 2001). In the only school shooting reported here that was perpetrated by a girl, Catherine Bush, 14, shot the head cheerleader at her school: "teased and harassed at her previous school" and "felt betrayed by the victim, who ostensibly had revealed to other students the contents of e-mails Catherine had sent her."

Evolutionary Psychology Explains Why Rejection Hurts

A good theory explains a lot of evidence with just a few ideas.

Groups are very important to us. They provide physical safety, emotional security, and the opportunity to interact with potential mates. School shooters (usually male) are frustrated by their inability to connect with groups, find a girlfriend or boyfriend, and enjoy emotional security. It's a tight place, emotionally.

Like herring conforming by maintaining a zone of repulsion (see Chapter 7), the **theory of optimal distinctiveness (ODT)** proposes humans desire the social acceptance of groups. But they also need to stand out as valued individuals within the group (see Baumeister & Leary, 1995; Brewer, 2011; Williams & Nida, 2011). Social rejection is especially difficult during adolescence as we're all striving to become adults with friends and partners who love us.

Social psychology helps us understand school shootings. Research on the effects of ostracism are just one avenue that provides some answers—and this area of study is ripe for more attention. Social psychology can also refine possible solutions.

Consider, for example, what it means to place metal detectors at school entrances. It sounds like a simple answer to a complex social problem. Here are a few social psychological questions worth asking before the school board invests money on metal detectors that could go to academic clubs or hiring more school psychologists:

- How might metal detectors affect people's moods and comfort as they start their day at school?

- Where will metal detectors encourage students to cluster as vulnerable groups as they enter the school?

- What social norm expectations are communicated by metal detectors?

DISCUSSION QUESTIONS

1. Describe at least one strength and one weakness of the case study approach to understanding school shootings. Can a single case study, or even several, really be generalizable to others? Or is each unique enough that it can't be truly prevented simply through psychological research?

2. Consider Lewin's famous prediction that behavior is a function of both the individual person and the environment. For problems like school shootings, what are two ways schools or communities can provide resources that address both individual needs and cultural environments that might help prevent such tragedies?

3. Leary et al. (2003) suggested that perpetrators of school shootings involve (1) social rejection, (2) personality problems, (3) interest in guns or explosives, and (4) fascination with death or other "dark" topics. Rank order these factors in terms of most to least influential, in your opinion, then explain your decision.

KEY TERMS

- **Interpersonal rejection**: Isolation or refusal to allow an individual into a group
- **Ostracism**: See *interpersonal rejection*
- **Rejection sensitivity**: The degree to which someone cares about social acceptance and/or rejection from groups they would like to join

- **Cyberbullying**: Taunts or threats that occur online or through digital venues
- **Inter-rater reliability**: The degree to which two or more people who code or analyze data agree with each other's assessments

- **Social-physical pain overlap**: The experience of emotions, such as grief, as physical pain
- **Cyberball**: A video game used in psychology experiments to test people's reactions to ostracism
- **Ostracism–aggression hypothesis**: The idea that social rejection leads people to feel anger, which in turn leads them to aggress against others

- **Gender role expectations**: The cultural norms put upon men and women regarding how they "should" think and act
- **Theory of optimal distinctiveness (ODT)**: The idea that humans want to be accepted into groups, but also desire to stand out as valued and respected individuals

---

8.3 ON THE SHOULDERS OF GIANTESSES: THE FIRST COMPUTER PROGRAMMERS

The Social Situation

The U.S. Army needed more computers.

That meant women, not machines. At the start of World War II, a "computer" was a job description, like "plumber," "painter," or "professor." You could be hired to be a computer—someone who applied a mathematical formula to a specific problem and then computed the solution.

The U.S. Army was hiring lots of computers to solve a specific problem: producing artillery firing tables that would inform gunners about the proper trajectory needed to send shells to their intended targets. The "computers" were kept busy calculating these complex sets of equations. Their calculations had to factor in many variables such as outside temperature and the amount of drag produced by the air around the shell.

The U.S. Army needed to speed up the calculating process. They wanted to find a way to reprogram mechanical calculating machines so that another roomful of female computers would not have to start from scratch with each new set of interacting variables. The solution was to build and program the ENIAC: the Electronic Numerical Integrator And Computer.

The (non-human) computers were physically huge at the start of the computer age. Jean Jennings (later Jean Jennings Bartik) described the 30-ton ENIAC as "the equivalent of about forty-five of the horses I had ridden and driven as a teenager on the farm in Missouri." She added that now, years later, "a silicon chip smaller than the tip of a pencil can hold the same capability" (Bartik et al., 2013, p. 2).

Theory and Method

Don't let modern stereotypes fool you: Computers were once considered best in the hands of women.

We normally think of a **group** as two or more people interacting with each other. But groups are also formed when two or more people are joined together by a common fate. Two random people in a town are not a group, but if they know each other and use the same bus line to get to work, then they can become a group.

The Creative Potential of Groups

Groups are bursting with creative potential.

Thanks to some common fate, "I" merges with "we." The common fate of both people having the same disease may nourish a friendship, motivate them to form a support group, or inspire a fundraiser. Enjoying crossword puzzles during wartime was a common fate that transformed women into a group of pioneering computer programmers. Becoming a group generates previously unconsidered opportunities for creativity.

The forward movement of science is also a group process, but it is a slow process that routinely transcends space and time. Sir Isaac Newton famously wrote, "If I have seen further, it is by standing on the shoulders of giants." The history of computing demonstrates a scientifically creative group process that has transcended space and time *and* gender, summarized in Walter Isaacson's (2014) book *The Innovators*.

The question embedded in every computer innovation is whether computers can think for themselves. So far, the answer seems still to be just beyond our fingertips. The most famous test of whether computers can think is Alan Turing's imitation game, called the **Turing Test**: A human and a computer are questioned by someone who does not know who is answering the questions. If the questioner cannot tell who is responding, then the computer deserves to be credited with thinking.

The Female Pioneers of Computing

In the 1830s, Ada Lovelace peered into the future.

She perceived a computing industry that did not yet exist. However, she did not believe that computers of the future ever would think for themselves (1843; see Krysa, 2012):

> The analytical engine [a computer] has no pretensions whatever to *originate* anything. It can do whatever we *know how to order it* to perform. It can follow analysis; but it has no power of *anticipating* any analytical relations or truths. Its province is to assist us in making *available* what we are already acquainted with.

Ada Lovelace envisioned programmable computers. She imagined computers that could be programmed to partner with humans rather than compete against humans. This case study is about the intergenerational group of creative women who crossed space and time to write the first computer program. The results of this group collaboration are the human–computer interactions that so many of us enjoy today.

The Six Women of ENIAC

They first met one another on a railroad platform.

Six women had been pulled from the 100 female computers working on shell trajectories: Fran Bilas, Jean Jennings, Ruth Lichterman, Kay MacNulty, Betty Snyder, and Marilyn Wescoff. They were traveling from Philadelphia to the Aberdeen Proving Grounds in Maryland. They were uncertain why they were selected and what they were being asked to do.

As a group, they were like many wartime groups: a clash of cultures that could have turned either creative or destructive. They would need group cohesion to succeed at a task that even the people who asked them to do it barely understood. It turned out to be critical to the war effort and then to the emerging computer industry.

Lichterman was from New York City, Jewish, and had studied math at Hunter College but never graduated. Wescoff was also Jewish but from Philadelphia; she had earned a bachelor's degree in education and sociology. Snyder was a Quaker from Philadelphia; her father and grandfather were both astronomers and high school teachers. MacNulty was an Irish Catholic whose father had been jailed for his activities in the Irish Republican Army. Jennings described herself as

> a red-haired, freckled farm girl from Missouri. None of the other four in the group had ever been around anyone quite like me before. By that I mean someone from my rural, Church of Christ background who was so wide-eyed about the world and so excited about everything we did and everywhere we went. (Bartik et al., 2013, p. 71)

Bilas, who joined the group later, came from an Austrian–German immigrant family now living in South Philadelphia. Some came from wealthy families; others from more modest homes. What they had in common was a love of intellectual stimulation—suggested by a love of crossword puzzles. Valuing education was the necessary starting point, but the group chemistry also had to work. Jennings remembered that

> we had a wonderful time . . . none of us had ever been in close contact with anyone from one of the others' religions. We had some great arguments . . . despite our differences, or perhaps because of them, we really liked one another. Of course, we had better like one another—we spent almost twenty-four hours a day together . . . then still wanted to be together in the evenings discussing everything about our lives. (Bartik et al., 2013, p. 97)

Results and Discussion

Their immediate mission was to make it easier to calculate artillery trajectories.

But the six women succeeded in programming the ENIAC by envisioning it as capable of doing much more. They became so familiar with its inner workings that they could debug the machine down to a failure in one of its 18,000 vacuum tubes. Isaacson (2014) observed that

> The main lesson to draw from the birth of computers is that innovation is usually a group effort, involving collaboration between visionaries and engineers, and that creativity comes from a drawing on many sources. Only in storybooks do

inventions come like a thunderbolt or a lightbulb popping out of the head of a lone individual in a basement or garret or garage. (Isaacson, 2014, p. 85)

They were a cooperative, hard-working group dedicated to a vision of achieving something greater than themselves. **Social facilitation** was high as they depended on each other, minimizing **coordination loss**. Their achievements as the world's first computer programmers were remarkable—and largely unrecognized. "In a perfect world," Jennings observed,

> The "Sensational Six"... would have ushered in an era of computer programming in which women led the way, or were at least on equal footing with men, and worked in equal numbers with them.... As for the ENIAC women, we were lost in the shuffle when World War II, which had ushered women into non-traditional roles, ended and the country reverted to its comfortable, male-dominated mode. (Bartik et al., 2013, p. xix)

Before she died, Betty Snyder was awarded the Ada Lovelace Award, perhaps the highest recognition from the Association for Women in Computing. Computer scientist and Rear Admiral Grace Hopper knew her work and described Snyder as "the best programmer she had ever met" (Bartik et al., 2013). "In a way," Jennings wrote,

> women became the first programmers by accident. If the ENIAC's administrators had known how crucial programming would be to the functioning of the electronic computer and how complex it would prove to be, they might have been more hesitant to give such an important role to women. (p. 123)

Group dynamics can be turned toward both destructive and creative purposes. The world's first computer program was the creative product of a scientific and cohesive group of creative women. Ada Lovelace in the 19th century was followed by more women in the 20th century that included the "Sensational Six" plus United States Rear Admiral Grace Hopper, Fran Bilas, Jean Jennings, Ruth Lichterman, Kay MacNulty, Betty Snyder, and Marilyn Wescoff. This group of visionaries and programmers within computer science knew each other in a way that existed beyond the constraints of space and time.

DISCUSSION QUESTIONS

1. Identify some other groups that transcend space and time. What holds them together? Analyze both their diversity and similarities.

2. Jean Jennings believed that the credit for being the first computer programmers was stolen from the "Sensational Six," partly due to sexism. If the six women had been given credit and had been more widely known, how might it have influenced the gender demographics among current computer programmers and other scientific fields?

3. What kind of personality traits make for the "best" group members—and what kind of personality traits make for the "best" group leaders? Explain your definition of "best," and why you have chosen certain traits for members and leaders. Can someone be both an effective member and leader simultaneously?

KEY TERMS

- **Groups**: Gatherings of two or more people because of shared space, interests, interactions, or a common fate
- **Turing Test**: A test in which a human tries to decide if they are interacting with a human or with a computer; it is considered a test of a computer's independent intelligence and/or thought
- **Social facilitation**: When the presence of others enhances our efforts or makes us work harder
- **Coordination loss**: Inefficiency or ineffectiveness in groups due to poor cooperation or communication
- **Group dynamics**: The interaction among group members and in the group as a whole, in helpful and productive ways or in harmful ways

Stereotypes, Prejudice, and Discrimination

9

9.1 ECONOMIC ANXIETY AND THE ILLEGAL DEPORTATION OF U.S. CITIZENS

The Social Situation

Repatriation is a polite word for cruelty.

It implies that families living in the United States wanted to "go back home." The cruelty was that the United States *was* their home, both legally and emotionally. From about 1930 to 1935, approximately 60% of the people sent on trains and buses to the Mexican border were U.S. citizens. This was a national moral panic, fed by the fears of economic disaster and the need for a scapegoat during the worst years of the Great Depression (see Balderrama & Rodriguez, 2006, pp. 67–71).

The 1929 stock market crash in October indicated an unexpected collision between dreams of fabulous wealth and losses of money, jobs, dignity, and self-esteem. The social comparison would be like falling through a trap door from high expectations to a bottom they were still hoping to touch. It did not help that government and private industry swiftly proved incapable of dealing with the crisis. The national mood became meaner as the unemployment rate moved toward 25%. Inept politicians and a confused public began looking for scapegoats.

Theory and Method

When we're frustrated, we often lash out at someone.

The story of this moral panic was told by historians Balderrama and Rodriguez (2006) in their book *Decade of Betrayal: Mexican Repatriation in the 1930s*. As predicted by **frustration–aggression theory**, the suffering caused by the Great Depression shifted many people's attention to a search for someone to blame. Scapegoating requires that we do not look too closely into the lives of those we blame. We might discover innocence or even sympathy that would make our own lives only more difficult.

The Big Three: Stereotypes, Prejudices, and Discrimination

It wasn't the first time—and it won't be the last.

In the 1930s, the "big three" (stereotypes, prejudices, and discrimination) became an ugly psychological conspiracy. Here's how it works: **Stereotyping** is an efficient way to

FIGURE 9.1

The Big Three: Stereotypes, Prejudices, and Discrimination

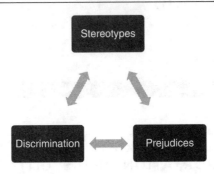

mentally categorize many different people into the same group. Stereotyping is emotionally convenient if we have pre-existing negative emotional **prejudices** about some group of people. If "they" are all alike, then we feel emotionally justified for acts of **discrimination** against all of them—based only on their membership in a group.

In the 1930s, stereotyping, prejudice, and discrimination were spreading like a bad case of poison ivy that the nation kept scratching. Balderrama and Rodriguez (2006) described how the social infection crawled into democratic social structures:

> For all Americans, the decade of the 1930s was one filled with frustration and disenchantment. The very tenets of our democratic/capitalistic system came under close scrutiny . . . some critics diagnosed the system's condition as terminal. . . . Americans, reeling from the economic disorientation of the depression, sought a convenient scapegoat. They found it in the Mexican community. (p. 1)

The result was mass deportation roundups, violence, and scare tactics. Those hated "Mexicans," including those who were in fact American citizens, were taking "American" jobs. It wasn't true or even logical, but many believed that

> getting rid of the Mexicans would create a host of new jobs . . . alleviating the unemployment situation would automatically end the depression. In a frenzy of anti-Mexican hysteria, wholesale punitive measures were proposed and undertaken by government officials at the federal, state, and local levels. Laws were passed depriving Mexicans of jobs in the public and private sector. (p. 2)

Institutional Discrimination

In a free, democratic society, institutional discrimination signals a deep sickness; categories of people are experiencing less freedom.

Institutional discrimination is the end result of stereotyping, prejudice, and discrimination. It does not need to be formally coordinated because the "big three" are mutually reinforcing. In the case of the moral panic against Mexicans in the 1930s, the institutional discrimination was open, but not always official. Local governments, labor organizations, veterans groups, the U.S. Department of Labor, and even news organizations conspired to feed the deportation monster. This officially unofficial cooperation made resistance so difficult that it sometimes led to self-deportation before things got even worse.

Results and Discussion

The private and public structures of society slowly collapsed.

The campaign of stereotyping, prejudice, and discrimination was "successful" at undermining American democracy:

> it removed many U.S. citizens with a Mexican heritage. Between 1930 and 1939, 46.3% of the people deported from the United States had some kind of historical connection to Mexico, even though Mexican immigrant families represented less than 1% of the total U.S. population at the time. The campaign did little to create jobs—and may have harmed the economy. (Balderrama & Rodriguez, 2006, p. 2)

Governmental Structures Collapsed

The U.S. government signaled its quasi-official stamp of approval of discrimination.

For example, they approved discrimination by their open cooperation with citizen groups. C. P. Visel was a spokesman for the Los Angeles Citizens Committee for Coordination of Unemployment Relief. He sent the following telegram to Colonel Arthur M. Woods, the U.S. Government Coordinator of Unemployment Relief:

> Four hundred thousand deportable aliens U.S. Estimate 5 percent in this district. We can pick them all up through police and sheriff channels. Local U.S. Department of Immigration personnel not sufficient to handle. You advise please as to method of getting rid. We need their jobs for needy citizens. (p. 67)

Many veterans' groups were outspoken racists. Both the Veterans of Foreign Wars and the American Legion advocated against Mexicans. The Legion formally assisted the removal of some 3,000 people from East Chicago, Indiana. They supplied guards to ride the trains, even though Mexican Americans "had served alongside them in the trenches in France during World War I" (p. 68).

Congressman Sam Hobbs of Alabama offered a bill (H.R. 4768). Balderrama and Rodriguez reported that the bill called "for the establishment of concentration camps for all aliens ordered deported and who were not out of the country within sixty days" (p. 69). Stereotypes were an easier way to think in a crisis. Stereotyped fears fed the prejudice and economic anxiety justified the discrimination. Immigration officials promoted fear to encourage self-deportation.

The psychological conspiracy was effective.

Immigration officials swept the streets of anyone who "looked Mexican," and one radio announcer recalled seeing "women crying in the streets when not finding their husbands" (Balderrama & Rodriguez, p. 70). Customs officials stopped Mrs. Angela Hernandez de Sanchez, an American citizen returning from visiting her relatives in Carrizal, Chihuahua. By law, she was not subject to deportation, and both of her children were born in the United States. However, customs officials demanded proof of citizenship and ordered tests of venereal diseases. The Department of Labor ordered both her and her children deported.

Nongovernmental Social Structures Collapsed

Nongovernmental organizations also collapsed during the moral panic.

The two most notable nongovernmental social structures to collapse were labor unions and freedom of the press. Labor unions were compromised in many ways. They were desperate to maintain memberships during a period when it was difficult to protect union jobs.

The American Federation of Labor turned against Mexican workers. The A.F.L. convinced its union members that getting rid of Mexicans would create more jobs. Mexicans were resented for two reasons. First, they would work for half the wages. Second, many employers believed that Mexican workers were loyal, worked harder, and often did better work. Like all **positive stereotypes**, this seemingly complimentary view still ended up having negative effects on the group.

Freedom of the press was also compromised by their need to sell newspapers to survive. Many newspapers played an important role in encouraging prejudice. They played on their audience's stereotypes in ways that openly encouraged discrimination and changed the positive content of stereotypes into the opposite:

Newspapers and journals had a field day in trumpeting charges and accusation that were seldom verified but were accepted at face value. Mexican families were accused of harboring ignoble, un-American sentiments and characteristics: slothfulness, shiftlessness, and lack of ambition. (Balderrama & Rodriguez, p. 41)

Any individual act of defiance:

produced dramatic press coverage. Newspapers underscored the fact that extended years spent contributing to the prosperity and economic development of the United States was not enough to gain Mexicans either permanent residence or acceptance . . . the Mexican worker and his family were ousted without any concern for citizenship status, length of residency, health conditions, or age factors. (p. 143)

There was significant resistance in several newspapers, but they mostly were overwhelmed by the conventional press:

Also fanning the flames . . . were influential newspapers and magazines. Among the most vociferous were the Hearst newspaper chain and the *Saturday Evening*

Post magazine. In the Midwest, the *Chicago Tribune* repeatedly called for the elimination of the alien horde. The biased articles appealed to the public's base fears and added to the hue and cry to get rid of the Mexicans. (p. 68)

How Do We Stop a Social Collapse?

Officials leading the psychological conspiracy did not view themselves in a negative light.

Mary Grace Wells from the Gary, Indiana, repatriation program believed that repatriation was a splendid success. Why? She asserted that "all [repatriates] were happy enroute and were delighted to set foot again on their native soil." This was likely another case of wishful thinking or confirmation bias because she had no evidence to support her claim—and for many, their "native" soil was Indiana and the United States.

> How Wells was able to surmise or arrive at that conclusion is a mystery, for she never made a trip to the border. . . . Only the younger children who did not fully comprehend what was happening to them viewed the trip with glee and good spirits. (p. 141)

Quite simply, Mary Grace Wells was wrong. Deportation was dangerous:

> *Excelsior*, one of Mexico City's leading newspapers, reported that on board one repatriation train twenty-five children and adults had died of illness and malnutrition during the trip to the border . . . a factor contributing to the sad plight of the repatriates was that vast numbers left the United States without ever contacting the Mexican consul in their respective districts . . . [and] arrived at the border without Certificates of Residency or any documentation needed to facilitate their processing. (Balderrama & Rodriguez, 2006, pp. 141–142)

Fear, feeding on itself, became a self-fulfilling prophecy that produced thousands of displaced citizens and tore apart families. Many states, and some federal policies, made use of institutional discrimination.

The Peak of Discrimination

The year 1931, during the Hoover administration, was the peak year for "repatriation."

Officially, 123,247 Mexicans were shipped home in 1931. A total of 345,839 were deported between 1930 and 1935. But self-deportation, out of fear and confusion, may have accounted for about two million Mexicans being "repatriated," more or less involuntarily. The cycle of economic fear and official scapegoating was psychologically effective, especially because it coincided with a period when the rule of law was weakened.

However, "as economic conditions in the United States slowly improved, the tide of repatriation receded. In 1935, according to the official count, only 16,196 Nationals were repatriated [that year]" (p. 150). The ill will toward U.S. citizens with roots in Mexico was declining. And all this happened in a nation of many people whose recent ancestors had come from "someplace else."

Refusing to Fear

The repatriation process continued into the Roosevelt administration.

President Franklin Roosevelt was inaugurated in 1933. He recognized that America's economic depression had boiled into a moral panic and a lost faith in democracy. American citizens were rapidly turning on one another, looking for and then finding scapegoats. So he opened his first presidential inaugural speech with words about the psychology of fear:

> So, first of all, let me assert my firm belief that the only thing we have to fear is fear itself—nameless, unreasoning, unjustified terror which paralyzes needed efforts to convert retreat into advance. (Roosevelt, 1933)

Roosevelt has been criticized for many decisions that sacrificed innocent lives, especially as Germany's murder of Jewish people became more apparent. And by the time America went to war with Germany, the target of ethnic hostilities refocused from Mexicans to Germans and the Japanese. But at this inaugural turning point in the American story, Roosevelt appealed to the opposite of fear: the "joy of achievement."

Even though Roosevelt's inaugural address was advocating for specific economic actions, he didn't appeal to materialism or greed or try to give the nation a pep talk about working harder:

> Happiness lies not in the mere possession of money; it lies in the joy of achievement, in the thrill of creative effort. The joy and moral stimulation of work no longer must be forgotten in the mad chase of evanescent profits. (Roosevelt, 1933)

Roosevelt was echoing what Abraham Lincoln also had proposed during his inaugural speech, during another time of severe national testing: an appeal to the "better angels of our nature." Whether it was luck, the looming war, appealing to our better angels, or just plain social exhaustion, Roosevelt seemed to be instrumental at dismantling the conspiracy of stereotyping, prejudice, and discrimination.

"We are not enemies," Abraham Lincoln had insisted, "but friends."

DISCUSSION QUESTIONS

1. Prejudice toward immigrants is still a problem in the United States and in many other countries. Can you find any evidence that this form of prejudice is correlated with either the perception of economic hardship or prosperity overall in a country or region? Explain how this correlation (if found) would be evidence supporting frustration–aggression theory.

2. This case study discussed how President Roosevelt was involved in changing people's views of "repatriation" efforts and prejudice toward other Americans. How much influence does any given U.S. president have on everyday citizens' views of each other, other countries, the future, and so on? Can you see evidence of your opinion in the current world in which you live?

3. Frustration–aggression theory is usually applied on a large-group level, such as how an entire nation responds to economic hardship. Can the theory be applied on an individual level? Do people's prejudices and aggressive behaviors increase when they are personally frustrated or when their lives are not going as planned?

KEY TERMS

- **Frustration–aggression theory**: The idea that when a social group is frustrated, often because of economic hardship, they find an outgroup to blame and act aggressively toward that outgroup
- **Stereotypes**: An oversimplified belief describing all members of a certain group
- **Prejudice**: Emotion-centered judgments or evaluations about people based on their perceived membership in a group

- **Discrimination**: Behaviors toward people because of their perceived membership in a group
- **Institutional discrimination**: Unfair treatment of individuals or certain groups by society or organizations through unequal selection, opportunity, or oppression
- **Positive stereotype**: A belief about a group of people with a positive frame or content, but that still has negative effects

9.2 INTERSECTIONALITY: SOJOURNER TRUTH

The Social Situation

The year 2019 was celebrated as the 100th anniversary of the 19th Amendment, granting women the right to vote.

It was certainly something to celebrate, and the struggle for women's rights had been hard. You've probably heard the names of famous women associated with the movement, such as Susan B. Anthony or Elizabeth Cady Stanton. Their achievement is impressive, and the 19th Amendment was the "single largest extension of democratic voting rights in American history" (Schuessler, 2019). One hundred years later, in 2019, this fight was honored with hundreds of local and national exhibits, events, and parties.

Here's the problem: The 19th Amendment *didn't* grant all American women the right to vote. While the wording of the Amendment stated that voting rights "shall not be denied or abridged by the United States or by any State on account of sex," in reality women of color were blocked from entering actual voting booths, sometimes through state laws.

It wasn't until 1965 that the Voting Rights Act secured the right of African American women to vote. And it was 10 years later when the federal government passed further amendments that prohibited voting discrimination against Asian Americans, Native Americans, and Latinas (see La Jeunesse, 2019).

Even though about one-third of the women who fought in the suffrage movement were women of color, their names aren't well known. This case study thus features one of the prominent women of color who proudly stood up for her rights, despite a culture of prejudice.

Theory and Method

Racism was prominent in the United States at the time when the Civil War was still in many people's memories. And many people pointed out that the 19th Amendment was supposed to decrease **sexism** in the country. But fewer people thought about the problems of the nation from a perspective that has now been labeled as **intersectionality**.

Intersectionality is the idea that we all live with social labels regarding group stereotypes our culture has formed and that how these overlap with each other results in different levels of privilege or prejudice. A gay man, for example, has male privilege but may also suffer from cultural homophobia or heterosexism. So women of color in the suffrage movement had the unique perspective of knowing what prejudice and discrimination were like on multiple levels.

Intersectionality helps us understand Sojourner Truth. She was born in 1797 with the slave-given name Isabella (Painter, 1994; Stowe, 1863). Her owner, a man named Dumont, had her marry another slave named Thomas. They had five children together, but all of them were sold as slaves to other families. Because she lived in New York, she was granted freedom by the New York Anti-Slavery Law of 1827. However, her safety as a free woman was not secured until the Civil War 35 years later. Once that happened, like many other former slaves, she chose a new name for herself: Sojourner Truth.

Truth devoted her adult life to fighting for abolition and women's suffrage. She is most well known for a speech she gave at the 1851 Women's Rights Convention in Akron, Ohio (Stowe, 1863). She hadn't written the speech down before giving it, so the only record we have are archival data retrieved from newspapers that reported it. The speech is now famously titled, "Ain't I a Woman?"

The need for the speech came from intersectionality. Apparently, many speeches were given on the first day of the convention regarding women's needs (Stowe, 1863). On the second day, Sojourner made it clear that she wanted to address the crowd. According to reports, several women in the room tried to stop her, worried that she would distract people from the main topic (voting rights for women) by talking about the rights of former slaves. From Truth's perspective, they already *were* the same thing. Here are some lines from the speech, as reported later (Stowe, 1863):

> That man over there says that women need to be helped into carriages, and lifted over ditches, and to have the best place everywhere. Nobody helps *me* any best place. And ain't I a woman? Look at me! Look at my arm. I have plowed, I have planted, and I have gathered into barns. And no man could head me. And ain't I a woman? I could work as much, and eat as much as a man—when I could get it—and bear the lash as well! And ain't I a woman? I have borne children and seen most of them sold into slavery, and when I cried out with a mother's grief, none but Jesus heard me. And ain't I a woman? . . . If the first woman God ever made was strong enough to turn the world upside down all alone, these women together ought to be able to turn it back and get it right-side up again.

Results and Discussion

For her entire adult life, anyone who met Sojourner Truth commented on her intelligence and bravery.

For several years, she befriended and worked with Frederick Douglass. That famous former slave also defied stereotypes and institutional discrimination. His published autobiography highlighted the horrors of slavery for both men and women (Patrick, 1994).

Yes, the United States has made progress since 1919 when the 19th Amendment was approved by Congress. But that constitutional opening exposed the deeper needs revealed by intersectionality in modern culture, politics, and economics. For example, the well-known "gender pay gap" means that on average, men are paid more than women for the same job. According to payscale.com, in 2020, for every $1.00 a man was paid, a woman was paid around 80 cents (*The State of the Gender Pay Gap*, 2020).

But that number is what the average *White* woman is paid, compared to the average White man. Compared to that $1.00, Asian American women earn 95 cents. Pacific Islander women earn 80 cents, and all other women of color make around 75 cents (*The State of the Gender Pay Gap*, 2020).

Intersectionality reveals even deeper unfairness related to prestigious or high-status jobs: the pay gap gets worse. For executives, women on average make only 69% of what men make—and statistics show that it's harder for women of color to advance to these higher-level jobs. People of color are also less likely to get raises when they ask.

The battle for equality in the United States, and arguably in every country, is still being fought. Insights into intersectionality highlight the complex and nuanced experience for many people in the fight. While it's important to celebrate milestones such as the passing of the 19th Amendment, it's also important to realize that not everyone gets to benefit from such milestones in the same ways.

DISCUSSION QUESTIONS

1. This case study mentioned voting rights and equal pay as two important examples of how intersectionality informs politics and economics. Identify at least two other examples of issues that benefit from an intersectional perspective, and explain why.

2. Two very different accounts of Truth's famous speech were published in a newspaper. In the one not quoted here, her language was represented as much more polished and "correct" (e.g., she was reported as asking, "Aren't I a woman?"). When history reports two different accounts, how can we tell which is more authentic? Does representing her speech as more polished make it more powerful, or less powerful, and why?

3. According to payscale.com, the jobs with the largest pay gaps between men and women include the following: anesthesiologists, electrical assemblers, farmers, fashion designers, computer operators, and waiters/waitresses. Analyze this list and suggest why these particular professions might lead to more pay difference between men and women, compared to other jobs. (You can see the full list at www.payscale.com/data/gender-pay-gap.)

KEY TERMS

- **Intersectionality**: The connection of multiple social categories such as race, gender, and class in a single person and how their overlap creates nuanced levels of advantage or discrimination for that individual

- **Racism**: Prejudice and discrimination toward someone because of their perceived race

- **Sexism**: Prejudice and discrimination toward someone because of their perceived sex or gender

---

9.3 ENVIRONMENTAL PSYCHOLOGY AND INSTITUTIONAL DISCRIMINATION: WHAT HAPPENED AT ERASMUS HIGH SCHOOL?

The Social Situation

Something special was happening at Erasmus High.

Erasmus Hall High School was founded as a private institution in 1786. It became a public high school 120 years later, in 1896. In the 20th century, Erasmus High flourished as the educational home for generations of immigrant children whose families got off the boat at Ellis Island and went no further than the Flatbush section of Brooklyn, New York. Erasmus was waiting for them, and they made the most of their opportunities. The Wikipedia entry lists more than 100 Erasmus graduates who demonstrated the immigrant story of success across many types of careers.

Diversity Encourages Creativity

The diversity among Erasmus students and their success after high school cannot be ignored.

George Troup was Governor of Georgia in the 1820s. James Meisner became a famous World War I flying ace. Eleanor Holm won Olympic gold in swimming. Bobby Fischer dropped out of Erasmus in 1960 but still became a world chess champion. Earl Graves became the publisher of *Black Enterprise*. And Jim Florio was Governor of New Jersey in the 1990s.

Several scientists came out of Erasmus. Eric Kandel won the Nobel Prize in 2000 but the second Erasmus graduate to be awarded the Nobel Prize in Medicine; Barbara McClintock won it in 1983. The immunologist William Paul lived well into the 21st century. Neurologist Lewis Rowland became president of the American Academy of Neurology. Julius Blank formed the Fairchild Semiconductor company. Harold Snyder founded Biocraft Laboratories, an early maker of generic drugs.

There were many writers. Dorothy Kilgallen became a journalist and was editor of the Erasmus school paper. She rejected a submission from Bernard Malamud who won the Pulitzer Prize in 1967 and wrote *The Natural* that became a popular movie. The detective novelist Micky Spillane created the character of Mike Hammer. Louis Begley's most recent (2016) novel *Killer, Come Hither* is a post-9/11 story of an injured soldier who begins writing while recuperating.

Erasmus also produced several famous sports figures including the Chicago Bears quarterback Sid Luckman, National Football League coach Sam Rutigliano, and boxing promoter Bob Arum. Hy Cohen played only seven baseball games for the Chicago Cubs. Tony Balsamo pitched 29 innings for the Cubs in 1962 and faced his boyhood idol Gil Hodges. (Balsamo walked Hodges on four nervous pitches.)

Jonah Goldman played baseball for 3 years with the Cleveland Indians, and Waite Hoyt was a dominant pitcher for the New York Yankees. Don McMahon was a major league relief pitcher for 18 years with eight teams including the Boston Braves and Houston Colts. Jerry Reinsdorf became part owner of the Chicago White Sox and the Chicago Bulls. Billy Cunningham was inducted into the basketball Hall of Fame. All of them spent much of their adolescence at Erasmus.

Erasmus alumni who became well-known artists include the painter Elaine de Kooning, pop singers Neil Diamond and Barbara Streisand, opera singer Beverly Sills, and folk singer Oscar Brand. Jeff Barry was for many years a hit-making machine with songs like "Do Wah Diddy Diddy," "Chapel of Love," and "Leader of the Pack." Art historian Arthur Sackler and Punk band drummer Markey Ramone came through Erasmus. Cartoonist Mort Drucker (*MAD Magazine*) and animator Joseph Barbera (*Tom and Jerry, The Flintstones, The Jetsons*) were Erasmus alumni. Rapper Special Ed must still have been attending Erasmus when he released his first album in 1989, when he was only 16.

Erasmus nurtured many actors. Clara Bow and Mary Anderson were stars in the era when silent films were sometimes accompanied by an organist following the action on screen. Barbara Stanwyck went from Erasmus to the Ziegfield Follies and then to a prominent film career. Actress Mae West ("Too much of a good thing can be wonderful.") was a pin-up girl with a salty sense of humor. She was joined by Moe Howard, one of an often-imitated but never-equaled comedy team: *The Three Stooges*.

Many of these high achievers were from first-generation immigrant families. They were Jewish, Black, Irish, Italian, Eastern European ... but it finally came to end. Erasmus High School closed in 1994. The buildings were broken up to serve five separate but smaller and more manageable schools.

So, what helped make Erasmus great, and why did it end?

Theory and Method

This case study uses interviews, historical records, and commentary.

One 1937 graduate described how the architecture at Erasmus communicated social norms: "I felt privileged attending Erasmus. The buildings themselves with their Gothic architecture, arches, the lawns and pathways, the statue of Erasmus, and the Old Building made me feel as though I was attending a college of lasting renown" (Kozol, 1991, p. 26).

Environmental Psychology

What your school looks like matters.

Environmental psychologists study how behavior is influenced by how the physical surroundings are experienced by its users. The physical environment at Erasmus communicated a social norm that expected excellence. Kozol's (1991) book *Savage Inequalities* examined the physical spaces in which many children learn. He highlighted the physical differences in schools from more and less privileged communities.

Dilapidated buildings and the absence of basic supplies such as books promote a different social norm and send a different message: "It's not worth the effort trying to educate people like you." According to Dickar (2006, p. 26), reassigning budgetary resources away from needy students is a form of institutionalized indifference.

Institutionalized Discrimination

Institutionalized indifference helped end the distinctive experience of Erasmus.

There was not one particular thing that brought an end to two centuries of educational excellence. Institutional discrimination is a systematic bias embedded in society in ways that privilege some people, while oppressing others. T. S. Elliot's poem, *The Hollow Men*, may have described what happened at Erasmus: "This is the way the world ends / Not with a bang but a whimper."

Discrimination is not, by strict definition, a bad thing—it means treating people differently based on their characteristics. It depends on *why* people are discriminating against a particular person or group. Professional sports teams are discriminating when, based on a player's talents and the team's needs, they offer a contract to one player over another. Teachers are discriminating when they offer different lesson plans to students of different needs.

In contrast, the legally sanctioned systemic **apartheid** in South Africa from 1948 through 1994 was institutional discrimination. It segregated Black South Africans from jobs, housing, and the right to vote. Likewise, the systemic practice that refused to let qualified baseball players from the Negro Leagues into the major leagues also was institutional discrimination. Every major league team was doing the same thing.

Types of Prejudice

There are two general categories of prejudices.

Overt or **old-fashioned prejudice** is explicit, purposeful prejudice that leads to the kind of discrimination that kept people of color out of baseball. When discrimination is based on anything unrelated to actual performance, then it is both prejudiced and, in the United States, now illegal. By contrast, **covert prejudice** is hidden from view, subtle, and expressed indirectly.

For many years, several prestigious colleges and universities did not allow women to earn graduate degrees. Their untested assumptions were that (a) women were not as intelligent, (b) educating women was a waste of time and resources, and (c) women would quit their jobs as soon as they became pregnant. That kind of discrimination has elements of both overt and covert sexism.

Results and Discussion

In the 1990s, New York City was still suffering from a long financial crisis.

New York City's financial crisis meant that Erasmus High School's physical campus had been neglected for almost 20 years. Now, lack of funding, overcrowding, and the city's other troubles conspired to destroy two centuries of educational excellence. The jewel of the city's public education system was now being called "rotting Erasmus."

Redlining

Banks began "redlining" the neighborhood around Erasmus.

The now-illegal practice of **redlining** referred to lending institutions that identify (with red lines on maps) certain neighborhoods as poor risk investments. They refuse to lend money to people who live within those areas. Redlining made it difficult for the people moving into the neighborhood around Erasmus to buy homes. So, landlords subdivided their buildings into many smaller, cheaper apartments. The neighborhoods grew denser and the schools became overcrowded.

Redlining was a subtle form of institutional discrimination. No single bank, city administrator, or borough council ever consciously decided to destroy Erasmus; bankers just stopped investing in the surrounding neighborhood. But somehow, during those same financially stressful years, "predominantly White schools were well maintained" (Kozol, 1991, p. 31).

Institutional indifference meant that instead of a grand entranceway, students entered Erasmus by a side door. Instead of noble archways, students passed through metal detectors. By the early 1990s, the dropout rate from the most famous high school in America was close to 50%, and its test scores were close to the bottom.

Educational Investments Yield Long-Term Social Dividends

The city of New York had placed an early bet on education—and not just at Erasmus.

Erasmus was the educational jewel that served thousands of immigrants pouring into Brooklyn. That bet paid off with decades of social dividends in the lives of Erasmus graduates. The city's educational investment also paid off with 15 more Nobel laureates from the City University of New York. Those are just the high-profile benefits; many thousands of others made less-noticed but still significant social contributions.

Erasmus was connected to another social investment in Flatbush that paid off in unanticipated ways. It played some of its games at nearby Ebbets Field, home of baseball's Brooklyn Dodgers. The Dodgers were the first team to crack baseball's wall of institutional discrimination when they signed Jackie Robinson.

That controversial investment in one player, Jackie Robinson, continues to pay significant social dividends. First, it opened the door for other people of color to participate in baseball, leading to higher expectations and higher salaries that helped individuals, families, and communities.

Second, it paid off for all baseball players. Jackie Robinson was one of the few players who stood by Curt Flood when he advocated for players' free agency. Curt Flood endured death threats by confronting the practice of baseball teams "owning" its players. Although he paid a high personal price, Flood liberated generations of baseball players in ways that dramatically increased their salaries and those they were able to help.

Third, the Jackie Robinson Foundation (JRF) has raised $90 million that it has reinvested in college scholarships (see Jackierobinson.org). The JRF provides specific guidance that helps students navigate the college experience. It appears to be working; JRF scholars have a 98% graduation rate.

Lack of Personal Responsibility

It is difficult to pinpoint the problems that ended the 200-year-old legacy.

The difficulty is caused, in part, by diffusion of responsibility that occurs when each person or agency with potential ownership of a problem assumes that some other person or agency will take responsibility. It is a common feature of institutional discrimination. When everyone is to blame, no one is to blame, and no one takes responsibility.

The problems at Erasmus were deeply embedded within self-sustaining economic and social structures. We may not want to be racist, feel particularly racist, or wish anyone else to suffer. But when our income or jobs depend upon continuing a policy that might have a racist edge, self-justifications come easily to mind. It is suddenly easy to explain why the social problems around are not really our problem. The end effect was institutional discrimination, and it helped deconstruct the most famous high school in America: Erasmus High.

Whose Future Is It?

The 21st century leadership at Erasmus High School is mindful of its extraordinary history.

Modern Erasmus High School is doing the harder work of undoing the effects of institutionalized discrimination. They are applying service learning and a relationship with Brooklyn College to help undo the conspiring history of stereotypes, prejudices, and discrimination that produced institutionalized racism. It can be done; will it?

As teachers, we are reminded that there is a new well-spring of creative potential that comes with every new class of students. Institutionalized discrimination can redirect their energy, but the potential will continue to bubble up regardless. Students *want* to succeed at something. That kind of creative potential found extraordinary release across two centuries of demographically shifting and unlikely collections of poor, immigrant children. It's a much longer legacy than the one imposed by institutional discrimination.

Erasmus High! Make it happen again.

DISCUSSION QUESTIONS

1. Can you identify examples of institutional discrimination in any institutions, organizations, or groups in your own life? Think about, for example, your town, high school, college or university, teams or clubs, and so on.

2. Attributional ambiguity occurs when you're not sure why someone else acted in the way they did toward you. If you didn't get a job, is it because you interviewed badly or because the interviewer was prejudiced against you? If you were complimented by someone, is it because you deserved the compliment or because they were trying to manipulate you? Identify at least two specific examples of attributional ambiguity from your own life experiences. How does not being sure of other people's motives make you feel?

3. People in socially privileged groups within a given society often benefit from historical

or cultural prejudice, even if they personally don't endorse or participate in the prejudice (e.g., male privilege, White privilege). Is it the responsibility of privileged groups to actively work against their own privilege and toward equality? Or, is it equally the responsibility of every citizen? Alternatively, is it unrealistic to believe that any society could ever truly be free of all forms of prejudice?

KEY TERMS

- **Environmental psychology**: The study of how behavior is influenced by our physical surroundings
- **Apartheid**: Institutional discrimination against Black people in South Africa between 1948 and 1994
- **Old-fashioned prejudice**: Blatant, explicit judgments that some groups are better or more worthy than others

- **Covert prejudice**: Subtle, hidden, or indirect feelings of negativity toward given social groups
- **Redlining**: Changing map designations of given neighborhoods for political and/or financial reasons, such as changing election districts

---

9.4 FOOTNOTE 11: AFTER THE DOLL STUDIES

The Social Situation

The decision was unanimous.

On May 17, 1954, Chief Justice Earl Warren read the Court's opinion in the case of *Brown v. Board of Education of Topeka*. The decision ended legal "separate but equal" segregated public schools. Children of all different races now could go to school together. Although "could" did not mean "would," or at least not right away, it was a ground-shifting legal change for what it meant to be American, a defining moment for the U.S. Constitution, and a crucial victory for civil rights.

The Supreme Court of the United States had concluded that "to separate [Black children] from others of similar age and qualifications . . . may affect their hearts and minds in a way unlikely ever to be undone." The Court came to this historic conclusion because of social psychological evidence referenced in the court document known as Footnote 11 (see Benjamin & Crouse, 2002).

Theory and Method

This case study describes how a psychological study influenced the Supreme Court.

The story behind Footnote 11 involves the husband–wife team of Kenneth and Mamie Phipps Clark, the first two African Americans to earn doctorates at Columbia University.

The methodology that produced their famous "doll studies" grew out of Mamie Phipps's master's thesis at Howard University (see Johnson & Pettigrew, 2005). The Clarks provided Black children with identical dolls, except that one was white skinned with blonde hair, and the other was brown skinned with black hair (Whitman, 1993).

Then they asked the children a series of questions about which doll they preferred: "Give me the doll you like to play with," " . . . you like best," " . . . is a nice doll," " . . . looks bad," " . . . is a nice color"—and finally, "which doll is most like you?" They compared the responses of children attending segregated schools in Washington, DC, and those of children attending racially integrated schools in New York.

The Clarks' research had deep psychological roots. **Social role theory** recognizes how stereotypes can dictate and limit the achievements of Black children. **Social learning theory** takes over when it passes those stereotypes through to the next generation. How? The messages are sent through media, toys, books, and language. Those first impressions imply halo effects that suggest that race-based "inferiority" applies to more than just not being good at some particular skill. The inferiority describes the whole person—and then to the entire community of dark-skinned people.

Racial prejudice easily becomes a confirmation bias so that (Black and White) children perceive only evidence that supports their expectations, and it ignores or explains away contradicting evidence. The result, far too often, is a self-fulfilling prophecy in which a child's belief became an adults' reality.

Results and Discussion

First, the obvious; second, the disturbing; third, the alarming.

First, some 90% of these 3- to 7-year-olds accurately indicated they were like the brown-skinned doll. Second, about two-thirds preferred the white doll! The preference for the white doll was more pronounced in the children from segregated schools in Washington, DC than to New York. Third, some of the children's reactions were alarming. One girl who had described the brown doll as "ugly" and "dirty" burst into tears. Others refused to continue the experiment. Some giggled self-consciously. One little boy tried to escape his dilemma by insisting that he had a suntan.

Social Psychological Explanations

Social psychologists understand most of the processes shaping these children.

However, those processes were historical long before they became a daily experience influenced by social psychological processes. The end of those historical processes was self-hatred, evidenced by how the children in the Clarks' studies perceived their dolls. They were only 3-to-7 years old, but they already had **internalized racism** that became a pivotal piece of information in the Court's decision.

The daily processes that got those children to that point were supported well by social psychological theory and experimental evidence. The various processes engaged a network of familiar social psychological theories and effects:

- social role theory
- stereotypes social learning theory

- first impressions
- halo effects
- confirmation bias
- self-fulfilling prophecy

The Historical Context

W. E. B. DuBois perceived the historical processes of psychological warfare.

DuBois traced the deeper history of psychological conflict in his 1903 publication of *The Souls of Black Folk*. The Black community was in a battle for community self-consciousness, as well as for self-respect and self-esteem. Their enemy was not just the conspiracy of daily expectations documented by social psychologists, but also "the red stain of bastardy, which two centuries of legal defilement of Negro women had stamped upon his race" (p. 12).

The response within the Black community was of a creativity born of desperation and the remnants of a shredded culture. For example, DuBois recognized that the music coming out of the Black church somehow produced a "plaintive rhythmic melody, with its touching minor cadences, which, despite caricature and defilement, still remains the most original and beautiful expression of human life and longing yet born on American soil" (DuBois, 1903/2008, p. 129).

That cultural creativity to support community self-esteem is documented also in Nia Crawford's (2018) doctoral dissertation, *More Than Hair: Building Self-Esteem in African-American Children's Books*. Brewer (2019) described how the Black church continues to contribute to community self-esteem by organizing events and awareness for social justice, political action, and public health initiatives.

A Complicated Legacy

Too bad this is not a story with a perfectly happy ending.

The story of Footnote 11 is complicated. The Clarks discovered that changing people's stereotypes and attitudes was far more difficult than changing the legal environment. The historic *Brown v. Board of Education of Topeka* legal decision did not automatically change hearts and minds (Nyman, 2010).

Riots broke out when some African American children, sometimes with armed guards, bravely walked into formerly segregated schools. One child in Little Rock, Arkansas, was "summarily expelled from school." The Clarks took her into their own home (Jones & Pettigrew, 2005, p. 650).

The American Psychological Association was disturbingly quiet in the aftermath of *Brown v. Board of Education of Topeka* (see Benjamin & Crouse, 2002). In 1970, Kenneth Clark was elected president of the American Psychological Association. In 1994, he was honored for his lifetime contributions to psychology.

The recognition was nice. But in his acceptance speech, Kenneth Clark admitted to personal disappointment. "Thirty years after *Brown*, I must accept the fact that my wife left this earth despondent at seeing that damage to children is being knowingly and silently accepted by a nation that claims to be democratic" (from Benjamin & Crouse, 2002, p. 48).

DISCUSSION QUESTIONS

1. Do you think that social psychological research should be used as evidence to persuade jurors, judges, or justices in court cases? Why, or why not?

2. Discuss at least two strengths and two limitations of the Clarks' procedure as a way to test internalized racism or the effects of school segregation with very young children. For each of the limitations you have identified, how would you design a study that would overcome these limitations or challenges?

3. Kenneth Clark's speech in 1994 expressed disappointment that the United States had not progressed further in eliminating prejudice and discrimination. Do you agree with his conclusion? Do you see progress between 1994 and now—or do you agree with some social psychologists that forms of discrimination have simply become more subtle or concealed?

4. Explain how the Clark doll studies can be used as evidence to support both social role theory and social learning theory.

KEY TERMS

- **Social role theory**: The idea that stereotypes are based on the roles different groups have in a culture, which are then reinforced through self-fulfilling prophecies
- **Social learning theory**: The idea that children imitate what they see other people doing, thus passing down ideas and behaviors from one generation to the next
- **Internalized racism**: Prejudice against one's own racial group, learned through cultural messages such as media, authority figures, and institutional discrimination

Helping and Prosocial Behavior

10

10.1 THE MISUNDERSTOOD MURDER OF KITTY GENOVESE: A CONTINUING CASE STUDY

The Social Situation

The scientific study of when people will—or won't—help others was partially instigated by a murder.

In Queens, New York, in 1964, Kitty Genovese was coming home from her closing shift as a bartender. It was around 3:00 am when a man she had never seen before chased her across the parking lot with a hunting knife. He stabbed her twice. She screamed for help at the bottom of her apartment complex, where dozens of people lived. The man ran away but came back a few minutes later. He stabbed her several more times, assaulted her, and robbed her. He left her in the entryway to her apartment building, bleeding. The total attack took over half an hour, and she died about an hour later.

Why did this particular murder become famous? Two weeks after Genovese's death, the *New York Times* ran a story with the headline, "37 Who Saw Murder Didn't Call the Police" (Gansberg, 1964). According to the story, 37 people in Kitty's apartment building heard her screams for help or saw it from their windows, but not a single one lifted a finger to help. The story claimed that one neighbor actually turned up his radio to avoid the annoying noise of the attack.

Several people—politicians, journalists, and social scientists—used Genovese's murder as evidence of society's increasing apathy and callousness. Citizens of New York were stereotyped as uncaring and jaded. Many people suggested their lack of response was because of **urban overload**, the idea that people in cities don't help those in need because they are overwhelmed with the sheer amount of need they encounter each day (Milgram, 1970).

The Kitty Genovese murder was one of the reasons the Emergency 911 system was created (Solomon et al., 2016). Bill Clinton referred to her death in a speech, noting that no one bothered to call the police. His conclusion was this: "It sent a chilling message suggesting that we were—each of us—not simply endangered, but fundamentally alone."

Did all of those people really choose to ignore a young woman who was being killed, just outside their door?

Theory and Method

There are a lot of explanations for the response to Kitty Genovese's murder—and the *New York Times* might have gotten a lot of things wrong.

The Bystander Effect

Two social psychologists were particularly interested in this case.

The wanted to explain the reported lack of response to Genovese's cries for help (Darley & Latané, 1968; Latané & Darley, 1970). Their series of studies assumed that the reporting was accurate. They wanted to know why those 37 neighbors didn't help. They didn't think the urban overload hypothesis was enough to explain each person's lack of response.

Latané and Darley didn't think New Yorkers were particularly callous and uncaring. In fact, they thought that several of the witnesses were probably quite disturbed by what they heard or saw. They proposed a new hypothesis: the **bystander effect**. When many people see someone in need of help, others see and hear what we see and hear—and assume that someone else will help. In some ways, it's an optimistic view of other people; of course someone else must have already called the police! So I don't have to—in fact, it might just be getting in the way if I do.

The bystander effect suggests that the likelihood of getting help in an emergency is negatively correlated with the number of people who are there to witness it. If lots of people are around, none of them will feel the individual responsibility to help. So those 37 people who supposedly saw the murder might have cared very much, but they didn't call the police because they assumed someone else already had.

The Five-Step Model of Helping

Latané and Darley didn't stop there.

Urban overload and diffusion of responsibility might explain why some people didn't help Kitty Genovese—but there are lots of other reasons people might not have helped. The pair of researchers eventually developed the **Five-Step Model of Helping** (Latané & Darley, 1970). Here, people might not help someone in need because of many situational factors. In fact, helping will only happen if a witness answers yes to all of the questions in their five steps:

1. Did I notice the event?
2. Did I interpret it as an emergency?
3. Did I feel responsible?
4. Did I know how to help?
5. Did I actually do something about it?

Consider, for example, Steps 1 and 2. Years after the Genovese murder, two films were produced regarding what really happened. Pul Grasten's 2016 film was called *37* and explored various reasons why people might not have helped. The film suggests that some of Genovese's neighbors might have said no to Step 1 because they didn't actually hear her cries due to other noises like children crying in their apartment. They also might have said no to Step 2 because they

- Interpreted her cries as a radio program from someone else's apartment

- Were suffering from mental illness or hearing problems

- Believed the noises of the attack were children playing a prank or drunk people returning from a party.

Another Answer: People Did Help

So now we had several hypotheses for why people didn't help:

1. They were apathetic, callous New Yorkers who just didn't care;

2. they assumed someone else would help; and

3. they didn't even realize someone needed help.

Any of these might be true for the neighbors who witnessed Genovese's murder and really didn't respond. But a second film suggests there might be another interpretation.

Kitty Genovese had several siblings, and she was particularly close to her little brother Bill. Haunted by the murder and the stories of people who didn't help his sister, Bill created a documentary called *The Witness* (Solomon et al., 2016). Years later, he returned to the scene of the crime to track down the neighbors and ask them for their own version of the story. And what he discovered shed a new light on this famous case study.

Results and Discussion

Bill was only 12 when his sister was killed.

So to track down the "37 witnesses" from the *New York Times*, he had to do some digging. Archival data provided the answer. First, the number itself turned out to be wrong. Bill found that it was actually 38 people, not 37, who were referred to in the newspaper articles. He got the police report from that fateful night and discovered that they had, indeed, interviewed exactly 38 people from the apartment about what they had seen, heard, and done. He also found the original transcript of the trial, in which five of those 38 people served as witnesses to the court. Bill wanted to talk to as many of them as possible, to find out why they didn't help his sister.

Many of the original 38 people listed in the police report had passed away. For the rest, he spent over a year finding their contact information. The first two people highlighted in the documentary admitted to not helping. One, the night elevator operator from the building across the street, said that he simply ignored the cries for help and went to sleep. One of her neighbors said he called his girlfriend to ask what to do, and she responded, "Don't get involved." He didn't.

Those two stories matched what the *New York Times* had reported. But there were other stories that turned out to be a surprise. In fact, several people *did* help, in various ways. In the court transcript, a neighbor named Robert Mozer testified that when he heard the first attack, he looked out the window and yelled down, "Hey, get out of there!" According to Mozer, his yells were the reason the attacker ran away after the initial stabbings. That makes sense; something had to explain why he ran away.

Another neighbor, Hattie Grund, told Bill that she *did* call the police that night. According to her, the police dispatcher cut her off quickly saying, "We already got the calls," and hung up. But according to the official police records, no one called until after Kitty was dead. So Grund's story is questionable; maybe she was just telling Bill what he wanted to hear, or remembering things in a way she can live with.

Perhaps most surprisingly, Sophie Farrar testified that she actually approached Kitty after the second attack. Farrar was still alive in 2016, and Bill spoke directly to her. Both Sophie and her brother remembered that Sophie ran to Kitty as she laid in the entry to their apartment. Sophie held her and comforted her as she died. It appears that Sophie, at least, helped—even if her help was a little late.

In the documentary, Bill Genovese also found one of the journalists. According to this man, several of the journalists all got the same information the day after the murder. That information included the fact that some of the neighbors heard the attack but thought it was a domestic violence—and that's why they didn't call.

In other words, even the people who admitted to not helping said they hadn't said yes to Step 2 of the model described above. But apparently, the journalists purposely left that information out when they reported what happened. Why? According to the reporter in Bill's documentary, "Because it would have ruined the story."

The sad Genovese murder instigated hundreds, if not thousands, of newspaper articles and psychology studies about people's motivations to help—or not help—others. This case study was originally used as an example of the social psychology of when people *won't* help. But now we can add to the story, noting that it appears a few people did help, but under specific circumstances. As we often find, the social situation is more complicated than it originally appears.

DISCUSSION QUESTIONS

1. Some people have criticized Bill Genovese's documentary conclusions that several neighbors did help. They argue that these witnesses may have faulty memories of an event that occurred decades ago, and that they were probably motivated to tell Bill Genovese a version of the story that put them in a better light. Do you think the people he interviewed so many years later can be considered reliable in what they say now? Why, or why not?

2. Part of this case study is the idea that the journalists who originally reported the murder purposely left out details of the case to make it more sensational. What is the obligation of journalists when reporting stories? Can you find other examples of stories that seem to twist facts to make the story better? Is the Kitty Genovese murder an early example of what we might now call "fake news?"

3. Consider people who live in a big city and are consistently confronted with people in need. Which of the five steps in the Five-Step Model of helping do you think is most commonly the point at which people say no and stop the process? Why did you pick that step?

KEY TERMS

- **Urban overload**: The hypothesis that the overwhelming stimuli of living in a busy city reduces the mental-emotional capacity to help others

- **Bystander effect**: The more people witnessing someone in need is negatively correlated with the probability of that person receiving help

- **Five-Step Model of Helping**: The probability of helping others in need requires a rapid, five-step evaluation of accurately (1) noticing, (2) interpreting, (3) feeling responsible, (4) knowing how to help, and (5) providing help

10.2 ZOMBIE WASPS AND ALTRUISTIC VAMPIRE BATS

The Social Situation

"In spite of everything, I still believe that people are really good at heart."

Anne Frank's famous diary declared her faith in human goodness. She was determined to believe despite layers of evidence including being hunted by Nazis for being Jewish, and the petty selfishness among the families who had joined them in having to hide in an attic from the Nazis.

"Good" and "evil" living together is one reason that many social psychologists are reluctant to apply the term *altruism* to human behavior. Among other objections, it implies that people are either good or evil rather than complicated. Every act of apparent goodness could be tinged with self-serving motives. Every act of apparent evil could mask an unseen moral dilemma or an unexamined social norm. A scientific approach can help us get past our wishes about human nature and possibly discover the forces pushing what looks like good and evil to the surface of our behaviors.

Theory and Method

Is there such a thing as pure altruism?

Sometimes, an indirect approach is the fastest path to our goal, just as a car sometimes has to drive in the wrong direction to get to a superhighway. Dugatkin (2007) explained why altruism is difficult to study:

The structure of an atom is not personal, and neither is studying, for example, night vision in mammals. Studying altruism can be personal, however, because we all want to understand the origins of goodness. (p. 1375)

This indirect approach to human nature explores apparent altruism in three non-human animals that are unlikely candidates for moral behavior. The first two are insects: the honeybee and the jewel wasp. Insects can teach us about human altruism because they are so different from big-brained human animals. The third is a bat: vampire bats. Honey-supplying bees, zombie-making jewel wasps, and blood-sucking Costa Rican vampire bats all display behaviors that may remind you of complicated, pro-social human behavior. If we can understand the "altruistic" behavior of these creatures, perhaps we can better understand it in ourselves.

Two Types of Altruism

Social psychologists distinguish between two types of altruism.

As a general concept, **altruism** refers to a selfless concern for the welfare of others. The first type of altruism, **pure altruism**, proposes that cooperative or self-sacrificing behaviors are performed with no selfish benefits. The second type, **egoistic altruism**, proposes that apparently selfless people still receive some kind of personal or social benefit from being a good person. Here are just a few subtly self-serving ways to be altruistic:

a. self-sacrificing to boost your own self-esteem,

b. donating your time to strengthen relationships with a group you want to join,

c. increasing the positive thoughts that others might have about you,

d. reinforcing the comforting belief that "what goes around comes around,"

e. trying to increase your reward in an afterlife,

f. reducing your sense of guilt for not having helped someone in need, and

g. building a reputation as a good person to increase social capital you can spend later.

Prosocial Behavior

Instead of *helping*, many social psychologists prefer the term *prosocial behavior*.

It is a more general description of the cooperative types of behavior that can by motivated by pure and egoistic altruism. The phrase "prosocial behavior" is a little clunky, in our opinion, and doesn't quite challenge humans to think more critically about their own motivations. So, like some others, we will use the terms *helping, altruism,* and *prosocial behavior* almost interchangeably and leave it to you to weigh the evidence of each case about pure versus egoistic altruism in humans and other animals.

The egoistic motives listed above make sense for humans—but what about other animals? Do insects worry about their self-esteem? It's difficult for many humans to imagine that insects or vampire bats might feel "guilt" about not helping or choose to help to boost their social reputation. So why do nonhuman animals seem to engage in selfless, prosocial behaviors that include making sacrifices to their own well-being to help others?

If insects don't need a moral code to be good, do humans?

Anthropomorphism

The usual human problem in animal research is anthropomorphism.

Anthropomorphism occurs when humans apply human characteristics to non-human creatures, objects, and events. It's a subtle bias that creeps up on you, partly because we find it entertaining. Children's books feature talking mice, cheerful birds, bumbling bears, well-dressed monkeys, and thoughtful dinosaurs. The animals around us are more than just comforting—we all want to think that our pets are "happy to see us" when we get home.

However, Marlene Zuk (2011) points out in *Sex on Six Legs* that even our anthropomorphism is biased. We humans easily project human characteristics onto creatures that can walk with two legs. It's a little more difficult to compare ourselves with four-legged creatures—but easier if they will at least stand up straight from time to time.

For example, Panda bears look cuddly and squirrels can act cute. There are plenty of mice in children's literature who dress up in clothes and debate whether it is better to live in the city or in the country. Four-legged creatures such as cats, dogs, and horses are often treated like humans, although some cultures are horrified at the thought of welcoming dogs into our homes, much less encouraging them to sleep on our beds.

But we don't usually anthropomorphize things with no legs or with way, way too many legs such as centipedes.

Results and Discussion

Insects? We generally don't like 'em.

And that's precisely why Zuk (2011) believes that insects can help us understand human altruism: Anthropomorphism doesn't come so easily when we think of cockroaches. Those six legs and two waving antennae are not things that we easily relate to. If insects are altruistic, then human goodness might not be such a remarkable achievement. We'll start with the slight exception to human's dislike of insects: the honeybee. Then we'll try to understand the zombie-making jewel wasp, and finish with the altruism of vampire bats, all to gain a better understanding of human altruism.

Altruistic Honeybees

Honeybees were a big problem for Charles Darwin.

Darwin was prepared to throw out his entire theory of **natural selection** if he could not explain the mystery of sterile male worker bees. Dugatkin (2007, p. 1375) described Darwin's dilemma:

> The worker bees that sacrifice themselves to protect their hives—the ultimate example of animal altruism—were deeply troubling to Darwin … altruists should disappear—and fast. But they did not disappear, and Darwin was so puzzled by this that he spoke of altruism as a problem that he feared was "one special difficulty, which at first appeared to me to be insuperable, and actually fatal to the whole theory" (Darwin, 1859, p. 236).

Sterile honeybees would seem to lack an evolutionary motivation. Nevertheless, they will defend their own hive in several ways, including stinging intruders (Downs & Ratnieks, 2000). Sometimes the intruders are skunks or a bear looking for a meal. But they also might be "robber bees" living in a nearby hive.

It's difficult to not think anthropomorphically about robber bees. Robber bees are like the bumbling human thieves parked outside a house they hope to rob in the film *Home Alone*. Robber bees "fly to-and-fro in front of the hive entrance with a characteristic swaying motion as though watching for an opportunity to enter the hive unchallenged by its guards" (Free, 1954, p. 233). In other words, they are acting suspicious by hanging out near the front door watching who is going in and out.

The altruistic guard bees will sniff robber bees, trying to use their aroma to learn about their intentions. And if the robbers try to enter the hive, then the guard bees will attack the intruder. If they attack by stinging, then they will die because their barbed stingers remain in their victims and rupture the bee's abdomen as it pulls away. Stingless bees reach the same end with what Shackleton and colleagues (2014) describe as "suicidal biting." These bees die to protect their hive.

Kinship selection is the kind of helping behavior that benefits near relatives more than distant neighbors. Kinship selection was the solution to Darwin's problem with sterile, altruistic honeybees. He wrote that the problem of altruistic honeybees

> disappears when it is remembered that selection may be applied to the family, as well as the individual and may thus gain the desired end (Darwin, 1859, p. 204).

The Zombie-Making Jewel Wasp

You can see both cruelty and kindness in the zombie-making jewel wasp.

The jewel wasp turns cockroaches and spiders into walking zombies. Zuk (2011) explains that the jewel wasp isn't paralyzing its insect victims into chemical zombies for its own amusement. Paralyzing victims rather than killing them keeps their prey tasty-fresh for the young jewel wasps back at the nest. But that creates a new problem: How do you get the heavy, paralyzed food back to the nest? Most mother wasps stagger

> under the weight of her groceries as she flies back to her young. Except, that is, in the case of the jewel wasp. . . . The female wasp . . . makes it into a zombie via a judicious sting inside the roach's head, so that its nervous system, and legs, still function well enough to allow it to walk on its own. (pp. 3–5)

The jewel wasp then grabs the zombie cockroach's antenna and leads it like a dog on a leash to its doom: fresh food for the rising generation of jewel wasps—whose females will also possess zombie-making powers.

These mama jewel wasps are working to feed their children, which many would consider one kind of altruism. Sacrificing your time, energy, and resources for children probably won't be "paid back" in any kind of direct way. So what is the mama getting out of this deal? From a Darwinian perspective, their interest in keeping their offspring alive ensures that their genes are passed to the next generation. Mama jewel wasps are as dramatic a case of altruism as sterile honeybees, but both are devoting their resources to help their larger community.

Altruistic Vampire Bats

Vampire bats famously feast on blood.

They usually land on large mammals such as wild pigs, cows, and horses (but rarely humans). They need a lot of blood. Vampire bats will drink about half their body weight during an uninterrupted feeding—so much that they sometimes have difficulty taking flight. Lisa DeNault and Don McFarlane (1995) discovered why vampire bats are so blood-thirsty. A vampire bat will die if it goes more than 48 to 72 hours without a blood meal.

Inclusive Fitness: Who "Deserves" Altruism?

But they also found altruism among vampire bats.

Both male and female vampire bats display awareness of their neighbors' needs—and they go even further. In an apparent act of altruism, a vampire bat with a sufficient blood meal will regurgitate and share it with starving neighbors.

This act of charity and self-sacrifice contradicts human stereotypes and fears about vampire bats. And the story of vampire bat altruism is even more sophisticated—perhaps in ways that indicate egoistic altruism at a group level. Vampire bats are selective in their sharing of blood.

When Wilkinson (1984) studied vampire bats in Costa Rica, he discovered that they were more likely to donate blood to those bats with the greatest need for a meal. Further-more, their altruistic food sharing was not limited to their immediate kin, which would have been predicted by the theory of kinship selection (see Dugatkin, 2007; Okasha, 2016). Instead, frequent roostmates were more likely to be the beneficiaries.

Sometimes the nearby social group is more important than the blood-related family group.

Reciprocal Altruism

Vampire bats are able to identify, remember, and *not help* certain vampire bats.

Wilkinson found that vampire bats were less likely to help other vampire bats that *had not* previously donated blood to other starving bats. In short, being selfish was pun-ished. There was an expectation among vampire bats of helping each other in times of need. If you left me high and dry (both metaphorically and literally in the case of thirsty vampire bats), then I won't help you when you are in need.

Among vampire bats, this **reciprocal altruism** has evolved into a sophisticated social norm, complete with punishment for those vampire bats that are less altruistic. Vampire bats are one of many other species that have evolved favor-trading—or maybe it's hold-ing a grudge (Van Vugt & Van Lange, 2006). There are at least three critical insights embedded in these observations about altruism among vampire bats:

- Assessing the blood needs of its own and of its neighbors suggests that the vampire bat is aware of itself as distinct from other bats: self-awareness.

- Mutual sharing suggests an ability to notice and remember favors given and received: reciprocal altruism.

- Making judgments about the relative worth of friends and neighbors suggests conscious decision making: social consciousness.

DISCUSSION QUESTIONS

1. When a parent sacrifices time, money, or other resources to feed their children, does that count as altruism? If so, is it pure altruism or egoistic altruism?

2. Find an example of a person in history who is seen as an altruistic hero. Discuss whether that person appears to have displayed pure altruism or egoistic altruism, and why.

3. Find evidence for at least one other nonhuman animal species that appears to display altruism and summarize those patterns of behavior. Make sure to properly cite any sources you use.

KEY TERMS

- **Altruism**: Selfless concern for the welfare of others
- **Pure altruism**: Cooperative, helping, or self-sacrificing behaviors done with no selfish benefits at all
- **Egoistic altruism**: Cooperative, helping, or self-sacrificing behaviors done because they somehow benefit the person performing them

- **Anthropomorphism**: Applying human-like characteristics to nonhuman animals, objects, or events
- **Kinship selection**: The theory that we're more likely to make sacrifices or help others who are genetically related to ourselves
- **Reciprocal altruism**: The expectation that if I help you now, you'll help me in the future

10.3 THE BACON TRUCE: COOPERATION DESPITE WAR

The Social Situation

The zig-zagging trenches were not part of the plan.

Long before it earned the title of "World War I," both sides presumed that the 1914 conflict would be (a) short and glorious, and (b) won by the fastest army. The infamous western front (in Europe) bogged down into 4 years of trench warfare because each army kept trying to outflank the other. When they finally bumped into the North Sea, the two armies had to settle down into what Ashworth (1980) called a "long, narrow zone of violence" (p. 3).

Many towns and villages not far from the western front barely knew the war existed. Only the occasional sounds of cannons plus the steady disappearance of their young men signaled that the conflict must be real. Trench warfare occurred because there was nowhere else for the two armies to go. Ashworth (1980) explained that

> the western front emerged as the infantries of each deadlocked army huddled in countless hastily dug and unconnected rifle pits, then joined these together into two continuous but parallel and opposing trench lines. (p. 4)

The Zig-Zag Trenches Created New Situations

They looked strange from the air.

The two webs of connecting lines occasionally passed each other but never connected with one another. They stretched almost 500 miles from the North Sea to Switzerland, across different countries, and through varied terrain. Between the two armies was no man's land that each side kept trying to fill with barbed wire to slow an attack from the other side.

Seen up close, the two sets of trenches zig-zagged across the landscape. They sometimes formed neat and orderly arrangements supported by timbers. But frequently, they were expanded shell pits, hastily dug and often collapsing. The purpose of the zig-zagging was to prevent the enemy from aiming their guns down a long, straight line of helpless soldiers.

However, the zig-zag pattern had created an unanticipated situation—and situations matter, especially during a war. The zig-zags created small bays that became homes for small groups of 7–20 soldiers. The zig-zags meant that

a. soldiers were informally reorganized into many small, independent groups;

b. it took much longer for messengers or high command to get from Point A to Point B;

c. top commanders were less likely to make it all the way to the front lines; and

d. the small groups could make more independent decisions.

There was a great deal of just waiting for something to happen. A restless soldier did not dare stick his head above the trench line—each side had long-range guns with powerful scopes. Each small, independent group took care of its members: brewing tea, frying bacon, and talking. They "chatted" with one another as they picked lice ("chats") off one another.

Living With Your Enemy

The little groups on both sides were not isolated.

Each side knew their neighbors in the connecting bay, of course. But the soldiers on both sides also could often hear, occasionally see, and sometimes smell their enemy. Their living situation created opportunities for deep social exchanges between young men struggling together through hours of boredom and miserable living conditions that could be interrupted by terror.

The proximity to their enemy made it possible to empathize with those they were ordered to kill. The frontline soldiers in WW I were sometimes physically and emotionally much closer to their sworn enemy than to their own commanding officers. There were social exchanges within groups, between groups within each army, and between the opposing armies.

The zig-zigs had produced unanticipated consequences: small, independent groups of men making life and death decisions about fighting people very much like themselves. In academic language, the zig-zags had created opportunities for **prosocial moral reasoning**.

Theory and Method

This case study relies mostly on archived writings by British soldiers in WW I.

Ashworth (1980) wanted to learn the gritty details that led enemies to cooperate. He looked for descriptions of informal peace-making between enemy soldiers on the Western front. As both a sociologist and historian, Ashworth chose to take an evidence-first, bottom-up approach to his research. He started with the details.

The Structure of the British Army

A battalion was the chief organizational unit of the British army.

A battalion was about 1,000 soldiers and 35 officers. It organized soldiers for battle, supplied food, paid salaries, delivered mail, and administered medical care. It included 64 sections made up of about 14 men each. That smallest grouping was approximately the number of soldiers who could fit into one, two, or three bays created by the zig-zagging trenches.

Four battalions made a brigade; three brigades made a division. The level of the division was how top military planners tried to strategically conduct the war. Perhaps surprisingly, Ashworth discovered data about informal truces from 56 (98%) of the 57 divisions that had experienced direct combat for at least 3 months. He collected an average of three documents from each division.

The Archived Materials

Ashworth sampled diaries, letters, and accounts.

Some accounts were written at the time, others were penned afterward. Ashworth did not, however, include official histories or official war diaries. Fraternization, or peace-making, was officially not allowed and was sometimes punished with execution. Ashworth also did not include his many interviews with surviving soldiers, unless they could provide some form of written confirmation of their stories. This conservative research approach suggests that Ashworth's estimates of the frequency of spontaneous peacemaking are an underestimate—making them all the more impressive.

Results and Discussion

The most famous truce in WW I was the Christmas Truce of 1914.

Soldiers celebrated by singing carols, playing football in no man's land, exchanging items, and taking photographs of one another before returning to the war. It involved nine divisions along 30 miles of the western front. It was verbally arranged, but trust had been built slowly from many previous, smaller truces and both explicit and implicit **social exchanges**. Opposing soldiers sometimes gave one another time to retrieve their dead and wounded from no man's land, and then began exchanging gifts and souvenirs.

The First Truce

The first truce probably was triggered by food.

The trenches were not roadways, and each side had to be fed. The armies could not drive horse-drawn food trucks through the long networks of trenches. It was a perfect opportunity for each side to shell the others' food trucks. Both sides delivered their rations to the frontlines at about the same time. One of the noncommissioned officers observed that

> I suppose the enemy were occupied in the same way; so things were quiet at that hour for a couple of nights, and the ration parties became careless because of it, and laughed and talked on their way back to their companies. (Ashworth, 1980, p. 24)

Ian Hay of the ninth division wrote that

> it would be child's play to shell the road behind the enemy's trenches, crowded as it must be with ration wagons and water carts, into a bloodstained wilderness . . . but on the whole there is silence. After all, if you prevent your enemy from drawing his rations, his remedy is simple: He will prevent you from drawing yours. (p. 26)

The Bacon Truce

Breakfast seemed the most likely time to trigger a truce:

> On December 1, 1914, a Private Hawkings from the 5th Division poked his head above the parapet of the trench when a sergeant suggested that the reason his "earnest curiosity had not been greeted with a shower of bullets was probably due to . . . Fritz enjoying his breakfast." (p. 25)

The soldier-historian Hart believed that breakfast truces were common, in part because

> unforgettable, too, is the homely smell of breakfast bacon that gained its conquest over the war reek of chloride of lime, and in so doing not only brought a tacit truce to the battlefront, but helped in preserving sanity. (p. 25)

A bacon truce! The diaries indicated many other triggers for truces. There were rain truces that allowed each side to repair their trench walls and straw truces that allowed both sides to fetch some hay in no man's land for warmth. There were informal truces for a German violinist, a British trumpeter, and even a drunken Scot who wandered, bottle in hand, into no man's land yet made it safely back to his trench.

Choose Between Two Philosophies

The war was still young in December of 1914 when the Christmas Truce evolved.

Already hundreds of thousands of soldiers had died. Many Germans spoke English, having worked in England before the war. There had been so many interchanges between combatants that the British high command issue a directive that forbid fraternizing with the enemy (see Weintraub, 2001). Fraternization

> [d]iscourages initiative in commanders, and destroys the offensive spirit in all ranks. . . . Friendly intercourse with the enemy, unofficial armistices and the exchange of tobacco and other comforts . . . are absolutely forbidden. (p. 3)

"Fraternization with the enemy" was not just frowned upon; some soldiers were executed for getting too friendly with the enemy. Nevertheless, the peacemaking persisted informally behind the backs of superior officers. Ashworth concluded that cooperation between enemies evolved not because some great healer, commanding general, or visionary politician brought it to pass.

Peacemaking between enemies was fueled by a simple social psychological philosophy: "Live and let live." The alternative philosophy, of course, was to "kill and be killed." Those philosophies regularly stumbled into conflict between soldiers on night patrols in no man's land. The diary of an officer in the 24th division reported discovering a German and a British soldier talking deep within a shell hole:

> I found Pte Bates . . . fraternizing with a German . . .

> Bates: "What rank are you in your army?" "I am a corporal," indicating stripes on his collar. "What rank are you?" "Oh," replied Bates, "I am Company Sergt Major." (Ashworth, 1980, p. 20)

How did Bates and the German soldier end up chatting amiably in a shell hole? Did they surprise one another on patrol, yet not fire their weapons? Before enlisting, most soldiers on both sides had been fed a constant diet of information that demonized the enemy. They had been enthusiastic volunteers for a grand cause that they believed in but could not articulate.

Then they had been sent off to war with songs, pride, parades, cheering women, and in the company of thousands of other young men who were equally enthusiastic. It had been a powerful, patriotic social norm. But now they found themselves in a muddy trench, often walking through water soiled by their own waste, suffering from trench foot, plagued by rats feeding on the corpses of their comrades, and fearful of lifting their heads above the rim of the trench.

These mortal enemies had a lot in common.

Reciprocal Altruism

The frontline soldiers knew each other's daily routines.

Reciprocal altruism gradually became a social norm, but it had to be taught. Ashworth (1980) described how a new recruit, Raleigh, was taken on a tour of the trenches and taught the informal rules of wartime sportsmanship by seasoned soldiers, one of them named Trotter:

Trotter: That's the Bosche front line. Bosche looking over this way now, maybe, just as we are—do you play cricket?

Raleigh: A bit.

Trotter: Could you chuck a cricket ball that distance?

Raleigh: I think so.

Trotter: Then you could do the same with a Mills bomb. . . . But you won't. Come on . . . let sleeping dogs lie. If we was to throw a bomb you can bet your boots the old Bosche would chuck one back, and Mr. Digby and Mr. 'Arris are both married men. Wouldn't be cricket would it? (p. 30)

The development of cooperation between enemies was the result of a live-and-let-live philosophy. It made more sense to many frontline soldiers than following the kill-and-be-killed orders of their superior officers. The impulse to survive was able to take root in part, because small, situational forces such as the aroma of bacon, the festive Christmas feeling, and the zig-zag pattern of the trenches encouraged social exchanges between sworn enemies.

DISCUSSION QUESTIONS

1. Many soldiers' lives may have been saved, at least for a few months, due to informal truces between enemies on the frontlines who wanted to preserve their own lives. However, this may have delayed the war and affected lives of private citizens back home. What are the ethical responsibilities of "everyday" soldiers when it comes to following orders from their superiors in cases such as this?

2. Have you ever experienced the slow development of trust with someone whom you originally considered an "enemy," or at least with someone whom you did not trust originally? What situational circumstances led to that development—and did it end with positive or negative results?

3. Ashworth's study of informal truces couldn't come from official war archives because this type of truce wasn't allowed. What does this teach us about sources of data for research purposes? Can archival data be trusted—why, or why not?

- **Prosocial moral reasoning**: Our ability to analyze moral dilemmas in which people's goals or needs conflict with each other

- **Social exchange**: Cooperative resource trading within a group or across groups that benefits everyone involved

10.4 THE SUBWAY SAMARITAN: THE MATHEMATICS OF RELATIVE ALTRUISM

The Social Situation

Subway routes in New York City are identified by letters and numbers.

"Take the A train" became a famous Duke Ellington song. The "C" and the "E" trains angle deep into Queens and Brooklyn. The "4" train can take you from north of Yankee Stadium in the Bronx, through Manhattan, and deliver you to the Brooklyn Botanic Gardens. The system can be confusing even for New Yorkers who usually take the same two or three trains to familiar destinations.

Cameron Hollopeter, from Littleton, Massachusetts, was waiting for the "1" train at 137th Street, a little north of Columbia University. Hollopeter experienced a seizure and fell onto the tracks. He got up and stumbled to the edge of the platform as two women rushed to help him. But he stumbled again and fell back between the tracks as the headlights of the downtown "1" train appeared. The train screeched its brakes but could not stop in time.

Wesley Autrey was a 51-year-old Navy veteran and construction worker. He also was waiting for the downtown "1" train with his two daughters (4 and 6 years old). Autrey left his girls with two strangers and jumped down onto the tracks. He tackled Hollopeter and held him down in what *CBS News* called "the murky, filthy water." He remained on top of him with a clearance of approximately 1 inch between his head and the five-car train rumbling over their heads.

Theory and Method

He was an instant hero.

This account was pieced together from reports from several sources: the Associated Press, the *New York Times,* television reports and interviews, and a CBS News interview in 2012 ("5 Years Later," 2012). The quotations vary slightly between sources but do not suggest any material difference in reporting—the facts are consistent across sources.

"The driver hit the horn so I knew from that sound he wasn't going to make it," Autrey told *CBS News* 5.

> Everybody started to freak so I yelled from underneath the train saying "excuse me everybody, be quiet, I am the father. Please let my girls know that I am OK."

It took about 40 minutes for rescuers to get them out. During that time:

Well, the kid, he was getting a little tight and I said, "We are underneath a train." He said, "Are we dead? Are we in heaven?" I said no. He kept asking . . . so many times, that I give him a pinch and said, "Dude, you're very much alive!"

Optimistic Bias

Hollopeter was taken to St. Luke's Roosevelt Hospital.

Autrey reported that nothing was wrong with him, so he continued his day and went to work. "I don't feel like I did something spectacular; I just saw someone who needed help. I did what I felt was right." But when he went to work the next day, his boss bought him lunch (a ham-and-cheese sandwich) and told him that he could "take yesterday off." While walking to his mother's apartment, a stranger put $10 in his hand. The media had tracked him down, dubbing him "the Subway Samaritan" and "Subway Superman."

"I'm still saying I'm not a hero," Autrey insisted, "'cause I believe all New Yorkers should get into that type of mode. You should do the right thing." Autrey was trying to deflect the unexpected rush of public acclaim.

"And if I had to do it again, I probably would," Autrey also told the hosts of CBS's *Early Show*. "I was like, 'Wow, I got to get this guy' . . . somebody's gotta save this guy but I was the closest one." He didn't feel any diffusion of responsibility, and assumed that anyone else would have done the same thing. He just happened to be "the closest one." Maybe he was right—or maybe he had an **optimistic bias**, when others would have done nothing.

Kinship Selection

Kinship selection is the evolutionary urge to favor those with genetic relatedness.

That means that you are more likely to be altruistic toward your brother than toward a stranger. You can see kinship selection at work in two ways: First, Autrey was careful to make sure his two daughters were cared for before he jumped on the tracks. Second, the welfare of his daughters was the first thing he asked about when the train came to a stop. However, that does not change the fact that Autrey risked his life for a stranger. Why would he do that?

Perhaps Autrey's training in the Navy somehow triggered his altruism. Firefighters are trained to risk their lives, if needed. It is expected of them. Perhaps the Navy had trained a social norm into Autrey that shaped his decision.

The Trolley Problem

Autrey's behavior can be studied experimentally.

No, we are not going to ask for volunteers to stumble onto subway tracks to see who might come to their aid. But there have been many experiments that mimic the situation that Hollopeter and Autrey lived through while waiting for the "1" train at 137th Street. The experiment is fundamentally a thought experiment—the trains and the dilemmas are only imagined.

Thompson and Fitzgerald (2017) described the classic **trolley problem**. A participant is asked to imagine an out-of-control trolley speeding toward five people tied to the tracks facing certain death. The participant in the study can

flip a switch that would change the direction of the tracks and lead the trolley down a different path; however, there is one person tied to the tracks on this second path. Therefore, the trolley problem asks the participant to choose between saving one life or five lives.

The trolley problem can be modified to see how it affects people's decisions. For example, you can specify who the people are on the tracks. Previous experiments found support for kinship selection. Participants were more likely to save the one person if that person were a close relative (see Bleske-Recheck et al., 2010). Thomson and Fitzgerald turned that philosophical scenario into a computer game that used stick figures that participants named after real family members.

The important difference is that the computer game version required the participant to decide within 1 second, just about the same amount of time that Autrey had to make his decision. That innovation in procedures improved the game's **experimental realism** because it was a controlled experiment that delivered a more authentic experience. It was much closer to what Autrey must have faced in his moment of decision.

Results and Discussion

The mayor congratulated Mr. Autrey.

The Chrysler company offered him a new car. He gave guest appearances on *Oprah, Ellen,* and late-night talk shows. He admitted to being nervous before he appeared on *The Late Show With David Letterman.*

When he met with President Bush, the president asked him, "You were scared of the audience but you weren't of a 32-ton train?!" Hollopeter's emotional father tried to read to the press from notes. "Mr. Autrey's instinctive and unselfish act . . . there are no words."

Empathy for his worried daughters was the first thing on Autrey's mind. That concern fit with the theory of kinship selection. But it doesn't explain why Autrey jumped in front of the train in the first place.

Hollopeter was 20 years old and came from a small Massachusetts town, about 25 miles north of Boston. His town had a population of just less than 9,000 people. Autrey was 51 years old, had been raised in Alabama, but had lived in Harlem for 3 decades. They didn't appear to have much in common—except their shared humanity.

DISCUSSION QUESTIONS

1. Autrey's actions might be used as an example of pure altruism, in which he made a sacrifice truly without expecting anything in return. Is that true, in your opinion? Or did he gain any kind of benefit from his actions?

2. Describe three small acts of kindness or helpfulness and any psychological rewards that the individual might receive.

3. On the surface, this case study might be used as evidence against strict evolutionary theories or explanations of altruism: Someone helped someone else who shared zero genetics. In other words, it might be evidence against ideas like kinship selection. What defense could evolutionary theories use in the face of this case study?

KEY TERMS

- **Optimistic bias**: The sometimes unrealistic belief that things will turn out well or as planned
- **Trolley problem**: A classic "thought experiment" in which an ethical dilemma can be analyzed regarding whom to save from a runaway trolley
- **Experimental realism**: Aspects of a research study that make it seem more realistic or authentic to participants

Aggression

11.1 DOLOREISA'S STORY: AGGRESSION, PROSTITUTION, AND SEX TRAFFICKING

The Social Situation

Doloreisa, a Central American woman, needed money.

Doloreisa (not her real name) took the advice of an acquaintance who turned out to be a recruiter for sex traffickers. She left her daughter with her mother and joined a group of women expecting to earn $200 per month working in a restaurant in the north. Instead, they were imprisoned in an apartment, repeatedly raped, and then sold and resold as prostitutes and slaves several times across Central and North America. Human trafficking is a large, dark, violent business.

Its products are its victims.

Theory and Methods

Sex trafficking is forcing or tricking someone into prostitution. The "trafficking" part is that it also involves moving victims away from their home, which makes them even more vulnerable.

The data for this case study come from oral histories, governmental reports, military histories, and interviews. Many of them were reported in Farr's (2005) summary of the industry titled *Sex Trafficking: The Global Market in Women and Children*.

Sex trafficking may be the fastest-growing crime in the world (see "Trafficking for Sexual Exploitation," 2020). Over 20 million people are currently living as kidnapped workers. The United Nations Office on Drugs and Crime estimates that 94% of the victims of sexual exploitation are women and girls. They are the products of a global, tax-free, multi-billion-dollar industry. They are usually poor and have little social power.

The Economic Incentives of Sex Trafficking

Personal economics make it difficult to combat sex trafficking.

The recruiters make a significant profit when they sell someone, usually a young girl (although boys are also victimized). The buyers are slaveowners who keep costs low by storing women in squalid conditions. Market forces put downward pressure on the age at which children are abducted into the commercial sex industry. An impoverished family may benefit by selling a daughter into prostitution, especially if she is a young virgin.

Slave Labor Is Profitable

Older sex slaves are also highly profitable commodities.

Depending on the country to which they have been sold, each woman represents a profit of $50,000 to $150,000 per year. The price of poor performance is a beating and sometimes death. As slaves, the women's work and income potential are not limited to paid-for sexual services. They may be a thank-you gift to a corrupt politician or be used to increase alcohol sales while soliciting customers. They also may work in the garden and kitchens when the brothel is not busy. The lack of taxes in a mostly unregulated industry is a significant structural support for an already highly profitable business.

The Debt-Bondage System Maintains the Labor Supply

The economic benefits do not trickle down to the sex worker.

Since the breakup of the Soviet Union, every year about 500,000 women from that region have been sold into prostitution every year. However, the sex trafficking **debt-bondage system** requires that women sold into prostitution repay the sex trafficker for inflated expenses (see Farr, 2005, p. 21). For example, a trafficker might tell a woman he's kidnapped that she actually owes him the money it cost to deliver her to another country—and that if she doesn't pay, she'll go to jail.

Luise White's (1990) **oral histories** provide a glimpse into the personal economics of prostitution in colonial Nairobi. In that paternalistic culture, women used prostitution to generate personal income that they typically send home to their rural families. Ironically, the risk of sexual violence was the price they paid to preserve their family structures (see Gilfoyle, 1999).

Farr (2005) traced supports for sex trafficking across centuries and cultures (see also Goldstein, 2001). Although some prostitutes have not been coerced into the business, Farr (2005) believes that arguing about the degree of personal choice misses the central point. Sex workers are unwilling targets of **aggression**, easily intimidated by almost anyone with social power: recruiters, traffickers, clients, and governments (Gil & Anderson, 1998).

Institutional Supports for Sex Trafficking

Governments have provided more than a knowing wink of support for sex trafficking.

For example, the military's "knowing wink" was based on a long and destructive history of losing soldiers to sexually transmitted diseases. The U.S. armed services created a set of persuasion posters intended to curtail soldiers' sexual behavior (see Gettelman & Murrmann, 2020). For example, one poster shows a curvy young woman and reads, "Booby Trap: Syphilis and Gonorrhea." The military—especially back then—recruited mostly young men, full of sexual energy, military minded, and then took them far away from home.

For example, the post–World War II military planners were aware of the volatile mixture of social forces around the Clark base in the Philippines: 25,000 (permanent) plus another 70,000 (rotating) troops in a small city. The young soldiers were in a city with more than 1,500 registered bars, brothels, and massage parlors—and 55,000 Filipino girls and women working as "entertainers."

An odd form of entertainment evolved prior to the 1992 closing of the U.S. Clark Air Force Base in Angeles City in the Philippines. "Foxy boxing" required women to fight one another—and they were refused payment "until they drew blood or showed bruises" (Farr, 2005, pp. 190–195). After the base closing, the region became a vacation destination for sex tourism (Barry, 1995; Kluge, 1986).

Japanese Comfort Women

The phrase *comfort women* doesn't sound like something terrible.

However, the phrase describes the sexual enslavement of 200,000 Asian women by the Japanese military between 1942 and 1945. About 80% were Korean women, but there were also Filipina, Chinese, Burmese, and Thai women abducted from their homes and communities, beaten into submission, and forced to live in "comfort stations" near Japanese military bases.

About 75% of these women "did not survive the violence they endured at the hands of the Japanese army" (Chai, 1993; Farr, 2005, p. 199). At war's end, the defeated Japanese opened their "comfort stations" to U.S. troops. The U.S. military asked that they build more.

The Honolulu Ladies of Hotel Street

The Ladies of Hotel Street demonstrate the human face of sex workers (see Stratton & Gire, 2016).

To control sexually transmitted diseases during World War II in Hawaii, the Honolulu Police Department registered 250 prostitutes as licensed "entertainers." The women were required to have regular medical exams, were not allowed to own property or a car, could not go out after 10:30 at night, and were not allowed to marry a member of the U.S. Army or Navy (see Bailey & Farber, 1992; Farr, 2005; Sturdevant & Stoltzfus, 1992).

"It was not hidden from view. Sailors on leave were required to wear their white uniforms. On a Friday or Saturday night, the lines waiting for prostitutes servicing sailors on Honolulu's notorious Hotel Street . . . looked like a slow-moving river of white . . . sometimes stretching around the block" (Stratton & Gire, 2016, pp. 50–51).

Then came the bombing of Pearl Harbor. A local reporter described the heroism of the ladies of Hotel Street on the day of the attack. Even as bombs were still dropping,

> the working women of Hotel Street became unexpected and much needed first responders, rushing to Hickam Field and Pearl Harbor . . . comfortable with intimate situations, bandaged and nursed the men and donated gallons of their blood (which the Army doctors knew was clean) . . . gave up their own rooms, turning the brothels into hospital wards . . . the Ladies of Hotel Street earned the

lasting admiration, respect, and loyalty of the men of the United States, Armed Forces. (Stratton & Gire, 2016, p. 138).

The respect was not official. When the Navy sent its most severely injured soldiers back to the U.S. mainland, several of the Hotel Street workers also left Hawaii. One soldier regretted the shabby way the heroic Ladies of Hotel Street were treated by the Navy.

They aided the nurses on board by changing the bed linens the men had soiled. They helped bathe them, feed them, encourage them, sitting by their bedsides, keeping vigil, cooling their forehead with washcloths, and keeping them company for the long voyage home. . . . When the women from Hotel Street asked if they could go with us to the hospital, just to visit awhile and say their goodbyes, the Navy personnel said no. . . . It wasn't right that they were treated so dismissively. To this day I feel bad about that. (Stratton & Gire, 2016, pp. 153–155).

Types of Aggression

Farr (2005) identified several forms of sex trafficking violence.

The aggression here is directed against people with little social power: mostly poor women and children. Violence and aggression can be direct—such as physically harming someone else—but it can also be indirect forms of abuse accompanied by sexual and emotional exploitation. Aggression and violence can also be broken down in other **typologies**, such as physical versus emotional, or instrumental versus hostile. The three examples below demonstrate physical, instrumental aggression: its purpose is control of another human being.

"Breaking-In" and Deterrent Violence

Breaking-in violence is a kind of "welcome to the industry" ritual.

It is used to suppress women and children who are initially resistant to becoming sexual slaves. It involves various forms of rape, starvation, and beatings. Deterrent violence are beatings most often administered as punishment for attempts to escape. Women forced into sexual slavery are reluctant to report violence, partly because they usually do not speak the local language, are unfamiliar with the local geography, and have no social support. Sometimes, police won't help because they are some of the traffickers' best customers.

Routine Control Violence

Violence by traffickers appears to be routine.

Based on sampled reports and interviews from rescued women, violence against sex workers by their controllers appears to be a standard way to maintain control: 89% in a study of approximately 1,000 women from Tajikistan, 73% of 37 women trafficked into the United States, 56% among a sample of 200 women from Kosovar, and 33% of 125 women returned to their native Albania (Doole, 2001; Farr, 2005; Kane, 1998; Raymond et al., 2001).

Results and Discussion

Reynolds (1986) described four ways in which societies have responded to prostitution:

- Laissez-faire governments treat prostitution as illegal but tolerated.

- A social control approach legally suppresses obvious prostitution.

- Zoning accepts illicit prostitution within a particular geographic area (e.g., a "red-light" district).

- Regulation closely monitors legalized prostitution.

Each approach has consequences in terms of aggression. For example, the laissez-faire, control, and zoning approaches encourage a prostitute not to report any aggression because

a. authorities turn a blind eye to prostitution (laissez-faire), or

b. reporting aggression invites legal prosecution (control and zoning).

Regulation, on the other hand, provides sex workers with protection from aggression and reduces the transmission of sexually transmitted diseases for both prostitutes and their clients. Within feminist circles, many people debate whether legalizing prostitution endorses the sexual objectification of women or provides safety and protection for women providing a consensual service that is simply never going away.

We opened this case study with the story of Doloreisa. Because of her trafficking victimization, she lost all contact with her family for several years. She reappeared in their lives about 15 years later, severely ill with an untreated sexually transmitted disease. She was shunned by them and died about a year later. This social rejection and ostracism from her former loved ones may have been one of the final forms of aggression she experienced during her brief lifetime.

DISCUSSION QUESTIONS

1. Prostitution has been called "the world's oldest profession." Should it be legalized, taxed, and regulated? This case provided just a start on the two sides of this debate. Discuss at least two advantages to legalizing prostitution, provide at least two disadvantages, and then state your opinion on the issue.

2. Sex trafficking often moves to wherever large groups of men are, such as following armies or setting up illegal brothels during the week of the Superbowl. Knowing this, what policies should military and government offices introduce that are likely to be effective at reducing the abuse of women by these men?

3. Create a typology—or use one that already exists in literature regarding aggression and violence—to categorize each of the forms of aggression that were discussed in this case

study. Identify at least two additional forms of aggression that you imagine victims of trafficking experience and add them to your typology.

4. Who should be given the harshest punishment when sex trafficking rings are brought down?

Possible choices are the person who originally led the victim into trafficking (the kidnapper), the person who bought the prostitute (the owner), the customer who pays to have sex, the prostitute herself, or others.

KEY TERMS

- **Sex trafficking**: Forcing or tricking someone into prostitution and moving them away from their home
- **Debt-bondage system**: A corrupt approach in which workers or slaves are held, usually against their will, because they are told they owe their controllers money

- **Oral histories**: Comprehensive autobiographical case studies in which people explain their lives so far
- **Aggression**: Intentional harm toward another person
- **Typologies**: Frameworks or structures for organizing ideas, such as listing types or categories

11.2 THE GREAT TRAIN ROBBERY: VIOLENCE AS ENTERTAINMENT

The Social Situation

"So, what do you want to watch?"

It can be a loaded—but also revealing—question whenever people decide to watch some movie. Viewers have come to expect entertainment violence, and they tend to approve of it. When participants in one study saw either a violent or nonviolent trailer for a movie, those watching the violent trailer anticipated greater enjoyment of the movie—especially if they were the kind of people who craved stimulation (high in **sensation seeking**; Xie & Lee, 2008).

Viewing aggression, however, promotes aggression, and it only requires minimal cues to do so. One randomized experiment (Dillon & Bushman, 2017) studied children who were 8 to 12 years old. Children who viewed a PG-rated movie containing guns played with a real gun longer, pulled the trigger more often, and were more likely to point the gun at real people (including themselves) compared to children who viewed the same movie with the guns cut out.

Gender might also be involved. Male children and adults are more likely to have aggressive dreams than female children and adults, a difference that appears to be temporarily suspended among teenagers (Zhang et al., 2020). Aggression can be a serious problem for any society. It creates controversy even when the aggression is socially approved, for example, by voters supporting the death penalty (Radelet & Phillips, 2018). The epidemic of gun violence in American schools has raised the stakes for understanding aggression, including how viewing media influences it.

Theory and Methods

This case study analyzes the violence in the first-ever film that told a story.

Viewing violence on television, in film, or while playing a video game is one of several variables that can promote aggressive behavior. Media violence, on its own, has what statisticians refer to as a small to moderate effect. That means that the effect is real but there is more to the story.

A more precise way to predict aggression is to use the **cumulative risk model**: add more predictors. When Anderson et al. (2017) added predictors already validated in previous studies, they found that their model held true across multiple cultures: Australia, China, Croatia, Germany, Japan, Romania, and the United States. As you would expect, they had a richer understanding of the causes of aggression by combining previously validated predictors of aggression: delinquency, violent media use, peer victimization, abusive parenting, neighborhood crime, and just being male.

Their model fit fairly well within the **General Aggression Model (GAM)**. The GAM recognizes that aggression is the result of how **distal variables** (biology, environment, personality) interact with **proximal variables** (the individual reacting to an immediate situation, such as being threatened). Media violence is one of many proximal variables that can influence aggressive behavior.

Results and Discussion

We have a behavioral epidemic of school shootings.

To resolve that public health crisis, we need to understand (a) the role of viewing media violence, and (b) that media violence is only one of several valid predictors of gun violence. This case study demonstrates that violent film entertainment has been present since the beginning of movie-making.

Every Plot Element Involved Violence

The Great Train Robbery was seen for the first time in 1903.

The 10-minute film was created by Edwin Porter and Thomas Edison and is available on YouTube. It is significant because it was the very first moving picture to tell a story. Porter and Edison use violence as entertainment at the beginning, middle, and end of a short, dramatic story.

Violence Engages the Audience

The film begins when a stationmaster is beaten unconscious.

He is immediately tied up by a gang who secretly board the train. Gang members exchange five shots with a guard before killing him, exploding a safe, and taking the loot. (The actor playing the dead guard wiggles around until he gets his arm in a more comfortable position, but he is *supposed* to be dead.)

The gang then takes over the steam engine. They achieve this by beating another train worker and carelessly throwing him off the train. Then they force the engineer to stop the train, line up all the passengers outside, and rob them. When one man foolishly tries to flee, they shoot him in the back.

That's one explosion, two beatings, two robberies, and three murders before history's first story film reached the 3-minute mark.

The Promise of More Violence Maintains Audience Interest

The gang exits the scene, shooting two more times into the air.

Cut to the stationmaster's daughter, delivering lunch to her father. The little girl discovers her father unconscious and tied up and prays that he is still alive. She cuts him loose with a large knife she happened to bring with her and prays again. Finally, she throws water in his face. (She misses and actually throws the water over his shoulder, but he revives anyway.)

Cut again to a square dance of ordinary, happy citizens—who periodically shoot their guns to keep the dancing lively (three more gunshots). The stationmaster bursts in with news of the robbery, and they form a posse. A chase scene produces 10 more gunshots and one more anonymous person killed.

Cut once more to a forest scene. The posse surprises the gang as they are splitting up their loot: about 25 gunshots and two more deaths.

The Violent Conclusion

The last 6 seconds present the most famous scene in this historically important film.

A rough-looking outlaw looks directly into the camera. He slowly pulls out his gun, aims it directly at the camera, and fires! Twice! The first audience to see the film famously ducked in their seats and started to leave the theater—until they remembered that it was only a film. Then they demanded three more showings—and still didn't want to leave.

The 10-Minute Total

Here's the 10-minute total of violence in *The Great Train Robbery*:

- One man tied up against his will

- One explosion

- One man thrown off a train (fate uncertain, probably dead)

- Two beatings

- Two competing gangs of armed civilians (outlaws and posse)

- Two robberies

- Five deaths

- About 50 gunshots

That averages to approximately one act of violence every 60 seconds and one gun-shot for every 12 seconds during history's first storytelling film—plus one little girl who knows how to pray and handle a large knife.

The Importance of "What Happened Next?"

The paying audience always wants to know "What happened next?" in the plot.

The social psychologist always wants to know "What happened next?" to the audience. Was the audience so charged up that they started a riot? Or did they simply find themselves a little irritable with slow trains, the local mayor, or why it took so long to get their supper?

Was there a **weapons effect** in which all the guns, knives, and violence primed the audience's thoughts toward aggression (as predicted by the General Aggression Model)? Or did watching fictional violence on film provide a more psychodynamic **catharsis** that left viewers more peaceful and cooperative because they had gotten so many frustrations out of their system?

Wilson and Hudson (2013) concluded that Americans love movies that depict violence. Their article cites several statistics from a study published in the journal *Pediatrics* that reviewed violence in PG-13 movies from 1950 to 2012 (see Bushman et al., 2013). Gun violence in PG-13 movies is worse than the gun violence in R-rated movies, and gun violence in movies has increased steadily since 1950.

We don't know what future research will tell us about how viewing aggression influences behavior. But now you know that it started with *The Great Train Robbery*.

DISCUSSION QUESTIONS

1. Explain whether you believe that the modern film industry would have evolved into something with fewer violent storylines if they had started with a dramatic story of a mother rescuing her children from a house fire, a documentary of sailboats, pictures of kittens playing, or some other nonviolent theme.

2. How might you devise an experiment (using random assignment to groups) that would test whether viewing this particular film encouraged viewers to act, think, or feel more aggressively? Would your procedures change from 1903 (when the film was released) to now? Why, or why not?

3. Propose a film plot that would be likely to *decrease* aggression among viewers.

KEY TERMS

- **Sensation seeking**: A tendency of some people to desire thrills and physiological arousal, sometimes due to fear (e.g., horror movies, carnival rides)

- **Cumulative risk model**: The idea that a given risk (e.g., health, aggression) is predicted better with each additional factor considered, adding to a total

- **General Aggression Model (GAM)**: The theory that aggression develops from biological responses to the environment, cognitive processing, and decisions about how to behave
- **Distal variables**: Factors that are further away in terms of time or physical space
- **Proximal variables**: Factors that are closer or more immediate in terms of time or physical space
- **Weapons effect**: A consistent finding that the mere presence of weapons in a room primes aggression
- **Catharsis**: The theory that venting aggression through small acts will reduce anger or violent feelings

11.3 THE CINDERELLA EFFECT

The Social Situation

Many of us grew up with classic fairytales.

As children, we might not have questioned some of the implicit cultural messages in *Snow White*, *Hansel and Gretel*, or *Beauty and the Beast*. As adults, we may not have considered how those childhood impressions may have shaped our adult expectations. But Maria Tatar (2003) was thinking about the powerful impressions communicated through fairytales.

For example, in one version (possibly the original) of Hans Christian Andersen's *The Little Mermaid*, Ariel not only lost her voice, but suffered agonizing pain with every step. Then, despite her sacrifices, her prince marries someone else, and she melts into sea foam. The original makes Disney songs like "Part of Your World" seem more like a vicious trick rather than a wonderful wish.

Adult Entertainment

Tatar (2003) wrote *The Hard Facts of the Grimms' Fairy Tales*.

She pointed out that the Brothers Grimm had to clean up the stories—a lot—before marketing them as nursery and household tales. The original versions were adult entertainment. These were the stories told in bawdy taverns and around late night campfires.

The plots of these meant-to-be-scary folk tales routinely featured murder, mutilation, cannibalism, infanticide, and incest. Their original violence often lies barely hidden beneath the still-disturbing plots made popular by the Disney Studios. Many of those plots featured disengaged or absent fathers and evil stepmothers.

The Evil Stepparent

Most stepparents do *not* harm their stepchildren.

Nevertheless, stepchildren on average are at greater risk for violence than biological children (but see Khan et al., 2020). Although the overall risk is low, Daly and Wilson (1985) found that stepchildren were 40 times more likely to be physically abused than biological children. Russell (1984) reported a similar pattern: Stepdaughters were seven times more likely to experience abuse than biological daughters. Wilson et al. (1995)

even found some support for the idea of the "evil" stepparent, but it was often the stepfather rather than the stepmother who was to blame.

Data from Canada and Britain about **familicide** (killing several people in one's family) support this prediction. Familicide is usually committed by a man, and stepchildren are *over*represented among the victims (meaning that stepchildren are much more likely to be killed than biological children). Furthermore, unlike other types of familicide, male perpetrators rarely commit suicide afterward if they kill a stepchild; suicide is more likely if they resort to killing a biological child (see Wilson et al., 1995).

Theory and Method

This case study explores the association between ancient fairy tales and family aggression.

One of the messages sent in several classic folk tales is that stepparents will not love their adoptive children as much as their own, biological children. The "evil stepmother" theme reappears across cultures and over time. Social psychologists refer to the increased risk of harm to stepchildren as the **Cinderella effect**.

Why might stepchildren be at higher risk? A universal pattern of human behavior suggests some common cause. Evolution only makes sense if a stepchild threatens to remove resources that otherwise would go to a biological child. But that is exactly what happens in the story of Cinderella. Furthermore, Daly and Wilson (1998) pointed out that the template for the Cinderella story evolved independently across cultures. Favoring biological children over stepchildren may be a universal pattern.

Parental Investment Theory

Japanese culture evolved a story uncannily similar to that of Cinderella.

Benizara is a gentle, honest, and humble girl, victimized by a cruel stepmother. Her beauty and virtue win the hearts of all those around her. Then, despite the trickery of an envious sister, Benizara eventually triumphs. How does she triumph? By winning the love of a wealthy nobleman.

A stepparent has no genetic stake in a stepchild, so evolutionary psychology makes the chilling prediction that, on average, stepchildren will be more vulnerable to violence than biological children. Parental investment in a child means that children not biologically related to the parent threaten to steal resources (such as marriage to a wealthy prince) from genetic offspring.

However, evolutionary psychology is not the only explanation.

The Family Stress Model

As usual, the best answer to the nurture–nature debate is both.

The **family stress model** recognized, for example, how economic and social pressures contributed to family violence during the Great Recession (see Koltai & Stuckler, 2020; Schneider et al., 2016). The National Center for Child Abuse and Neglect (1997) recognized that there are subcultures in which violence toward children is more common.

For example, D'Alessio and Stolzenberg (2012) found that rates of child abuse among stepchildren were more extreme when the family had scarce resources. But why should being poor increase any form of violence? This is possibly because merely witnessing violence creates violent expectations, and living in a densely populated, distressed section of a city provides more opportunities to witness interpersonal violence than living in an isolated rural county.

Social Learning Theory

Social learning theory makes some obvious predictions supported by data.

For example, Farver et al. (1999) found disturbing patterns in the reports by mothers of 64 inner-city 4-year-old children. Most mothers heard gunshots on a *weekly* basis. They witnessed or experienced for themselves gang activity, drug deals, police pursuits, arrests, weapons, and being physically threatened, assaulted, robbed, or having their homes broken into. That's a lot of violence for any 4-year-old (or adult) to witness.

Witnessing violence is associated with (but not necessarily a cause of) personal distress and lower cognitive performance (see Attar et al., 1994; Cooley-Quille et al., 1995; Farver et al., 2005; Raia, 1996; Taylor et al., 1994).

Social Role Theory: Gender Socialization

Social role theory proposes that social roles create expectations.

Those expectations can become self-fulfilling prophecies (see Eagly, 1997; Eagly et al., 2000). Boys, for example, may be more biologically inclined to be overtly aggressive, but also expected to be more "assertive" (Kim et al., 2010). Girls are more often socialized to be pleasant, passive, polite, and dependent in ways that lead to "anxious expectations of rejection" (Downey et al., 2004, p. 13) that also lead to other forms of conflict (see Campbell et al., 1993; Harmon et al., 1992; Underwood, 2004; Zahn-Waxler, 2000).

Results and Discussion

Nature and nurture are at it again.

Evolutionary impulses and cultural patterns reflect and reinforce the social role expectations expressed so artfully in *Cinderella, Snow White, Hansel and Gretel*, and many other fairy tales. Stepmothers are routinely depicted as jealous, scheming, murderous opportunists of the worst kind. And the original stories are far more vicious, brutal, and perverted with rape and cannibalism.

Fairy Tales: The Brutal Past

For example, Alison Maloney (2017) described the original version of *Sleeping Beauty*.

It was written by the Italian writer Giambattista Basile in the 17th century. In that version, the comatose princess is

> being repeatedly raped by the king who comes across her and then giving birth to his children, all while still asleep. She finally wakes up when one of her children sucks an enchanted splinter out of her finger and, in revenge, the queen attempts to get the king to EAT his kids. The king then murders his wife so he can be with Sleeping Beauty. (Maloney, 2017)

Those are probably not the sweet dreams that parents hope will help their children drift off into a gentle sleep. Perhaps the cleaned-up versions still being told contribute to self-fulfilling prophecies we would prefer not to live with. The Cinderella effect demonstrates how some of the most disturbing violence within families can be explained by interacting combinations of biological, evolutionary, and, yes, cultural influences such as fairy tales.

The Next Wave of Gender Socialization in Children's Books

Why not start new social influences—or expand on the ones that already exist?

Maybe some psychology major with a flair for story-telling will understand the stakes and write alternative tales. These stories have been changed many times already. And there is a smaller stockpile of tales that feature real dangers but with positive role models. Think *Anne of Green Gables* rather than *Snow White; Nancy Drew* rather than *The Little Mermaid;* or the biographical value tales featuring Sacagawea and Harriet Tubman rather than Grimm's Fairy Tales featuring Hansel and Gretel.

Anna Roberts (2018) reported the results of a marketing survey of 2,000 parents. About 25% of parents reading fairy tales to their children were changing the plots of fairy tales, leaving out details, or changing the endings. Parents raised several objections that reflect social psychological research. Some of the concerns reported by parents were

- The *Ugly Duckling* encourages body shaming.

- *Sleeping Beauty* should not be kissed by Prince Charming without her consent.

- *Cinderella* should not be doing all the household cleaning.

- *The Little Mermaid*'s Ariel gave up her fins and her voice for a man who apparently fell in love with her just for her looks.

DISCUSSION QUESTIONS

1. This case study argued that at least some fairytales teach children the implicit lesson that stepparents will not love them as much as biological parents. Identify two other specific examples of other messages about social relationships (in families, romantic relationships, friendships, etc.) that are taught in fairytales. Do you think these lessons are healthy for children to learn? Why, or why not?

2. Some research has argued that romantic myths glorify traditional, sexist, or out-of-date roles for men and women. These myths are endorsed by mainstream culture through children's stories, television, movies, and books. They may not sound bad at first glance, such as "Men will protect women." and "Women should be innocent and beautiful." But they reinforce unrealistic expectations for modern intimate relationships. Do you agree or disagree—and why?

3. This case study mentions that across cultures, stepparents engage in more violence toward children than biological parents; however, there are other variables at play. One example is that growing up in poverty may also increase violence because of additional stressors. What other situational or personality variables would affect familial relationships? How would you set up a research study to test your hypotheses?

KEY TERMS

- **Familicide**: Murder of several people in one's immediate family (i.e., parents, spouse, or children)
- **Cinderella effect**: The idea that parents are more likely to be aggressive or violent toward stepchildren than biological children
- **Family stress model**: Predicts that violence will occur in a family when economic and/or social pressures cause stress

Intimate Relationships

12.1 RELIGION AND MARRIAGE COUNSELING

The Social Situation

It's not easy to peek inside a marriage.

Experienced marriage and family therapists, however, are in a privileged position to observe influences on intimate relationships. One of those influences is religion. Case studies (with the informed consent of the participants) are one useful way to understand how religion affects a marriage.

But what if you are among the 15 million mostly young "new atheists"? Cragun (2015, pp. 195, 210) points to the widespread influence of the following three books: Sam Harris's (2004) *The End of Faith*, Richard Dawkins's (2006) *The God Delusion*, and David Dennett's (2007) *Breaking the Spell*. It may take some time for research to catch up with the growing base of atheists around the world to see if marriage counseling needs to accommodate their needs (see D'Andrea & Sprenger, 2007).

It seems that, so far, atheists are just as likely to have marriage troubles as people of any given religion (no more, no less). So, atheists also may benefit from Steve Johnson's (2013) three case studies described below. His purpose was to extract, from a particular theoretical approach, any common benefits from marriage counseling to couples coming from three different religious traditions.

Theory and Method

This case study explores how a theory can guide marriage counseling.

Johnson (2013) used **rational emotive behavior therapy** (REBT; see Ellis, 2000) to navigate a tricky situation within couples counseling. The goal was to "help address marital issues . . . in a way that supports the couples' religious values but decreases disturbance associated with religious issues" (p. 84). REBT helps people by identifying irrational, self-defeating patterns of thought. Therapy sessions help clients change their thoughts and attributions to more rational, healthy, productive patterns.

Johnson recognized that religion is much more than a particular set of private beliefs. His review clarified that religion is both an expression and a product of complex cultural expectations about the meanings of marriage. Those religious cultures create assumptions about what husbands and wives expect of themselves and of one another after they step inside the hidden intimacy of a long-term marriage. In his paper, he examined how REBT helped couples from three different religions get through troubled times.

Ira and Rachel: Jewish Expectations of Marriage

The geographical origin of American Jews is mostly from Eastern Europe.

They represent a burst of immigration that began at the start of the 20th century. Many American Jews now represent the second to fifth generations living in the United States. Johnson (2013) explains the strong Jewish emphasis on marriage and family as partly a result of their history of extreme discrimination, a sense of their own history, the role of children as giving purpose to life, and religious commandments.

There are three major branches of modern religious Judaism (Orthodox, Conservative, and Reform); they all reinforce a strong Jewish identity. The Orthodox are the most visible and religiously traditional. The Reform movement is the most liberal. But there is really a fourth category: many Jewish people are "cultural" Jews. They do not identify especially with any organized religion but embrace a secular appreciation for Jewish life and culture based on their ethnicity.

Ira and Rachel were a conservative Jewish couple who had been married for 24 years and had one 22-year-old son (Johnson, 2013). Their counseling revolved around their son's recent announcement that he was gay and had started a relationship with another man. Ira took an argumentative approach that damaged his relationship with both his son and wife. Rachel exhibited several signs of depression and felt hopeless about her sense of loss regarding not having a grandchild. Ira and Rachel had grown even more distant.

Across eight sessions of REBT, the emerging pattern featured several concept words prominent within REBT. Ira and Rachel displayed *demandingness* that their son *must not* be gay and *should* stop his relationship with another man. They believed that it would be *awful* for them not to become grandparents. Both parents displayed *self-downing* (like self-criticism), but also *downing of one another* as a way to blame the other's poor parenting skills for their son "turning out" gay.

The therapist first affirmed their Jewish values and desire to be grandparents. But the therapist also helped them tone down their extreme and irrational belief that life would became meaningless if they did not become grandparents. The alternative was to express appropriate and authentic, but not exaggerated, disappointment. By the end of therapy, the couple was considering alternative ways to help disadvantaged children and leave a meaningful legacy.

Tom and Susan: Christian Expectations of Marriage

Like Judaism, Roman Catholicism in the United States grew dramatically due to European immigration starting in the early 20th century.

Catholics were more likely to come from countries such as Ireland, Poland, and Italy. Before that, the earliest Protestant version of Christian faith in the Americas was Puritanism. The Puritan belief in a divine calling to Christianize the native peoples helped precipitate the infamous Salem witch trials and two brutal wars with Native Americans: King Philip's War and King William's War. Many Puritans believed that dark-skinned people from anywhere, but especially the Native Americans who fought them, were actual devils (see Norton, 2002).

The Protestant churches continue to be subdivided into many denominations, sects, and independent churches, usually organized around shared cultural values rather than nuanced doctrinal beliefs. The traditional Christian view of marriage is that it transforms two people into one entity that models Jesus' relationship to the church. However, there are important distinctions between Protestant and Catholic views of marriage. Although marriage is an institution created by God for both, the Roman Catholic view adds that marriage is a sacrament. The practical consequence for long-term marriages was that it was more difficult for Catholics to get divorced.

Tom and Susan had been married for 4 years and had a 2-year-old daughter and a 5-month-old son (Johnson, 2013). They were in conflict over baptism. Tom had been raised as a Catholic, and Susan as an evangelical Protestant. They had partially resolved their conflicting cultural and religious expectations by alternating attendance at a Catholic and conservative Protestant church. How to baptize their children was an aggravating marital conflict, already stirred by the expectations of their disapproving families.

The same word-concepts of REBT that helped Ira and Rachel were introduced by the therapist and helped them identify aggravating, irrational thought patterns. REBT therapists are trained to listen for words and emotions that express unreasonable demandingness about how other people should behave. Expressions such as *should, must, have to, ought, supposed to,* and *awful* signal a belief system that is probably self-harming.

The therapist helped Tom and Susan to recognize that each was *demanding* that the other partner *must* accept their religious practices. They each made a *false inference* that the other's *unwillingness to change* over the baptism issue was a symptom of an insincere love. Each was, in fact, willing to change and compromise. The therapist helped them think about baptism as a preference rather than a demand.

Across four sessions, the REBT therapeutic approach affirmed their religious preferences. Therapy also focused on how their own demandingness was at odds with their religious views of how God viewed them. Their *demandingness* and *downing of the other* implied that God's decision to allow them a free will had been a mistake—each had the free will to make a different choice. Tom and Susan worked out another compromise by learning to assert their preferences without demanding that the other obey them. They reached a practical compromise. They could follow both the infant baptism advocated by Catholicism and the later baptism advocated by Protestantism.

Abdullah and Khadijah: Muslim Expectations of Marriage

There are two major origins of Muslims in the Americas (Tweed, 2004).

The first origin was Muslims who immigrated either by force (as part of the first slave ship, for example, in 1619) or by choice (predominantly Syrians) during the 20th century migrations. The second origin is Muslim sects that developed among African Americans in the late part of the 20th century.

The 2018 estimates by the Pew Research Center identify the total percentage of Muslims in the United States today at only about 1% (Mohamed, 2018). Nevertheless, the *New England Journal of Medicine* reported that efforts to restrict immigrants from Muslim countries have harmed American health care (Masri & Senussi, 2017). Like previous immigrants to the United States, many Muslims are fleeing desperate circumstances.

Muslims around the world, and especially in the United States, are facing significant strains. "Many Islamic countries are facing the challenges of modernity and social change" (Leeman, 2009, p. 743). The formal Muslim laws of marriage are different from traditionally Jewish and Christian marriages. Islamic law describes marriage as a contract between a man and a woman. A Muslim woman may only marry a Muslim man, but a Muslim man is free to marry a Jewish, Christian, or Muslim woman.

A Muslim man may, according to shari'ah law, marry four women, but only if he can financially support all of them and treat them equally. In Islamic traditions, many people accept **arranged marriages** coordinated and planned by family members, but it is preferred that both people getting married consent to it. Like other religious faiths, the marriage contract is central to preserving a sense of identity and the authority of the faith.

Abdullah and Khadijah were second-generation Arabs in the United States and had married 7 years earlier, in their early 20s (Johnson, 2013). The marriage had not been arranged, but their families had been influential in connecting them. Their emerging conflict was that Abdullah had decided that Khadijah should stop working and become a stay-at-home mother. She disagreed, believing that it would become an intellectually unsatisfying life.

The REBT therapist was familiar with Islamic laws and customs and encouraged them to discuss their decision with an Islamic scholar. The scholar, for the most part, sided with the wife. Abdullah became worried that his reputation as a strong male leader would be stained. In short, he was experiencing a cascade of *irrational demands* made more severe by the cultural struggles of Muslims in America. For example, in keeping with Arab culture, Abdullah was *demanding* that his wife behave as he instructed, that it would be *awful* to have his peers think less of him, and that she *must* do what he said was right.

The therapeutic REBT approach affirmed the importance to Abdullah of being respected by his friends. But his demandingness was now moderated. He understood that others' beliefs did not—and could not—determine his manhood without his permission. Abdullah was able to tell himself that the goal of going to Mosque was to worship, not to gain the approval of his peers.

Results and Discussion

You probably noticed that the theme of "demandingness" showed up across all three experiences of marriage counseling (Johnson, 2013).

This was the product of looking at each case through the theoretical lens (and language) of REBT. Were you satisfied with the endings of these therapy sessions? They were all relatively brief, and they were able to apply the REBT principles to specific beliefs. The participants were all practicing religionists whose faith traditions and beliefs were important to them. Increasingly, counselors and therapists are encouraged to include cultural competency and respect of diversity in their training.

Several studies have indicated positive benefits of religious participation on the quality of a marriage. One review (Mahoney et al., 2001) indicated small but reliable positive effects. But was it the actual religion or something else? Is this a case of "correlation does not imply causation?"

Religious participation provides significant emotional, financial, and practical social supports that can increase **satisfaction** (subjective happiness) and **commitment** (the cognitive decision to stay in a given relationship). However, as the authors (Mahoney et al., 2001) caution, there are many alternative (i.e., nondivine) explanations for a strong association between religious activity and marriage. In addition, there are many ways in which religious participation and subcultures may harm as well as help individuals and marriages.

These particular therapeutic interventions, based on REBT, appear to have been successful, at least in the short term. But is there validation and replication? Maybe the benefits were the consequences of troubled couples finally taking the time to work on their problems and listen to each other's needs. Maybe any form of therapy would have helped, because it meant finding compromises and respecting each other. Each couple had modest goals and achieved modest gains. Will they come back to therapy, or have they achieved their own happily ever after?

DISCUSSION QUESTIONS

1. Does thinking about marriage and counseling from a religious perspective help to consider the needs and motives of the clients involved— or does it only stereotype them and attempt to mold them into a relationship deemed acceptable by their religious perspective?

2. Do you think that your own religious or spiritual views affect the way you act in relationships or the people you prefer to have as partners? How do you plan to respond to things like family planning or relationship dynamics if your partner is of a different religious faith or culture than your own?

3. Some people have argued that *all* couples would benefit from occasionally visiting a couples counseling session—even couples who are not experiencing any major troubles. Theoretically, it offers a chance to check in with each other, air any grievances before they become resentments, and so on. Do you agree—or do you think that this type of session might only make a "mountain out of a molehill," meaning that people might bring up small issues they would otherwise simply let go?

KEY TERMS

- **Rational emotive behavior therapy** (REBT): Helps clients change irrational, unhealthy patterns of thought to more rational, healthy patterns instead

- **Arranged marriage**: One organized and planned by family members, often based on compatibility and mutual benefit

- **Satisfaction**: Subjective perceptions of happiness in a relationship, or the belief that a relationship provides more benefits than costs

- **Commitment**: The cognitive and conscious decision to stay in a given relationship

12.2 MALE VICTIMS OF RELATIONSHIP ABUSE

The Social Situation

Perhaps the greatest contradiction in human relationships is when one lover abuses another.

Within a committed relationship, your partner is supposed to be the person who supports and cares for you the most, so when that person becomes your abuser, it's hard to understand. The stereotype of **relationship violence** is "wife battery," when a man controls a woman using both physical and emotional power tactics. This scenario is, unfortunately, more common than most people would like to admit. Well-respected studies have estimated that as many as one in every three women will at some point be victimized. It could be physical or mental abuse, stalking, or sexual assault by a man she is currently or was formerly dating (National Intimate Partner and Sexual Violence Survey, 2010).

Many anti-abuse organizations and researchers argue that violence from men toward women within relationships is the most common form of relationship abuse. Their worry is that paying attention toward any other form of violence takes potentially valuable resources away from these terribly victimized women (see Campbell, 2002; Johnson, 2007; Kilpatrick, 2004; Klein et al., 1997).

It is true that prevalence rates of male-to-female relationship violence are extremely troubling. The ideal number of cases, of course, would be zero. However, there *are* other forms of relationship violence.

For example, violence within same-sex relationships is also much more common than anyone would like. Gay and lesbian victims may also fear that reporting violence will further enforce negative views of gay couples from outsiders as unhealthy or dysfunctional (Elliot, 1996; Hart, 1986). Still, violence in same-sex couples is prevalent; one study (Straus, 1979) reported the highest rates of violence within lesbian couples (48%), then gay male couples (38%), then heterosexual couples (28%). Note, however, that these numbers are several years old; more research and public attention must be given to relationship violence in all forms.

And violence does occur by women toward men. Denying the existence of female-to-male relationship abuse is disrespectful to the thousands of men who have to experience relationship violence every day. Research has also shown that the stigma and embarrassment that male victims of violence feel makes them less likely to report what's happening and therefore less likely to get any help (see Arnocky & Vaillancourt, 2014).

Theory and Method

This case study explores the experience of a man who was abused by his wife for many years.

Their relationship qualifies as what Johnson (1995, 2007) calls "**intimate terrorism**." It includes emotional, psychological, sexual, and physical violence that increased over time, both in frequency and in severity. One partner is controlling the other through fear and intimidation. Eventually, the victim of the abuse sought help and was able to escape from his wife and very unhealthy marriage.

Qualitative research expert Jacqueline Allen-Collinson (2009) published a case study of an "abused heterosexual male victim" (p. 22). In the opening paragraph of her article, she noted that research on the experiences of female victims of abuse has provided valuable insights into their experience, but that research trying to show a man's perspective of victimization has been met with "controversy and hostility" (p. 22).

Despite that hostility, the case she presents is of a man who kept a diary record of his wife's physical and emotional abuse of him over 20 years. In many ways, the man did not fit the common stereotype of victims of violence: He was White, middle-aged, had a high-paying professional job—and of course, he was male. He started keeping a diary during the last 2 years of his 20-year marriage, as he attempted to confront what was happening to him and build up the courage to escape.

The man, who went by the initials NH to maintain his anonymity, wrote his diary in third person, "finding it too emotionally-charged and embarrassing to write in the first [person]" (Allen-Collinson, 2009, p. 26). So, instead of writing, "I woke up today," NH wrote, "He woke up today," referring to himself as a character in his own life. Writing one's story can be cathartic and therapeutic; doing so with the help of a mental health professional is called **narrative therapy**.

NH notes that over their long marriage, his wife's abuse and control tactics increased in severity. Often, her abuse took the form of emotional manipulation:

> He is lying in bed on Sunday morning feeling ill. His domestic situation is worrying him and his work situation is worrying him. He is feeling despondent because of these things. His wife enters the room. "Why are you still in bed?" "I'm just tired," he replies. "Yes," she says, "guilt does make you tired." She leaves the room. (Allen-Collinson, 2009, p. 30)

He also wrote about how he would often simply try to avoid his wife instead of dealing with her constant criticism:

> He finishes work by 11:30. Phew. Rings three times from the office . . . to see if he can bring anything home for Christmas. She tells him off for having been at work. He brings home the turkey but gets into trouble because there is not the right stuffing at the butcher's. Once home, she tells him to "get out of the house" until [5:30 p.m.], when her parents are coming round. How does this fit with him never doing anything to help? He sits in the car on the common for three hours, getting more cold and more tired. What a way to spend Christmas Eve, he thinks. (p. 30)

Sometimes, his wife's physical behavior toward him could be interpreted in more than one way. If she pressures him for sexual intimacy, is that abusive? Does the answer change if it's a woman pressuring a man versus the other way around? In one diary entry, he writes that his wife began poking, scratching, and violently pulling on parts of his body (such as ears and genitals) in an attempt to get him to have sex with her. What happened next?

Then, when he is distressed by the aggression, she turns 180 degrees to feign comfort—attempts at stroking and cuddling . . . which are really only another form of aggression, invading his space when he needs it to recover. Along with this, dogged insistence on her part—"I won't leave you alone until I have had a cuddle." (Allen-Collinson, 2009, p. 28)

And at other times, her physical aggression is less subtle:

More beatings tonight and facial bleeding and cuts ready for his senior management away day tomorrow. He is finding it increasingly difficult to blame the dog. . . . She picks herself up and fists him in the face. . . . He goes upstairs to get out of the way. She follows, scratches, pokes, thumps and what he hates most now, puts both of her hands inside his mouth and pulls it open further than it will naturally go. (p. 32)

Results and Discussion

In her article about NH, Allen-Collinson (2009) notes that many male victims of heterosexual relationship violence are either not believed or are simply judged for being "wimps."

Surely, a man who is physically bigger and stronger than his wife or girlfriend couldn't really be hurt, right? She notes that in many cases, the men struggle with how to defend themselves without physical retaliation that would, in turn, hurt their partner (Allen-Collinson, 2009, pp. 33–35). A common concern with male victims of female perpetrators is fear that if the violence comes from both parties, he will be labeled as the primary aggressor even in self-defensive situations.

Unfortunately, NH also had to deal with this struggle. In his diary, he writes,

He holds his arms up against his chest to defend himself. She loses her balance and falls back, hitting her head on the sofa. She accuses him of hitting her. This is significant as he is now [deemed to be] the violent party in the relationship. He has been waiting for this moment—that she will injure herself as a result of him defending himself and then he will become the guilty one. This point is now reached. (p. 34)

Escaping an abusive partner is much more challenging and complicated than many outsiders believe. It can provoke the victim-blaming question of, "Why don't they just leave?" Several studies have examined the psychological, social, and practical barriers to leaving, such as finding housing, access to finances, and overcoming social stigma (e.g., Kirkwood, 1993; Metz et al., 2019; Rosen & Stith, 1997).

These barriers exist for almost every victim of violence. But they are especially challenging for victims who are low income, have religious reasons to stay in a marriage, believe they have to stay to protect children from abuse, or cannot access resources such as emergency shelters. Again, most shelters and government-provided services are intended to help women, and so men may have a harder time gaining access to them.

Fortunately, NH was eventually able to leave his abusive relationship safely. He divorced his wife and was able to rent a modest home and maintain his professional career. Happy, safe endings need to be more commonly found for all victims of relationship violence, so that they can become survivors and begin to heal from their physical and psychological wounds.

DISCUSSION QUESTIONS

1. Many researchers and practitioners who work with victims of relationship violence debate over how serious the problem of female-to-male abuse really is. What is your opinion on this subject? Do you think that more attention and resources should be given to male victims (of either heterosexual or homosexual violence)? Or, do you agree that the problem is much greater for female victims and that they should be the focus of help?

2. Discuss how gender roles and stereotypes have influence in abusive relationships. How do perpetrators of violence—either male or female—use cultural norms, traditional values, the legal system, or any other institutional paradigms to their advantage?

3. People doing research to understand the dynamics of relationship violence have made use of both qualitative data (such as case studies and diaries) and quantitative data (such as statistics from police records or court cases). What are the advantages and disadvantages to each method when they are being applied to something so personal and potentially traumatic as relationship violence?

KEY TERMS

- **Relationship violence**: Intentional aggression toward a romantic partner including sexual, emotional, psychological, and physical abuse
- **Intimate terrorism**: A form of relationship abuse in which one partner uses aggression to control another through fear and manipulation

- **Narrative therapy**: A counseling technique in which a client writes their autobiography as a way to process traumatic past events

12.3 THE INFLUENCE OF DATING TECHNOLOGY

The Social Situation

Technology has advantages and disadvantages.

Just ask the many people who use apps to meet others for dates or sexual encounters. They are not all young (or single). Online dating is exploding in popularity across ages and socioeconomic backgrounds (Finkel et al., 2012; Valkenburg & Peter, 2007). As of 2020, 30% Americans had used some kind of online or mobile dating site or app (Pew Research Center, 2020). The general public's acceptance of online dating has rapidly increased, even for people who don't use these sites.

Online dating allows users to meet a wider range of people. It also offers a distinct advantage, compared to traditional dating methods (like trying to meet people in bars, social groups, or social events). By looking through online profiles, you can immediately learn a lot about potential partners (Finkel et al., 2012).

If you know what you're looking for (e.g., level of college education, whether they are a smoker, if they want kids), then you can immediately select for those traits and, theoretically, be more efficient. Some dating services even boast that they have computer algorithms that will do your "matching" work for you. Now, at least in theory, you sit back and wait for the matches to roll in.

The risk of virus transmission during the COVID-19 pandemic has influenced technological screening and sexual practices. One study found "less sex but more sexual diversity" (Lehmiller et al., 2020). Another found changes in tongue-kissing (Ruiz-Eugenio et al., 2020). COVID-19 has placed more pressure on relationships unrelated to sexuality. The pandemic has created social, emotional, and financial stressors (Coop-Gordon & Mitchell, 2020). The general recognition seems to be that technology during COVID-19 has created mostly obstacles, but also opportunities for relationships (Dewitte et al., 2020).

Theory and Method

This case study discovers what is known about how technology has changed cultural expectations about dating.

Online dating means different things to different people. This discussion includes **sexual hookups**, "brief uncommitted sexual encounters among individuals who are not romantic partners" (Garcia et al., 2012, p. 162). Such hookups, however, range from simply kissing to sexual intercourse. Hookups have become ubiquitous in popular culture (movies, music, and so on). Dating apps like Tinder and Grindr make hookups both more convenient and more socially acceptable as more people join.

One of the most popular apps for meeting potential new relationship partners is Tinder, which boasts about 50 million users (Iqbal, 2020). Users create a profile for themselves, and then they can browse from profiles within a given proximity (typically 100 miles). Profiles include a photograph, as well as basic information such as age, employment, and education.

The setup is almost like a game: Users can "swipe left" to make unappealing profiles disappear, or "swipe right" if they are interested. Tinder then creates lists of "matches" when both people have shown interest, and they can send messages to each other. While users can theoretically be looking for relationships of any type, Tinder is usually considered a way to meet sexual hookups (Sales, 2015).

One qualitative study examined motivations and experiences with Tinder users among people aged 18–34 (LeFebvre, 2018). They completed online surveys about their Tinder experience, including answers to open-ended questions such as

- Why did you start using Tinder?

- What are your reasons for "swiping right" (indicating interest)?

- What are your reasons for "swiping left" (indicating no interest)?

- Why did you delete Tinder (or stop using it)?

Examples of responses from the participants in this study can be seen in Table 12.1. Of course, people's experiences varied, but it is an insightful view into one way to initiate communication and potential intimacy with someone else in the modern age.

Other studies focused on Grindr and Jack'd, apps specifically designed for same-sex interactions. The mixed experiences Tinder users reported are similar to frustrations that people find within Grindr and Jack'd. For example, one study discovered that gay men who want long-term, emotionally intimate relationships sometimes turn to these apps to accelerate communication and self-disclosures (Yeo & Fung, 2018).

Unfortunately, the apps often lead only to short-term and/or sexual encounters, which are inevitably disappointing to many users. For these men, the apps focus on physical attractiveness. Immediate judgment of others based on their appearance may lead to negative body esteem (Penney, 2014). Here are some quotations from a case study regarding these advantages and disadvantages (Yeo & Fung, 2018):

- "Nowadays everyone, regardless of age and class, always has a phone in their hands. So the speed of knowing a guy has increased exponentially" (p. 6).

- "The phone is with you everywhere. You can [chat] when you go out, or even when you are sitting on a toilet" (p. 6).

- "Everything happens very quickly. You chat with someone for a bit, and then meet up, and then have sex" (p. 6).

- "The good thing about Jack'd is its speed, but its downside is that it can easily become a platform for 'fun' and instant relationships" (p. 7).

- "When you meet someone at a bar, perhaps you'll chat a little . . . you can play a game or have a drink, and you have more time to develop. You'll have more opportunities to get to know a person. But when you're on an app . . . there isn't much depth in the communication. . . . It's harder to get to know a person" (pp. 7–8).

TABLE 12.1

Reasons People Provide for Why and How They Use Tinder

Adapted from LeFebvre (2018). Statements in the table are examples from the study.

Why Did You Start Using Tinder?
"I chose to download the Tinder app because it feels like a culture I should be part of since so many of my peers use it. It also seems fun!"
"It's user-friendly, quick, visually appealing, and anonymous enough."
"I like to connect with people, and I like to have sex."
"It was just an opportunity to meet people nearby that are interested in dating."
What Are Your Reasons for Swiping Right?
"Their face either took my breath away or they were somewhat attractive with great things in their bio."
"If I like the bio and information the person provides and I think they're attractive, I want to let them know."
"I never message first so I swipe right to everyone."
"I get more matches [that way] and then sift through them."
"It's a game to me. It is entertaining."
What Are Your Reasons for Swiping Left?
"Because sometimes it's 100% obvious, right off the bat, that the user is a waste of my time. Plenty to choose from and I have a limited amount of right swipes."
"I just went with what felt right to me. Follow my gut."
"If someone has a no shirt pic... that is a red flag for me right off the bat, I'll avoid that person."
"Sometimes I close my eyes and just swipe and see what I land on."
Why Did You Stop Using Tinder?
"I found the selection abysmal."
"It's overwhelming, and I wasn't getting anywhere with finding what I wanted. I want a relationship, not a one-night-stand."
"I just created one to see if my spouse had one."
"Too many dick pics."
"I have a very nosy and jealous ex-girlfriend."

Source: LeFebvre (2018).

Results and Discussion

We have learned quite a bit about the effects of dating technology.

Tinder and Grindr facilitate individual experiences that vary widely. Some use them for short-term excitement, while others search for longer-term love and relationships. The variety of applications is not too surprising for a techno-savvy generation. A deeper potential insight is that apps appear to have modified the culture's **sexual scripts**—assumptions about how sexual encounters will progress (Gagnon & Simon, 1973; Goodfriend, 2012).

Communication between two people has never been easier. But there are both advantages and disadvantages to being able to reach someone almost instantaneously, around the clock. And better phone technology has created better communication interfaces such as private messaging, texting, and sending photos (which may or may not be edited).

Cell technology has made **sexting** possible, or sending sexually explicit words, images, or photographs through phones or online (Hasinoff, 2013). Sexting can range from icons that indicate sexual acts or body parts (such as an eggplant for men or taco for women) to photographs of genitals or breasts. The ability of people to "sext" offers both risks and opportunities (Livingstone, 2008).

Possible problems with sexting, especially for teenagers, are abundant. Teenage girls may legitimately fear that real or modified images of their bodies will be distributed without their consent (Powell, 2010; Ringrose et al., 2012). When that happens, it not only hurts the individual girls, but it also contributes to the objectification and sexualization of women and girls in general (Ringrose et al., 2012). On the other hand, there may be benefits for people who sext.

Some teens report enjoying the excitement of texting and say that they learn about their own sexual identity (Cupples & Thompson, 2010; Lenhart, 2009). It appears that just participation in sexting is not correlated with either risky sexual behaviors or with psychological well-being (Gordon-Messer et al., 2013). The anonymity of exploring sexuality through phone apps may help LGBTQ (lesbian, gay, bisexual, transgender, queer) teens gain from safety and distance, as well as avoid stigmas or bullying (Hasinoff, 2013; Thurlow & Bell, 2009).

Finally, girls are sometimes socialized to be shy or even embarrassed about sexual interests; exploring sexuality through sexting can help them communicate sexual needs or desires with partners in a "fun" and peer-accepted way (Fine & McClelland, 2006; Tolman, 2009). This benefit works for older women as well: One 50-year-old study participant reported that (Leshnoff, 2009):

> It makes you a little more brave. It takes your fear away, your inhibitions. I might be a little more bold in a text message than I would be over the phone or in person. . . . I would rather talk on the phone. But I'm also comfortable with hiding behind texting if I want to say something dirty. (p. 1)

No matter how (or if) you use dating apps or digital communication, it's important to consider the expectations of others and whether your personal safety and privacy are ensured.

DISCUSSION QUESTIONS

1. Phone apps like Tinder encourage users to immediately judge others based on physical appearance. What changes would users experience if they didn't get to see a photograph of someone until after "swiping right" based on informational facts, such as their personal interests, education, or career? Would users like that formatting more or less? Why?

2. The dating app Bumble is different from most others in that for heterosexual matches, women are required to make the first move. What are the advantages and disadvantages to both men and women for this change in social norms?

3. Some people believe free dating apps will produce lower-quality potential matches because "you get what you pay for." Other people believe that apps you have to pay for aren't worth it because there are so many free options. Do you think the users of each type of platform (free versus not free) are significantly different from each other? How could you test your hypothesis?

KEY TERMS

- **Sexual hookups**: Brief, uncommitted encounters involving some kind of sexual contact ranging from kissing to intercourse
- **Sexual scripts**: Culture-based assumptions about how sexual encounters will progress
- **Sexting**: Sending sexually explicit words, images, or photographs through phones or online

12.4 HAPPILY EVER AFTER: INGREDIENTS TO A LONG, HAPPY MARRIAGE

The Social Situation

"Happily ever after."

Most of us grew up on stories with this kind of happy ending. These same stories also trained us to believe in "love at first sight," "soulmates," and that "somewhere, out there" love would lead us to "that special someone." Chirping birds and fields of wildflowers are just around the corner, if only we can find "Mr. or Ms. Right."

But what if that belief is wrong?

Most people quickly discover that intimate relationships aren't so simple. We struggle to find mutual attraction right at the beginning. And if we're lucky enough to find someone with whom to engage in a committed, monogamous relationship, it's often fraught with arguments, resentments, and hurt feelings. When one complicated person starts living with another complicated person, they start breeding even more complicated complications.

So, how can research help to explain the mysterious ingredients that make up happy, long-term relationships? The *how* part of discovering the answer is not complicated: Talk to people in happy, long-term relationships. The *what* part is fairly easy as well: We'll give you lists that others have made. The *doing it* part of long-term relationships is another story.

Theory and Method

These case studies use the investment model to understand long-term relationships.

The **investment model** (Rusbult, 1980) states that commitment will be predicted by high satisfaction, high **investments**, and low **alternatives**. Most relationship studies explore the initiation, progression, and frequent dissolution of relationships. But the participants in these studies have often been college students or young people of similar age (between 18 and 30 years old).

There is a practical reasons for studying younger couples: convenience. Many researchers are faculty at colleges and universities. They can ask students to participate in studies as a class assignment or for extra credit. To save time, effort, and money, researchers take advantage of a **convenience sample** of students. But to really understand relationships that endure over decades, more samples from varied populations are required.

Results and Discussion

Case 1: Experienced Assessment of Conference Attendees

In 1990, clinicians and researchers attended a "Healthy Families" conference (see Kaslow & Robison, 1996).

The theme of the conference that year was "basic dimensions of a strong, healthy family" ("Healthy Families," 1990, p. 8). The attendees created a list of nine criteria they believed make up such happy families, based on years of research and working directly with clients in therapeutic settings. Here's their list:

- Adaptive ability (flexibility in dealing with stress)
- Commitment to family (recognition of individual effort and investment in the family as a group)
- Communication (honest and frequent exchanges)
- Encouragement of individuals (a sense of belonging, but not codependency)
- Expression of appreciation (consistent signs of positivity and caring)
- Religious or spiritual orientation (common to family members, but no particular type or sect of religion)
- Social connectedness (family participates in larger groups, such as the local community)
- Clear roles (each family member understands his or her responsibilities during both normal times and times of crisis)
- Shared time (simply being together; includes both quality and quantity)

Case 2: A Survey of Older Couples (25–46 Years)

Kaslow and Hammerschmidt (1993) compared this "Healthy Families" list against survey responses from 20 couples. These couples had been married between 25 and 46 years. When their participants were given open-ended questions and asked about the essential ingredients to what made their relationships last over time, they identified eight similar criteria (p. 35):

- Trust in each other

- Good coping skills

- Permanent commitment

- Good communication

- Enjoy time together

- Shared value system and interests

- Mutual appreciation and reciprocity

- Deep love

Case 3: Comparing Older (40–50 Years) and Much Older (60+ Years) Couples

Conflicts represent another way to understand successful long-term relationships.

This approach was taken by a third set of researchers (Levenson et al., 1993). These researchers compared "middle-aged" couples—in which spouses were 40–50 years old and had been married about 15 years—to "older" couples, in which spouses were 60–70 years old and had been married at least 35 years.

The "younger" couples (together for at least 15 years) were most likely to note disagreements about children (26% of the sample) or money (26%). Older couples (together for at least 35 years) were more likely to say they fought over communication (19% of the sample) or what to do for recreation (16%). Of course, it seems likely that the older participants might have fought about children and money earlier in their marriages.

Case 4: Marriage in Pakistan

Replication of findings can help establish their **external validity**, the degree to which findings from any particular study apply to other people and circumstances. Case studies can be helpful; we can use detailed, qualitative analyses to see into the lives of a few individuals (or couples). The three studies summarized above were all conducted with heterosexual, American couples in mind. Exploring other people, cultures, and types of relationships will help clarify the external validity of what started at the Healthy Families conference.

One case study investigated a marriage based on interviews with a woman from Pakistan. The 25-year-old woman became a wife through an arranged marriage, and considered herself quite happy (Fatima & Ajmal, 2012). Her experience is limited compared to a 35-year marriage, but that does not automatically invalidate her perceptions of what makes for a happy marriage.

Her interview showed the same essential components for a happy relationship. For example, both the lists above noted that shared value systems or religious orientations make things easier. The woman in this case agreed, noting,

> Sectarian difference proves to be a hurdle . . . because you do not have to compromise with the habits and personality but with the whole set of beliefs of the person. . . . Also children of such parents remain confused throughout life. (Fatima & Ajmal, 2012, p. 39)

Another overlap was the need for mutual appreciation and shared caring for each other. While the woman in this case study might express caring for her husband in what is considered a very "traditional" way by some people in the United States and similar cultures, the motives behind her actions are clearly those of giving selflessness—and she expects the same from her husband:

> Serving him food, being dressed according to his choice, taking care of his likes and dislikes . . . shows that you care for him and love him and in turn he is even more caring and loving for you. (p. 39)

The woman in this case study also emphasizes the importance of communication and trust, other criteria listed in both studies mentioned above:

> I think good understanding lay the foundation for a happy marriage . . . it is really hard to live with the person who doesn't trust you because he/she makes your life like hell. So, partners should learn to trust each other. . . . If you communicate properly then your spouse would know better about you and effective communication makes your relationship stronger. (pp. 39–40)

So, many of the criteria found in a western sample reappeared in this Pakistani case study. This modest **replication** increases our confidence that our findings might generalize (or apply to) other populations. Interestingly, the participant in this case study also pointed out additional elements of what made her marriage happy. These included forgiveness, that at least one of the members of the couple should be even-tempered, and that the happiest couples have children.

She also reported that having happy, healthy relationships with one's in-laws are a large factor in a lasting marriage. These particular criteria didn't make it to the lists we saw earlier. But it's likely that many heterosexual American couples would agree with her.

Case 5: Satisfaction in Gay Marriages

We also can compare American heterosexual couples to American same-sex couples.

With legal recognition in the United States, there are now many more same-sex marriages, in addition to the many long-term relationships that have always existed. One study compared heterosexual and gay relationships that had lasted an average of 30 years (the minimum to participate was 15 years; Mackey et al., 2004). Using semi-structured interviews, 216 participants answered a series of questions about what made them satisfied in their relationship. Again, there were many similarities found between the two types of couples.

One lesbian couple (who had been together for 25 years) talked about their conflict management; they acknowledged their ability to overcome disagreement and misunderstanding. This was one of the criteria listed earlier, so on this point, replication was found. One partner noted,

> When there was something that needed to be talked about, that was a little hot, I would tend to retreat. . . . As we've been together over time, I've become more assertive about getting my opinion and my feeling out. (Mackey et al., 2004, p. 122)

And her wife followed up with,

> We were always very civilized with each other but our styles are vastly different. I am confrontational . . . in the middle of the most horrific, mud-slinging campaign, she was able to remain calm. . . . We learn one thing and we keep learning it again and again. There is no easy way. (p. 122)

Another lesbian couple talked about the importance of psychological intimacy. One of the gay men in the sample described how over the 20 years of their relationship, sexual intimacy had waned in favor of simple companionship. These points had not been explicitly mentioned in the other studies—but again, it is very likely that any two people who are in a relationship would be happier with consistent psychological and physical intimacy.

Regardless of sexual orientation, the couples in their sample said that quality of communication, conflict management, decision making, and physical affection were the most significant predictors of happiness. They also analyzed quantitative data comparing heterosexual couples, gay couples, and lesbian couples. They found that *neither* sexual orientation nor gender of the participant had a significant influence on the results. *Relationships* are difficult, not the category of the participants in the relationship.

Several studies have tried to find the mysterious components to "happily ever after" when it comes to love. These five case studies have represented diverse couples at different ages and living in different cultures. The observations vary but also demonstrate overlapping themes, some of which are stated plainly and others inferred.

While many of us struggle to find someone with whom we can attain the components, the specific ingredients listed here probably don't offer much in the way of surprises. We can logically understand that things like good communication, consistent shows of love and support, and mutual trust are likely to make us happy in love.

The "doing it" is the difficult part. Do not be shocked when long-term relationships require conflict resolutions skills you don't yet have, consistent communication habits that may be new to you, and levels of physical and emotional effort you had not anticipated. Long-term relationships will change you in many ways.

We do not have a magical summary or how-to list. Even if we did, a satisfying relationship always seems much harder to achieve in the harsh light of day or the dark recesses of night. But couples over time, across cultures, and within different circumstances keep discovering the benefits of eventually finding someone who gives us the kindness, love, and respect we deserve.

DISCUSSION QUESTIONS

1. When you look at the lists of criteria from "Healthy Families" (1990) and from Kaslow and Hammerschmidt (1993), are there any surprises? Are there important things left off of these lists that were either added by the two studies described later or that you can identify yourself? Of the criteria on these two lists, which two or three "ingredients" do you think are the most important?

2. Here, you were asked to compare the two lists of criteria to two other studies that served, at least in some form, as replications. One comparison was an individual woman from another culture, and one comparison was with gay couples. Do you think these are appropriate comparisons? Why, or why not? Does replication only really count if the samples are the same type of people? If an individual case study fails to find the exact same results, does that mean one or the other research attempt was invalid?

3. Levenson et al. (1993) compared couples who were middle-aged to those who were older and found some differences in what couple members said were most important in terms of leading to happiness. In this particular study, they did not include participants who were younger (high school or college aged). For younger participants who are just starting to form committed, long-term intimate relationships, what do you think are the two or three most important criteria for satisfaction and happiness? And what do you think might be the two or three most common areas of conflict?

4. Make your own list of what supports a satisfying, long-term relationship.

KEY TERMS

- **Investment model**: Predicts that relationship commitment is associated with high satisfaction, low alternatives, and high investments from each partner

- **Investments**: Time, effort, and shared resources put into a relationship that would be lost if a relationship ended

- **Alternatives**: Other partners one could date, or the option of being single, if someone ended their current romantic relationship
- **Convenience sample**: Finding participants for a study through some easy or inexpensive method instead of using random sampling
- **External validity**: Testing whether findings from any particular study apply to other people and circumstances
- **Replication**: Discovering the same or similar findings in a new sample of participants

References

5 years later New York City subway hero Wesley Autrey is still the man. (2012). *CBS*. http://newyork.cbslocal.com/2012/02/21/5-years-later-new-york-city-subway-hero-wesley-autrey-is-still-the-man/

Aajami, Z., Kebriaeezadeh, A., & Nikfar, S. (2019). Direct and indirect cost of managing Alzheimer's disease in the Islamic Republic of Iran. *Iranian Journal of Neurology, 18*(1), 7.

Agthe, M., Spörrle, M., & Maner, J. K. (2010). Don't hate me because I'm beautiful: Anti-attractiveness bias in organizational evaluation and decision making. *Journal of Experimental Social Psychology, 46*(6), 1151–1154.

Ajzen, I., & Fishbein, M. (1977). Attitude-behavior relations: A theoretical analysis and review of empirical research. *Psychological Bulletin, 84*(5), 888–918.

Allen-Collinson, J. (2009). A marked man: Female-perpetrated intimate partner abuse. *International Journal of Men's Health, 8*(1), 22–40.

American Academy of Pediatrics. (1998). *Auditory integration training and facilitated communication for autism.* AAP News and Journals Gateway. http://pediatrics.aappublications.org/content/102/2/431.info

American Psychological Association. (2003). *Facilitating communication: Sifting the psychological wheat from the chaff.* http://www.apa.org/research/action/facili tated.aspx

Ancel, P. Y., Goffinet, F., & the EPIPAGE-2 Writing Group. (2015). Survival and morbidity of preterm children born at 22 through 34 weeks' gestation in France in 2011: Results of the EPIPAGE-2 cohort study. *JAMA Pediatrics, 169*(3), 230–238.

Anderson, C. A., Suzuki, K., Swing, E. L., Groves, C. L., Gentile, D. A., Prot, S., Lam, C. P., Sakamoto, A., Horiuchi, Y., Krahe, B., Jelic, M., Liuqing, W., Toma, R., Warburton, W. A., Zhang, X-M., Tajima, S., Qing, F., & Petrescu, P. (2017). Media violence and other aggression risk factors in seven nations. *Personality and Social Psychology Bulletin, 43*(7), 986–998.

Appignanesi, L. (2008). *Mad, bad, and sad: Women and the mind doctors.* W. W. Norton.

Arbilly, M., & Laland, K. N. (2017). The magnitude of innovation and its evolution in social animals. *Proceedings of the Royal Society B: Biological Sciences, 284*(1848), 20162385.

Arnocky, S., & Vaillancourt, T. (2014). Sex differences in response to victimization by an intimate partner: More stigmatization and less help-seeking among males. *Journal of Aggression, Maltreatment & Trauma, 23*(7), 705–724.

Ashworth, T. (1980). *Trench warfare, 1914–1918: The live and let live system.* Pan Macmillan.

Attar, B. K., Guerra, N. G., & Tolan, P. H. (1994). Neighborhood disadvantage, stressful life events, and adjustment in urban elementary-school children. *Journal of Clinical Child Psychology, 23*(4), 391–400.

Axelrod, R. (1984). *The evolution of cooperation.* Basic Books.

Bailey, B., & Farber, D. (1992). Hotel Street: Prostitution and the politics of war. *Radical History Review, 1992*(52), 54–77.

Balderrama, F. E., & Rodríguez, R. (2006). *Decade of betrayal: Mexican repatriation in the 1930s.* University of New Mexico Press.

Barlow, D. H. (2010). Negative effects from psychological treatments: A perspective. *American Psychologist, 65*(1), 13–20.

Barry, K. (1995). *The prostitution of sexuality.* New York University Press.

Bartik, J. J., Rickman, J. T., & Todd, K. D. (2013). *Pioneer programmer: Jean Jennings Bartik and the computer that changed the world.* Truman State University Press.

Bartlett, F. C. (1932). *Remembering: A study in experimental and social psychology.* Cambridge, UK: Cambridge University Press.

Baumeister, R. F., & Leary, M. R. (1995). The need to belong: Desire for interpersonal attachments as a fundamental human motivation. *Psychological Bulletin, 117*(3), 497–529.

Baumrind, D. (1964). Some thoughts on the ethics of research: After reading Milgram's "Behavioral study of obedience." *American Psychologist, 19*, 421–423.

Beard, G. (1882). *The psychology of the Salem witchcraft excitement and its practical application to our own time.* G. P. Putnam.

Becker, E. (1973). *The denial of death.* Academic Press.

Beer, J. S., John, O. P., Scabini, D., & Knight, R. T. (2006). Orbitofrontal cortex and social behavior: Integrating self-monitoring and emotion-cognition interactions. *Journal of Cognitive Neuroscience, 18*(6), 871–879.

Begley, L. (2016). *Killer come hither.* Random House.

Benjamin, L. J., & Simpson, J. A. (2009). The power of the situation: The impact of Milgram's obedience studies on personality and social psychology. *American Psychologist, 64*(1), 12–19.

Benjamin, L. T., & Baker, D. B. (2014). *From séance to science: A history of the profession of psychology in America.* University of Akron Press.

Benjamin, L. T., & Crouse, E. M. (2002). The American Psychological Association's response to *Brown v. Board of Education*: The case of Kenneth B. Clark. *American Psychologist, 57*(1), 38–50.

Berman, T., & Balthaser, J. (2012, January 6). *Michigan family alleges harrowing misconduct by prosecutors, police.* ABC News. http://abcnews.go.com/Health/michigan-family-alleges-harrowing-misconduct-prosecutors-police/story?id=15299991

Best, J. (2013). *Social problems* (2nd ed.). W. W. Norton.

Bigelow, H. J. (1850). Dr. Harlow's case of recovery from the passage of an iron bar through the head. *American Journal of the Medical Sciences, 20*, 13–22.

Biklen, D. (1990). Communication unbound: Autism and praxis. *Harvard Educational Review, 60*(3), 291–314.

Biringer, F., & Anderson, J. R. (1992). Self-recognition in Alzheimer's disease: A mirror and video study. *Journal of Gerontology, 47*(6), P385–P388.

Bisaro, A., & Hinkel, J. (2016). Governance of social dilemmas in climate change adaptation. *Nature Climate Change, 6*(4), 354–359.

Blank, R. H. (2019). End-of-life decision making for Alzheimer's disease across cultures. In R. H. Blank (Ed.), *Social & public policy of Alzheimer's disease in the United States* (pp. 121–136). Palgrave Pivot.

Blass, T. (2004). *The man who shocked the world.* Basic Books.

Bleske-Rechek, A., Nelson, L. A., Baker, J. P., Remiker, M. W., & Brandt, S. J. (2010). Evolution and the trolley problem: People save five over one unless the one is young, genetically related, or a romantic partner. *Journal of Social, Evolutionary, and Cultural Psychology, 4*, 115–127.

Bliss, S. (1853). *Memoirs of William Miller.* JV Himes.

Blomqvist, J. (2007). Self-change from alcohol and drug abuse: Often-cited classics. In H. Klingemann & L. C. Sobell (Eds.), *Promoting self-change from addictive behaviors: Practical implications for policy, prevention, and treatment* (pp. 31–57). Springer.

Boyce, P., & Parker, G. (1989). Development of a scale to measure interpersonal sensitivity. *Australian and New Zealand Journal of Psychiatry, 23*(3), 341–351.

Boyer, P., & Nissenbaum, S. (Eds.). (1993). *Salem-Village Witchcraft: A Documentary Record of Local Conflict in Colonial New England.* UPNE.

Brewer, L. C. (2019). We've come this far by faith: The role of the Black church in public health. *American Journal of Public Health, 109*(3), 385–386.

Brewer, M. B. (2011). Optimal distinctiveness theory: Its history and development. In P. A. M. Van Lange, A. Kruglanski, & E. T. Higgins (Eds.), *Handbook of theories of social psychology, Vol. 2* (pp. 81–98). SAGE.

Brody, E. M., Kleban, M. H., Lawton, M. P., & Silverman, H. A. (1971). Excess disabilities of mentally impaired aged: Impact of individualized treatment. *The Gerontologist, 11*(2, Pt. 1), 124–133.

Brown v. Board of Education of Topeka, 347 U.S. 483 (1954).

Buchthal, S., & Comment, B. (2010). *Fragments: Poems, intimate notes, letters by Marilyn Monroe.* Farrar, Straus & Giroux.

Burr, G. L. (1914/2002). *Narratives of the New England witchcraft cases: 1648–1706*. Scribner.

Bushman, B. J., Jamieson, P. E., Weitz, I., & Romer, D. (2013). Gun violence trends in movies. *Pediatrics, 132*(6), 1014–1018.

Buss, D. M., & Schmitt, D. P. (1993). Sexual strategies theory: An evolutionary perspective on human mating. *Psychological Review, 100*(2), 204–232.

Campbell, A., Muncer, S., & Gorman, B. (1993). Sex and social representations of aggression: A communal-agentic analysis. *Aggressive Behavior, 19*(2), 125–135.

Campbell, J. C. (2002). Health consequences of intimate partner violence. *The Lancet, 359*(9314), 1331–1336.

Carrington, M. B., & Carnevale, P. J. (1984). Physical attractiveness and self-esteem: Attributions for praise from an other-sex evaluator. *Personality and Social Psychology Bulletin, 10*(1), 43–50.

Chai, A. Y. (1993). Asian-Pacific feminist coalition politics: The choˇngshindae/ju-gunianfu ("comfort women") movement. *Korean Studies, 17*(1), 67–91.

Chang, S., Kenney, N. J., & Chao, Y. Y. (2010). Transformation in self-identity amongst Taiwanese women in late pregnancy: A qualitative study. *International Journal of Nursing Studies, 47*(1), 60–66.

Chen, Q., Feng, Y., Liu, L., & Tian, X. (2019). Understanding consumers' reactance of online personalized advertising: A new scheme of rational choice from a perspective of negative effects. *International Journal of Information Management, 44*, 53–64.

Chernew, A. (2018). In defense of Milgram experiments. *SPICE: Student Perspectives on Institutions, Choices and Ethics, 13*(1), 6.

Chessick, R. (1983). Marilyn Monroe: Psychoanalytic pathography of a preoedipal disorder. *Dynamic Psychotherapy, 1*, 161–176.

Claidière, N., & Whiten, A. (2012). Integrating the study of conformity and culture in humans and nonhuman animals. *Psychological Bulletin, 138*(1), 126–145.

Clements-Nolle, K., Marx, R., & Katz, M. (2006). Attempted suicide among transgender persons: The influence of gender-based discrimination and victimization. *Journal of Homosexuality, 51*, 53–69.

Clifford, M. M., & Walster, E. (1973). Research note: The effect of physical attractiveness on teacher expectations. *Sociology of Education, 46*(2), 248–258.

Cohen, S. (2002). *Folk devils and moral panics: The creation of the Mods and Rockers*. Psychology Press. (Original work published 1973)

Connell, S. D. (2000). Is there safety-in-numbers for prey? *Oikos, 88*(3), 527–532.

Cooley-Quille, M. R., Turner, S. M., & Beidel, D. C. (1995). Emotional impact of children's exposure to community violence: A preliminary study. *Journal of the American Academy of Child & Adolescent Psychiatry, 34*(10), 1362–1368.

Cooley, E., Payne, B. K., Cipolli III, W., Cameron, C. D., Berger, A., & Gray, K. (2017). The paradox of group mind: "People in a group" have more mind than "a group of people." *Journal of Experimental Psychology: General, 146*(5), 691.

Cooper, J. (2019). Cognitive dissonance: Where we've been and where we're going. *International Review of Social Psychology, 32*(1), article 7.

Cragun, R. T. (2015). Who are the "new atheists"? In L. G. Beaman & S. Tomlins (Eds.), *Atheist identities— Spaces and social contexts* (pp. 195–211). Springer International Publishing.

Crawford, N. (2018). *More than hair: Building self-esteem in African-American children's books* [Doctoral dissertation, Bowie State University].

Critcher, C. (2008). Moral panic analysis: Past, present and future. *Sociology Compass, 2*(4), 1127–1144.

Crum, A. J., & Phillips, D. J. (2015). Self-fulfilling prophesies, placebo effects, and the social-psychological creation of reality. In R. A. Scott, S. M. Kosslyn, & N. Pinkerton (Eds.), *Emerging trends in the social and behavioral sciences* (pp. 1–14). Wiley.

Cupples, J., & Thompson, L. (2010). Heterotextuality and digital foreplay: Cell phones and the culture of teenage romance. *Feminist Media Studies, 10*(1), 1–17.

D'Alessio, S. J., & Stolzenberg, L. (2012). Stepchildren, community disadvantage, and physical injury in a child abuse incident: A preliminary investigation. *Violence and Victims, 27*(6), 860–870.

Daly, M., & Wilson, M. (1985). Child abuse and other risks of not living with both parents. *Ethology & Sociobiology, 6*(4), 197–210.

Daly, M., & Wilson, M. (1998). *The truth about Cinderella: A Darwinian view of parental love.* Yale University Press.

Damasio, A. (2010). *Self comes to mind: Constructing the conscious brain.* Pantheon/Random House.

D'Andrea, L. M., & Sprenger, J. (2007). Atheism and non-spirituality as diversity issues in counseling. *Counseling and Values, 51*(2), 149–158.

Darley, J. M., & Latané, B. (1968). Bystander intervention in emergencies: Diffusion of responsibility. *Journal of Personality and Social Psychology, 8*(4, Pt.1), 377–383.

Darwin, C. (1859). *On the origin of species.* J. Murray.

D'Avanzato, C., Joormann, J., Siemer, M., & Gotlib, I. H. (2013). Emotion regulation in depression and anxiety: Examining diagnostic specificity and stability of strategy use. *Cognitive Therapy and Research, 37*(5), 968–980.

Dawkins, R. (2006). *The God delusion.* Random House.

De Las Cuevas, C., & de Leon, J. (2019). Development and validation of the patient's health belief questionnaire on psychiatric treatment. *Patient Preference and Adherence, 13,* 527–536.

DeNault, L. K., & McFarlane, D. A. (1995). Reciprocal altruism between male vampire bats, Desmodus rotundus. *Animal Behaviour, 49*(3), 855–856.

Dennett, D. C. (2007). *Breaking the spell: Religion as a natural phenomenon.* Penguin.

Dewing, J. (2007). Values underpinning help, support and care. In R. Neno, B. Aveyard, & H. Heath (Eds.), *Older people and mental health nursing: A handbook of care* (pp. 40–52). Blackwell.

Dewitte, M., Otten, C., & Walker, L. (2020). Making love in the time of corona—considering relationships in lockdown. *Nature Reviews Urology.* https://doi.org/10.1038/s41585-020-0365-1

Dickar, M. (2006). Reading place: Learning from the savage inequalities at Erasmus Hall. *Educational Studies: Journal of the American Educational Studies Association, 40*(1), 23–39.

Dillon, K. P., & Bushman, B. J. (2017). Effects of exposure to gun violence in movies on children's interest in real guns. *JAMA Pediatrics, 171*(11), 1057–1062.

Doole, C. (2001, April 17). *Albania blamed for human trafficking: Gangs use Albania to lure women into prostitution.* BBC News Online. http://news.bbc.co.uk/2/hi/europe/1281816.stm

Downey, G., Irwin, L., Ramsay, M., & Ayduk, O. (2004). Rejection sensitivity and girls' aggression. In M. M. Moretti, C. L. Odgers, & M. A. Jackson (Eds.), *Girls and aggression: Contributing factors and intervention principles* (pp. 7–25). Kluwer/Plenum.

Downs, S. G., & Ratnieks, F. L. (2000). Adaptive shifts in honey bee (Apis mellifera L.) guarding behavior support predictions of the acceptance threshold model. *Behavioral Ecology, 11*(3), 326–333.

DuBois, W. E. B. (1903/2008). *The souls of Black folk.* Oxford University Press.

Dugatkin, L. A. (2007). Inclusive fitness theory from Darwin to Hamilton. *Genetics, 176*(3), 1375–1380.

Dugatkin, L. A., & Wilson, D. S. (1993). Fish behaviour, partner choice experiments and cognitive ethology. *Reviews in Fish Biology and Fisheries, 3*(4), 368–372.

Eagly, A. H. (1997). Sex differences in social behavior: Comparing social role theory and evolutionary psychology. *American Psychologist, 52*(12), 1380–1383.

Eagly, A. H., Wood, W., & Diekman, A. B. (2000). Social role theory of sex differences and similarities: A current appraisal. In T. Ekes & H. M. Trautner (Eds.), *The developmental social psychology of gender* (pp. 123–174). Erlbaum.

Elder, G. H., Johnson, M. K., & Crosnoe, R. (2003). The emergence and development of life course theory. In J. T. Mortimer & M. J. Shanahan (Eds.), *Handbook of the life course* (pp. 3–19). Springer.

Elder, G. H., & Rockwell, R. C. (1979). The life-course and human development: An ecological perspective. *International Journal of Behavioral Development, 2*(1), 1–21.

Elliot, P. (1996). Shattering illusions: Same-sex domestic violence. *Journal of Gay & Lesbian Social Services, 4*(1), 1–8.

Ellis, A. (2000). Can rational emotive behavior therapy (REBT) be effectively used with people who have devout beliefs in God and religion? *Professional Psychology: Research and Practice, 31*(1), 29–33.

Eshbaugh, E. M., & Gute, G. (2008). Hookups and sexual regret among college women. *The Journal of Social Psychology, 148*(1), 77–90.

Etcoff, N. (1999). *Survival of the prettiest: The science of beauty.* Anchor/Doubleday.

Farr, K. (2005). *Sex trafficking: The global market in women and children.* Worth.

Farr, K. (2019). Trouble with the other: The role of romantic rejection in rampage school shootings by adolescent males. *Violence and Gender, 6*(3), 147–153.

Farver, J. M., Natera, L. X., & Frosch, D. L. (1999). Effects of community violence on inner-city preschoolers and their families. *Journal of Applied Developmental Psychology, 20*(1), 143–158.

Farver, J. M., Xu, Y., Eppe, S., Fernandez, A., & Schwartz, D. (2005). Community violence, family conflict, and preschoolers' socioemotional functioning. *Developmental Psychology, 41*(1), 160–170.

Fatima, M., & Ajmal, M. A. (2012). Happy marriage: A qualitative study. *Pakistan Journal of Social and Clinical Psychology, 9*(2), 37–42.

Fawkner, H. J., & McMurray, N. E. (2002). Body image in men: Self-reported thoughts, feelings, and behaviors in response to media images. *International Journal of Men's Health, 1*(2), 137–161.

Feingold, A. (1992). Good-looking people are not what we think. *Psychological Bulletin, 111*(2), 304–341.

Fenton, T., Nasser, R., Eliasziw, M., Kim, J., Bilan, D., & Sauve, R. (2013). Validating the weight gain of preterm infants between the reference growth curve of the fetus and the term infant. *BMC Pediatrics, 13*(1), 1–10.

Fernald, D. (1984). *The Hans legacy.* Erlbaum.

Fernández-Cabana, M., García-Caballero, A., Alves-Pérez, M. T., García-García, M. J., & Mateos, R. (2013). Suicidal traits in Marilyn Monroe's fragments: An LIWC analysis. *Crisis: The Journal of Crisis Intervention and Suicide Prevention, 34*(2), 124–130.

Festinger, L., Riecken, H. W., & Schachter, S. (2008). *When prophecy fails: A social and psychological study of a modern group that predicted the destruction of the world.* Minneapolis, MN: University of Minnesota Press. (Original work published 1956)

Fine, M., & McClelland, S. (2006). Sexuality education and desire: Still missing after all these years. *Harvard Educational Review, 76*(3), 297–338.

Finkel, E. J., Campbell, W. K., Brunell, A. B., Dalton, A. N., Scarbeck, S. J., & Chartrand, T. L. (2006). High-maintenance interaction: Inefficient social coordination impairs self-regulation. *Journal of Personality and Social Psychology, 91*(3), 456–475.

Finkel, E. J., Eastwick, P. W., Karney, B. R., Reis, H. T., & Sprecher, S. (2012). Online dating: A critical analysis from the perspective of psychological science. *Psychological Science in the Public Interest, 13*(1), 3–66.

Fishbein, M., & Ajzen, I. (2010). *Predicting and changing behavior: The reasoned action approach.* Psychology Press.

Fisher, K., & Szreter, S. (2003). "They prefer withdrawal": The choice of birth control in Britain, 1918–1950. *Journal of Interdisciplinary History, 34*(2), 263–291.

Fisher, M. L., Worth, K., Garcia, J. R., & Meredith, T. (2012). Feelings of regret following uncommitted sexual encounters in Canadian university students. *Culture, Health & Sexuality, 14*(1), 45–57.

Fisher, T. D. (1986). Parent-child communication about sex and young adolescents' sexual knowledge and attitudes. *Adolescence, 21*, 517–527.

Fishman, P., Coe, N. B., White, L., Crane, P. K., Park, S., Ingraham, B., & Larson, E. B. (2019). Cost of dementia in Medicare managed care: A systematic literature review. *The American Journal of Managed Care.* https://www.ajmc.com/journals/issue/2019/2019-vol25-n8/cost-of-dementia-in-medicare-managed-care-a-systematic-literature-review? p=4

FiveThirtyEight. (2020). *Should parents be afraid to let their kids play football?* FiveThirtyEight. https://fivethirtyeight.com/features/should-parents-be-afraid-to-let-their-kids-play-football/

Fleming, J. S., & Courtney, B. E. (1984). The dimensionality of self-esteem: II. Hierarchical facet model for revised measurement scales. *Journal of Personality and Social Psychology, 46*(2), 404–421.

Flyvbjerg, B. (2006). Five misunderstandings about case-study research. *Qualitative Inquiry, 12*(2), 219–245.

Fourati, M., & Hayek, D. (2019). Are Muslim immigrants really different? Experimental evidence from Lebanon and Australia. https://novafrica.org/wp-content/uploads/2019/10/Lebanese_Experiment.pdf

Fransen, M. L., Fennis, B. M., Pruyn, A. T. H., & Das, E. (2008). Rest in peace? Brand-induced mortality salience and consumer behavior. *Journal of Business Research, 61*(10), 1053–1061.

Free, J. B. (1954). The behaviour of robber honeybees. *Behaviour, 7*, 233–240.

Freud, S. (1927/1961). (J. Strachey, Trans., Ed.). *The future of an illusion*. W. W. Norton.

Fried, S. (2018). *Rush: Revolution, madness, and the visionary doctor who became a founding father*. Broadway Books.

Frieze, I. H., Olson, J. E., & Russell, J. (1991). Attractiveness and income for men and women in management. *Journal of Applied Social Psychology, 21*(13), 1039–1057.

Gagnon, J., & Simon, W. (1973). *Sexual conduct: The social sources of human sexuality*. Aldine.

Gagnon, J. H., & Simon, W. (1987). The sexual scripting of oral genital contacts. *Archives of Sexual Behavior, 16*(1), 1–25.

Gansberg, M. (1964). Thirty-seven who saw murder didn't call the police. *New York Times, 27*.

Gao, S., Assink, M., Cipriani, A., & Lin, K. (2017). Associations between rejection sensitivity and mental health outcomes: A meta-analytic review. *Clinical Psychology Review, 57*, 59–74.

Garcia, J. R., Reiber, C., Massey, S. G., & Merriwether, A. M. (2012). Sexual hookup culture: A review. *Review of General Psychology, 16*(2), 161–176.

Gettelman, E., & Murrmann, M. (2020). *The enemy in your pants: The military's decades-long war against STDs*. MotherJones.com. https://www.motherjones.com/media/2010/05/us-military-std-posters/

Gil, V. E., & Anderson, A. F. (1998). State-sanctioned aggression and the control of prostitution in the People's Republic of China: A review. *Aggression and Violent Behavior, 3*(2), 129–142.

Gilfoyle, T. J. (1999). Prostitutes in history: From parables of pornography to metaphors of modernity. *The American Historical Review, 104*(1), 117–141.

GLAAD. (2017) *Accelerating acceptance 2017: A Harris Poll survey of Americans' acceptance of LGBTQ people*. https://www.glaad.org/files/aa/2017_GLAAD_Accelerating_Acceptance.pdf

Global Witness. (2017). Home. https://www.globalwitness.org/en/

Goldstein, J. S. (2001). *War and gender: How gender shapes the war system and vice versa*. Cambridge University Press.

Goode, E., & Ben-Yehuda, N. (2009). *Moral panics: The social construction of deviance* (2nd ed.). Wiley-Blackwell.

Goodfriend, W. (2012). Sexual script or sexual improv? Nontraditional sexual paths. In M. Paludi (Ed.), *The psychology of love* (Vol. 1, pp. 59–71). Praeger.

Gordon-Messer, D., Bauermeister, J. A., Grodzinski, A., & Zimmerman, M. (2013). *Sexting among young adults*. Journal of Adolescent Health, 52(3), 301–306.

Grabe, S., & Hyde, J. S. (2006). Ethnicity and body dissatisfaction among women in the United States: A meta-analysis. *Psychological Bulletin, 132*(4), 622–640.

Greenberg, J., Pyszczynski, T., & Solomon, S. (1990). Anxiety concerning social exclusion: Innate response or one consequence of the need for terror management? *Journal of Social and Clinical Psychology, 9*(2), 202–213.

Grey, D. J. (2013). "Liable to very gross abuse": Murder, moral panic and cultural fears over infant life insurance, 1875–1914. *Journal of Victorian Culture, 18*(1), 54–71.

Grigorovici, D., Nam, S., & Russill, C. (2003). The effects of online syllabus interactivity on students' perception of the course and instructor. *The Internet and Higher Education, 6*(1), 41–52.

Gross, M. (2011). *Model: The ugly business of beautiful women*. HarperCollins.

Guimarães Jr, P. R., Pires, M. M., Jordano, P., Bascompte, J., & Thompson, J. N. (2017). Indirect effects drive coevolution in mutualistic networks. *Nature, 550*(7677), 511–514.

Gunnell, J. J., & Ceci, S. J. (2010). When emotionality trumps reason: A study of individual processing style and juror bias. *Behavioral Sciences & The Law, 28*(6), 850–877.

Halonen, J. S., Buskist, W., Dunn, D. S., Freeman, J., Hill, G. W., & Enns, C. (2013). *APA guidelines for the undergraduate psychology major* (Version 2.0). American Psychological Association.

Harlow, J. (1868). Recovery from the passage of an iron bar through the head. *Publications of the Massachusetts Medical Society, 2*, 327–347.

Harlow, J. M. (1993). Recovery from the passage of an iron bar through the head. *History of Psychiatry, 4*(14), 274–281.

Harmon, J. A., Stockton, S., & Contrucci, C. (1992). *Gender disparities in special education* (Research Rep. No. 143). Retrieved from ERIC database. (ED358631)

Harris, S. (2005). *The end of faith: Religion, terror, and the future of reason.* W. W. Norton.

Hart, B. (1986). Lesbian battering: An examination. In K. Lobel (Ed.), *Naming the violence: Speaking out about lesbian battering* (pp. 173–189). Seal Press.

Harvard Business School. (2014). *The HBS case method.* www.hbs.edu/mba/academic-experience/Pages/the-hbs-case-method.aspx

Hasinoff, A. A. (2013). Sexting as media production: Rethinking social media and sexuality. *New Media & Society, 15*(4), 449–465.

Haslam, S. A., Reicher, S. D., Millard, K., & McDonald, R. (2015). 'Happy to have been of service': The Yale archive as a window into the engaged followership of participants in Milgram's 'obedience' experiments. *British Journal of Social Psychology, 54*(1), 55–83.

Healthy families featured in Washington conference. (1990, July/August). *Family Therapy News*, p. 8.

Heinzen, T., Lilienfeld, S., & Nolan, S. A. (2015). *The horse that won't go away.* Worth.

Hempelmann, C. F. (2007) The laughter of the 192 Tanganyika epidemic. *Humour: International Journal of Humour Research, 20*(1), 49–71.

Henry, J., & Meadows, J. (2008). An absolutely riveting online course: Nine principles for excellence in web-based teaching. *Canadian Journal of Learning and Technology, 34*(1), [online].

Hill, F. (2002). *Delusions of Satan: The full story of the Salem witch trials.* Da Capo Press.

Hirschman, E. C. (1990). Secular immortality and the American ideology of affluence. *Journal of Consumer Research, 17*(1), 31–42.

Hoffman, R. R., Crandall, B., & Shadbolt, N. (1998). Use of the critical decision method to elicit expert knowledge: A case study in the methodology of cognitive task analysis. *Human Factors, 40*(2), 254–276.

Houlihan, P. R., Stone, M., Clem, S. E., Owen, M., & Emmel, T. C. (2019). Pollination ecology of the ghost orchid (Dendrophylax lindenii): A first description with new hypotheses for Darwin's orchids. *Scientific Reports, 9*(1), 1–10.

How will the pandemic change higher education? (2020). *The Chronicle Review.* https://store.chronicle.com/a/downloads/-/4b6496c00998212b/ab9ea5ea2b1e8a5f

Hughes, P. (1964, March 30). "WILD ONES" INVADE SEASIDE—97 ARRESTS. *Daily Mirror*, p. 3D.

ICI (2020). Institute on Communication and Inclusion at Syracuse University. https://ici.syr.edu/

Iqbal, M. (2020, April 24). *Tinder revenue and usage statistics.* BusinessofApps. https://www.businessofapps.com/data/tinder-statistics/

Isaacson, W. (2014). *The innovators: How a group of hackers, geniuses, and geeks created the digital revolution.* Simon & Schuster.

Jennings, N., Clifford, S., Fox, A. R., O'Connell, J., & Gardner, G. (2015). The impact of nurse practitioner services on cost, quality of care, satisfaction and waiting times in the emergency department: A systematic review. *International Journal of Nursing Studies, 52*(1), 421–435.

Johnson, J. M., & Pettigrew, T. F. (2005). Kenneth B. Clark (1914–2005). *American Psychologist, 60*(6), 649–651.

Johnson, M. P. (1995). Patriarchal terrorism and common couple violence: Two forms of violence against women. *Journal of Marriage and the Family, 57*(2), 283–294.

Johnson, M. P. (2007). The intersection of gender and control. In L. O'Toole, J. R. Schiffman, & M. L. K. Edwards (Eds.), *Gender violence: Interdisciplinary perspectives* (2nd ed., pp. 257–268). New York University Press.

Johnson, S. (2006). *The ghost map: The story of London's most terrifying epidemic—and how it changed science, cities, and the modern world.* Riverhead Books.

Johnson, S., Burrows, A., & Williamson, I. (2004). 'Does my bump look big in this?' The meaning of bodily changes for first-time mothers-to-be. *Journal of Health Psychology, 9*(3), 361–374.

Johnson, S. A. (2013). Using REBT in Jewish, Christian, and Muslim couples counseling in the United States. *Journal of Rational-Emotive & Cognitive-Behavior Therapy, 31*(2), 84–92.

Jones, J. M., & Pettigrew, T. F. (2005). Kenneth B. Clark (1914–2005). *American Psychologist, 60*(6), 649–651.

Jong, J., Halberstadt, J., & Bluemke, M. (2012). Foxhole atheism, revisited: The effects of mortality salience on explicit and implicit religious belief. *Journal of Experimental Social Psychology, 48*(5), 983–989.

Jussim, L., & Harber, K. D. (2005). Teacher expectations and self-fulfilling prophecies: Knowns and unknowns, resolved and unresolved controversies. *Personality and Social Psychology Review, 9*(2), 131–155.

Kalamägi, J., Lavikainen, P., Taipale, H., Tanskanen, A., Tiihonen, J., Hartikainen, S., & Tolppanen, A. M. (2019). Predictors of high hospital care and medication costs and cost trajectories in community-dwellers with Alzheimer's disease. *Annals of Medicine, 51*(5/6), 294–305.

Kane, J. (1998). *Sold for sex.* Ashgate.

Kaposi, D. (2017). The resistance experiments: Morality, authority and obedience in Stanley Milgram's account. *Journal for the Theory of Social Behaviour, 47*(4), 382–401.

Kaslow, F. W., & Hammerschmidt, H. (1993). Long term "good" marriages: The seemingly essential ingredients. *Journal of Couples Therapy, 3*(2–3), 15–38.

Kaslow, F. W., & Robison, J. A. (1996). Long-term satisfying marriages: Perceptions of contributing factors. *American Journal of Family Therapy, 24*(2), 153–170.

Kasser, T., & Sheldon, K. M. (2000). Of wealth and death: Materialism, mortality salience, and consumption behavior. *Psychological Science, 11*(4), 348–351.

Kennair, L. E. O., Bendixen, M., & Buss, D. M. (2016). Sexual regret: Tests of competing explanations of sex differences. *Evolutionary Psychology, 14*(4), 1474704916682903.

Khan, R., Brewer, G., & Archer, J. (2020). Genetic relatedness, emotional closeness and physical aggression: A comparison of full and half sibling experiences. *Europe's Journal of Psychology, 16*(1), 167–185.

Kilpatrick, D. G. (2004). What is violence against women? Defining and measuring the problem. *Journal of Interpersonal Violence, 19*(11), 1209–1234.

Kim, S., Kim, S. H., & Kamphaus, R. W. (2010). Is aggression the same for boys and girls? Assessing measurement invariance with confirmatory factor analysis and item response theory. *School Psychology Quarterly, 25*(1), 45.

Kirkwood, C. (1993). *Leaving abusive partners: From the scars of survival to the wisdom for change.* SAGE.

Kirsch, I., & Sapirstein, G. (1998). Listening to Prozac but hearing placebo: A meta-analysis of antidepressant medication. *Prevention & Treatment, 1*(2), 1–16.

Kitwood, T. (1990). *Concern for others: A new psychology of conscience and morality.* Taylor & Frances/Routledge.

Kitwood, T. (1997). The experience of dementia. *Aging & Mental Health, 1*(1), 13–22.

Klein, E., Campbell, J., Soler, E., & Ghez, M. (1997). *Ending domestic violence: Changing public perceptions/halting the epidemic.* SAGE.

Klein, G. (2003). *The power of intuition.* Random House.

Kluge, P. F. (1986). Why they love us in the Philippines: The American naval bases provide cash and jobs. *Playboy,* 88.

Knight, G. R. (2010). *William Miller and the rise of Adventism.* Pacific Press.

Koltai, J., & Stuckler, D. (2020). Recession hardships, personal control, and the amplification of psychological distress: Differential responses to cumulative stress exposure during the US Great Recession. *SSM-Population Health, 10,* 100521.

Kozol, J. (1991). *Savage inequities.* Crown.

Krinsky, C. (2013). Introduction: The moral panic concept. *The Ashgate research companion to moral panics.* Routledge.

Kritsky, G. (1991). Darwin's Madagascan hawk moth prediction. *American Entomologist, 37*(4), 206–210.

Krysa, J. (2012). 100 Notes, No. 055, Ada Lovelace. In *Documenta und Museum Fridericianum Veranstaltungs-GmbH.* Kassel University Press.

Kwok, Y. L. A., Gralton, J., & McLaws, M. L. (2015). Face touching: A frequent habit that has implications for hand hygiene. *American Journal of Infection Control, 43*(2), 112–114.

La Jeunesse, M. (2019, Aug. 16). *The 19th Amendment only really helped White women.* TeenVogue. https://www.teenvogue.com/story/19th-amendment-anniversary-benefited-white-women

Latané, B., & Darley, J. (1970). *The unresponsive bystander: Why doesn't he help?* Century Psychology Series. Appleton-Century Crofts.

Laumann, E. O., Gagnon, J. H., Michael, R. T., & Michaels, S. (1994). *The social organization of sexuality: Sexual practices in the United States.* University of Chicago Press.

Leary, M. R., Kowalski, R. M., Smith, L., & Phillips, S. (2003). Teasing, rejection, and violence: Case studies of the school shootings. *Aggressive Behavior, 29*(3), 202–214.

Le Bon, G. (1896). *The Crowd. Tr. fr. the French.* Fisher Unwin.

LeDoux, J. (1998). Fear and the brain: Where have we been, and where are we going? *Biological Psychiatry, 44*(12), 1229–1238.

Leeman, A. B. (2009). Interfaith marriage in Islam: An examination of the legal theory behind the traditional and reformist positions. *Indiana Law Journal, 84,* 743–771.

LeFebvre, L. E. (2018). Swiping me off my feet: Explicating relationship initiation on Tinder. *Journal of Social and Personal Relationships, 35*(9), 1205–1229.

Lehmiller, J. J., Garcia, J. R., Gesselman, A. N., & Mark, K. P. (2020). Less sex, but more sexual diversity: Changes in sexual behavior during the COVID-19 coronavirus pandemic. *Leisure Sciences.* https://www.tandfonline.com/doi/full/10.1080/01490400.2020.1774016

Lenhart, A. (2009). Teens and sexting. *Pew Internet & American Life Project, 1,* 1–26.

Leshnoff, J. (2009). C* U* 2night: Sexting not just for kids. *AARP Magazine.* https://www.aarp.org/relationships/love-sex/info-11-2009/sexting_not_just_for_kids.html

Lev, A. I. (2004). *Transgender emergence: Therapeutic guidelines for working with gender variant people and their families.* Haworth.

Levenson, R. W., Carstensen, L. L., & Gottman, J. M. (1993). Long-term marriage: Age, gender, and satisfaction. *Psychology and Aging, 8*(2), 301–313.

Lewin, K. (1951). *Field theory in social science: Selected theoretical papers* (D. Cartwright, Ed.). Harpers.

Lifshin, U., Greenberg, J., Soenke, M., Darrell, A., & Pyszczynski, T. (2018). Mortality salience, religiosity, and indefinite life extension: Evidence of a reciprocal relationship between afterlife beliefs and support for forestalling death. *Religion, Brain & Behavior, 8*(1), 31–43.

Lilienfeld, S. O. (2007). Psychological treatments that cause harm. *Perspectives on Psychological Science, 2*(1), 53–70.

Lilienfeld, S. O. (2010). Can psychology become a science? *Personality and Individual Differences, 49*(4), 281–288.

Livingstone, S. (2008). Taking risky opportunities in youthful content creation: Teenagers' use of social networking sites for intimacy, privacy and self-expression. *New Media & Society, 10*(3), 393–411.

Lovelace, A. (1843). *Sketch of the Analytical Machine Invented by Charles Babbage, Esq. With Notes by the Translator.* Richard and John E. Taylor.

Luciano, R., & Fisher, D. (1982). *The umpire strikes back.* Bantam.

Lunn, P. D., Belton, C. A., Lavin, C., McGowan, F. P., Timmons, S., & Robertson, D. A. (2020). Using behavioral science to help fight the coronavirus. *Journal of Behavioral Public Administration, 3*(1), [online].

MacDonald, G., & Leary, M. R. (2005). Why does social exclusion hurt? The relationship between social and physical pain. *Psychological Bulletin, 131*(2), 202.

Mackey, R. A., Diemer, M. A., & O'Brien, B. A. (2004). Relational factors in understanding satisfaction in the lasting relationships of same-sex and heterosexual couples. *Journal of Homosexuality, 47*(1), 111–136.

Macmillan, M. (2000). *An odd kind of fame: Stories of Phineas Gage.* MIT Press.

Mahoney, A., Pargament, K. I., Tarakeshwar, N., & Swank, A. B. (2001). Religion in the home in the 1980s and 1990s: A meta-analytic review and conceptual analysis of links between religion, marriage, and parenting. *Journal of Family Psychology, 15*(4), 559–596.

Malinowski, B. (1948). *Magic, science and religion and other essays.* Doubleday.

Maloney, A. (2017). *Not so happily ever after. The Sun.* https://www.thesun.co.uk/fabulous/3106480/sleeping-beauty-raped-sleep-real-endings-disney-fairy-tales/

Mandeville, B. (1714). *The fable of the bees: Or, private vices, public benefits.* J. Roberts.

Mannheim, K. (1923/1952). The problem of generations. In P. Kecskemeti (Ed), *Essays on the sociology of knowledge* (pp. 276–322). Routledge & Kegan Paul.

Marrow, A. J. (1977). *The practical theorist: The life and work of Kurt Lewin.* Teachers College Press.

Marsh, H. W., & Richards, G. E. (1988). Tennessee self-concept scale: Reliability, internal structure, and construct validity. *Journal of Personality and Social Psychology, 55*(4), 612–624.

Marshall, D. A. (2020). The biological logic of human action: On the (considerable) difference between "rational" and "adaptive." In R. Giovagnoli & R. Lowe (Eds.), *The Logic of Social Practices* (pp. 49–67). Springer.

Masri, A., & Senussi, M. H. (2017). Trump's executive order on immigration—Detrimental effects on medical training and health care. *New England Journal of Medicine, 376*(19), e39.

Mather, C. (1693). *The wonders of the invisible world: Being an account of the tryals of several witches lately executed in New-England and of several remarkable curiosities therein occurring.* John Dunton.

Mather, I. (1684). *An essay for the recording of illustrious providences, wherein an account is given of many remarkable and very memorable events, which have happened in this last age, especially in New-England.* Reproduced in Burr, 1914/2002.

Meichenbaum, D., & Lilienfeld, S. O. (2018). How to spot hype in the field of psychotherapy: A 19-item checklist. *Professional Psychology: Research and Practice, 49*(1), 22–30.

Mendoza, R. L. (2019, April). Why any seatbelt mandate is an infinitely iterated Prisoner's Dilemma: A health economics perspective. *Forum for Social Economics, 48*(2), 194–215.

Merton, R. K. (1948). The self-fulfilling prophecy. *Antioch Review, 8*(2), 193–210.

Merton, R. K. (1987). A simple model of capital market equilibrium with incomplete information. *The Journal of Finance, 42*(3), 483–510.

Merton, R. K. (1994). Durkheim's division of labor in society. *Sociological Forum, 9*(1), 17–25.

Metz, C., Calmet, J., & Thevenot, A. (2019). Women subjected to domestic violence: The impossibility of separation. *Psychoanalytic Psychology, 36*(1), 36–43.

Milgram, S. (Director). (1962). *Obedience* [Documentary]. United States: Yale University.

Milgram, S. (1963). Behavioral study of obedience. *The Journal of Abnormal and Social Psychology, 67*(4), 371–378.

Milgram, S. (1970). The experience of living in cities. *Science, 167*(3924), 1461–1468.

Milgram, S. (1974). *Obedience to authority: An experimental view.* Harper & Row.

Milinski, M., Pfluger, D., Külling, D., & Kettler, R. (1990). Do sticklebacks cooperate repeatedly in reciprocal pairs? *Behavioral Ecology and Sociobiology, 27*(1), 17–21.

Mischkowski, D., Crocker, J., & Way, B. M. (2016). From painkiller to empathy killer: Acetaminophen (paracetamol) reduces empathy for pain. *Social Cognitive and Affective Neuroscience, 11*(9), 1345–1353.

Mizock, L., & Lewis, T. K. (2006). Trauma in transgender populations: Risk, resilience, and clinical care. *Journal of Emotional Abuse, 8*, 335–354.

Mohamed, B. (2018, Jan. 3). *New estimates show U.S. Muslim population continues to grow. Fact Tank.* https://www.pewresearch.org/fact-tank/2018/01/03/new-estimates-show-u-s-muslim-population-continues-to-grow/

Montee, B. B., Miltenberger, R. G., & Wittrock, D. (1995). An experimental analysis of facilitated communication. *Journal of Applied Behavior Analysis, 28*(2), 189–200.

Moore, C. N. (2011). "A diamond is forever": The construction of secular immortality and De Beers diamond advertising 1939–1958. New Mexico State University.

Moulton, C., Regehr, G., Lingard, L., Merritt, C., & MacRae, H. (2010). Slowing down to stay out of trouble in the operating room: Remaining attentive in automaticity. *Academic Medicine, 85*(10), 1571–1577.

Muiño, R., Carrera, P., & Iglesias, M. (2003). The characterization of sardine (Sardina pilchardus Walbaum) schools off the Spanish-Atlantic coast. *ICES Journal of Marine Science, 60*(6), 1361–1372.

National Center on Child Abuse and Neglect. (1997). *Fifth forum on federally funded child abuse and neglect research: Fiscal year 1996 projects.* Author.

National Intimate Partner and Sexual Violence Survey. (2010). *NISVS summary reports.* https://www.cdc.gov/violenceprevention/nisvs/index.html

Neill, S., & Cullen, J. M. (1974). Experiments on whether schooling by their prey affects the hunting behaviour of cephalopods and fish predators. *Journal of Zoology, 172*(4), 549–569.

Nichol, F. D. (1944). *The midnight cry: A defense of William Miller and the Millerites.* Review and Herald.

Nietzsche, F. (1996). *On the genealogy of morals: A polemic.* Oxford World Classics. (Original work published 1887)

Norton, M. (2002). *In the devil's snare: The Salem witchcraft crisis of 1692.* Knopf.

Nowak, M. A. (2006). Five rules for the evolution of cooperation. *Science, 314*(5805), 1560–1563.

Nowak, M. A., & Sigmund, K. (1992). Tit for tat in heterogeneous populations. *Nature, 355*(6357), 250–253.

Nyman, L. (2010). Documenting history: An interview with Kenneth Bancroft Clark. *History of Psychology, 13*(1), 74–88.

Okasha, S. (2016). On Hamilton's Rule and inclusive fitness theory with nonadditive payoffs. *Philosophy of Science, 83*(5), 873–883.

O'Reilly, P. (1988) The impact of sex-role stereotyping on human development. *Monograph, 3*(1). Ohio State Department of Education.

Oro, D. (2020). *Perturbation, behavioural feedbacks, and population dynamics in social animals: When to leave and where to go.* Oxford University Press.

Otgaar, H., Howe, M. L., Patihis, L., Merckelbach, H., Lynn, S. J., Lilienfeld, S. O., & Loftus, E. F. (2019). The return of the repressed: The persistent and problematic claims of long-forgotten trauma. *Perspectives on Psychological Science, 14*(6), 1072–1095.

Oullier, O., de Guzman, G. C., Jantzen, K. J., Lagarde, J., & Kelso, J. S. (2008). Social coordination dynamics: Measuring human bonding. *Social Neuroscience, 3*(2), 178–192.

Owens, L., Shute, R., & Slee, P. (2000). "Guess what I just heard!": Indirect aggression among teenage girls in Australia. *Aggressive Behavior: Official Journal of the International Society for Research on Aggression, 26*(1), 67–83.

Painter, N. I. (1994). Representing truth: Sojourner Truth's knowing and becoming known. *The Journal of American History, 81*(2), 461–492.

Pan, W., & Bai, H. (2009). A multivariate approach to a meta-analytic review of the effectiveness of the DARE program. *International Journal of Environmental Research and Public Health, 6*(1), 267–277.

Panksepp, J., Herman, B., Conner, R., Bishop, P., & Scott, J. P. (1978). The biology of social attachments: Opiates alleviate separation distress. *Biological Psychiatry, 13*, 607–618.

Paris, B. (2019). *Lessons left to learn: A school shooting case study.* https://digital.library.txstate.edu/handle/10877/8136

Penney, T. (2014). Bodies under glass: Gay dating apps and the affect-image. *Media International Australia, 153*(1), 107–117.

Pessoa, F. (2002). *The book of disquiet.* Penguin.

Pew Research Center. (2020, Feb. 6). *The virtues and downsides of online dating.* https://www.pewresearch.org/internet/2020/02/06/the-virtues-and-downsides-of-online-dating/

Pilcher, J., (1994). Mannheim's sociology of generations: An undervalued legacy. *British Journal of Sociology 45*(3), 481–495.

Pitcher, T. J. (1993). Stewardship and sustainability of Pacific fishery resources: The need for critical insight and an encyclopedia of ignorance. In *Our common shores and our common challenge: Environmental protection in the Pacific. Proceedings of the Fourth International Symposium of the Conference of Asian and Pan-Pacific University Presidents.* University of Alaska Sea Grant.

Pitcher, T. J., Misund, O. A., Fernö, A., Totland, B., & Melle, V. (1996). Adaptive behaviour of herring schools in the Norwegian Sea as revealed by high-resolution sonar. *ICES Journal of Marine Science, 53*(2), 449–452.

Poldrack, R. A., & Yarkoni, T. (2016). From brain maps to cognitive ontologies: Informatics and the search for mental structure. *Annual Review of Psychology, 67*, 587–612

Porter, E. S. (Producer), & Porter, E. S. (Director). (1903). *The great train robbery* [Motion picture]. Warner Bros.

Powell, A. (2010). Configuring consent: Emerging technologies, unauthorized sexual images and sexual assault. *Australian & New Zealand Journal of Criminology, 43*(1), 76–90.

Provine, R. R. (1996). Laughter. *American Scientist, 84*(1), 38–45.

Pyszczynski, T. (2019). The role of death in life: Exploring the interface between terror management theory and evolutionary psychology. In T. K. Shackelford & V. Ziegler-Hill (Eds.), *Evolutionary perspectives on death* (pp. 1–24). Springer.

Radelet, M. L., & Phillips, S. (2018). Capital punishment/death penalty. In A. J. Trevino (Ed.), *The Cambridge Handbook of Social Problems, Vol. 2* (pp. 433–447). Cambridge University Press.

Raia, J. A. (1996, March). Perceived social support and coping as moderators of effects of children's exposure to community violence. *Dissertation Abstracts International, 56*, 5181.

Rasmussen, J., & Langerman, H. (2019). Alzheimer's disease–why we need early diagnosis. *Degenerative Neurological and Neuromuscular Disease, 9*, 123.

Raymond, J., Hughes, D., & Gomez, C. (2001). *Sex trafficking of women in the United States: Links between international and domestic sex industries.* Coalition Against Trafficking in Women. www.catwinternational.org

Reicher, S. D., Haslam, S. A., & Smith, J. R. (2012). Working towards the experimenter: Reconceptualizing obedience within the Milgram paradigm as identification-based followership. *Perspectives on Psychological Science, 7*, 315–324.

Ren, D., Wesselmann, E. D., & Williams, K. D. (2018). Hurt people hurt people: Ostracism and aggression. *Current Opinion in Psychology, 19*, 34–38.

Reynolds, H. (1986). *The economics of prostitution.* Charles C Thomas.

Ricks, S. (1985). Father-infant interactions: A review of empirical research. *Family Relations, 34*, 505–511.

Riggle, E. D., Rostosky, S. S., McCants, L. E., & Pascale-Hague, D. (2011). The positive aspects of a transgender self-identification. *Psychology & Sexuality, 2*(2), 147–158.

Rindfleisch, A., & Burroughs, J. E. (2004). Terrifying thoughts, terrible materialism? Contemplations on a terror management account of materialism and consumer behavior. *Journal of Consumer Psychology, 14*(3), 219–224.

Ringrose, J., Gill, R., Livingstone, S., & Harvey, L. (2012). *A qualitative study of children, young people and "sexting": A report prepared for the NSPCC.* National Society for the Prevention of Cruelty to Children.

Roach, M. K. (2013). *Six women of Salem.* Da Capo Press.

Roberts, A. (2018). Fairytale ending. *The Sun.* https://www.thesun.co.uk/fabulous/6263918/parents-traditional-fairy-talespc/

Robins, L. N. (1993). Vietnam veterans' raid recovery from heroin addiction: A fluke or normal expectation? *Addiction, 88*(8), 1041–1054.

Rolls, J. A. (2010). Tales from broken hearts: Women and recovery from romantic relationships. *Storytelling, Self, Society: An Interdisciplinary Journal of Storytelling Studies, 6*(2), 107–121.

Romenskyy, M., Herbert-Read, J. E., Ward, A. J., & Sumpter, D. J. (2017). Body size affects the strength of social interactions and spatial organization of a schooling fish (Pseudomugil signifer). *Royal Society Open Science, 4*(4), 161056.

Roosevelt, F. D. (1933, March 4). *First inaugural address.* Washington, DC.

Rosen, K. H., & Stith, S. M. (1997). Surviving abusive dating relationships: Processes of leaving, healing and moving on. In G. Kantor & J. Jasinski (Eds.), *Out of the darkness: Contemporary perspectives on family violence* (pp. 170–182). SAGE.

Rosenthal, R. (1994). Interpersonal expectancy effects: A 30-year perspective. *Current Directions in Psychological Science, 3*(6), 176–179.

Rosenthal, R. (2002). Covert communication in classrooms, clinics, courtrooms, and cubicles. *American Psychologist, 57*(11), 839–849.

Rosenthal, R., & Fode, K. (1963). The effect of experimenter bias on the performance of the albino rat. *Behavioral Science, 8*(3), 183–189.

Rosenthal, R., & Jacobsen, L. (1968). *Pygmalion in the classroom: Self-fulfilling prophecies and teacher expectations.* Holt, Rhinehart, and Winston.

Routledge, C., Abeyta, A. A., & Roylance, C. (2018). Death and end times: The effects of religious fundamentalism and mortality salience on apocalyptic beliefs. *Religion, Brain & Behavior, 8*(1), 21–30.

Ruiz-Eugenio, L., Torras-Gómez, E., López de Aguileta-Jaussi, G., & Gutiérrez-Fernández, N. (2020). Changes in tongue kissing in hook-ups after COVID-19. *Sustainability, 12*(16), 6309.

Rusbult, C. E. (1980). Commitment and satisfaction in romantic associations: A test of the investment model. *Journal of Experimental Social Psychology, 16*(2), 172–186.

Russell, D. E. (1984). The prevalence and seriousness of incestuous abuse: Stepfathers vs. biological fathers. *Child Abuse & Neglect, 8*(1), 15–22.

Sabat, S. R. (1994). Excess disability and malignant social psychology: A case study of Alzheimer's disease. *Journal of Community & Applied Social Psychology, 4*(3), 157–166.

Sagan, C. (1995). *Demon-haunted World: Science as a candle in the dark.* Random House.

Sales, N. J. (2015). *Tinder and the dawn of the "Dating Apocalypse."* Vanity Fair. http://vanityfair.com

Schneider, D., Harknett, K., & McLanahan, S. (2016). Intimate partner violence in the Great Recession. *Demography, 53*(2), 471–505.

Schuessler, J. (2019, Aug 15). *The complex history of the women's suffrage movement.* New York Times. https://www.nytimes.com/2019/08/15/arts/design/womens-suffrage-movement.html

Seligman, M. E. P. (2002). Positive psychology, positive prevention, and positive therapy. In C. R. Snyder, & S. J. Lopez (Eds.), *Handbook of positive psychology* (pp. 3–9). Oxford University Press.

Shackleton, K., Al Toufailia, H., Balfour, N. J., Nascimento, F. S., Alves, D. A., & Ratnieks, F. L. (2015). Appetite for self-destruction: Suicidal biting as a nest defense strategy in Trigona stingless bees. *Behavioral Ecology and Sociobiology, 69*(2), 273–281.

Sherry, M. (2016). Facilitated communication, Anna Stubblefield and disability studies. *Disability & Society, 31*(7), 974–982.

Shryock, R. (1971). The medical reputation of Benjamin Rush: Contrasts over two centuries. *Bulletin of the History of Medicine, 45*, 507–552.

Sleegers, W. W., Proulx, T., & Van Beest, I. (2017). The social pain of Cyberball: Decreased pupillary reactivity to exclusion cues. *Journal of Experimental Social Psychology, 69*, 187–200.

Smith, K. (2005). Prebirth gender talk: A case study in prenatal socialization. *Women and Language, 28*(1), 49–54.

Solomon, J. D., Genovese, W., Jacobson, M., & Valva, M. (Producers), Solomon, J. D. (Director). (2016). *The witness* [Motion picture]. FilmRise.

Solomon, S., Greenberg, J., & Pyszczynski, T. (1991). Terror management theory of self-esteem. In C. R. Snyder, & D. R. Forsyth (Eds.), *Handbook of social and clinical psychology: The health perspective* (pp. 21–40). Pergamon.

Spoto, D. (1993). *Marilyn Monroe: The biography.* Rowman & Littlefield.

The state of the gender pay gap 2020. (2020). *Payscale.com.* https://www.payscale.com/data/gender-pay-gap

Sternberg, R. J. (2008). *An ethnographic approach to studying practical intelligence: A review of gang leader for a day.* Penguin.

Stratton, D., & Gire, K. (2016). *All the gallant men.* Harper Collins.

Straus, M. A. (1979). Measuring intrafamily conflict and violence: The conflict tactics (CT) scales. *Journal of Marriage and The Family, 41*(1), 75–88.

Stowe, H. B. (1863). Sojourner Truth. *Atlantic Monthly, 473*, 481. http://www.kyphilom.com/www/truth.html

Sturdevant, S. P., & Stoltzfus, B. (1992). *Let the good times roll: Prostitution and the U.S. military in Asia.* New Press.

Sun, W. (2017). Bridal photos and diamond rings: The inequality of romantic consumption in China. *The Journal of Chinese Sociology, 4*(1), article 15.

Tatar, M. (2003). *The hard facts of the Grimms' fairy tales.* Princeton University Press.

Taylor, L., Zuckerman, B., Harik, V., & Groves, B. M. (1994). Witnessing violence by young children and their mothers. *Journal of Developmental and Behavioral Pediatrics, 15*(2), 120–123.

Taylor, S. (2019). *The psychology of pandemics: Preparing for the next global outbreak of infectious disease.* Cambridge Scholars Publishing.

Tchalova, K., & Eisenberger, N. I. (2016). The shared neural substrates of physical and social pain. In K. D. Williams & S. A. Nida (Eds.), *Ostracism, exclusion, and rejection* (pp. 71–90). Routledge.

Thomas, W. I., & Thomas, D. S. (1928). *The child in America.* Knopf.

Thompson, J. A., & Fitzgerald, C. J. (2017). Nepotistic preferences in a computerized trolley problem. *Current Research in Social Psychology, 25,* 36–44.

Thompson, K. (1998). *Moral panic.* Routledge.

Thompson, S. (1975). Gender labels and early sex role development. *Child Development, 46,* 339–347.

Thurlow, C., & Bell, K. (2009). Against technologization: Young people's new media discourse as creative cultural practice. *Journal of Computer-Mediated Communication, 14*(4), 1038–1049.

Toledo, A. H. (2004). The medical legacy of Benjamin Rush. *Journal of Investigative Surgery, 17*(2), 61–63.

Tolman, D. L. (2009). *Dilemmas of desire: Teenage girls talk about sexuality.* Harvard University Press.

Trafficking for sexual exploitation. (2020). *EqualityNow .org.* https://www.equalitynow.org/trafficking

Tweed, T. A. (2004). *Islam in America: From African Slaves to Malcolm X.* National Humanities Center. http://nationalhumanitiescenter.org/tserve/twenty/tkeyinfo/islam.htm

Twitchell, J. B. (2000). *Twenty ads that shook the world: The century's most groundbreaking advertising and how it changed us all.* Broadway Books.

Underwood, M. K. (2004). Glares of contempt, eye rolls of disgust and turning away to exclude: Non-verbal forms of social aggression among girls. *Feminism & Psychology, 14*(3), 371–375.

United Nations General Assembly. (2019). Convention on the prevention and punishment of the crime of genocide. 9 December 1948, United Nations, Treaty Series, Vol. 78.

Valkenburg, P. M., & Peter, J. (2007). Who visits online dating sites? Exploring some characteristics of online daters. *CyberPsychology & Behavior, 10*(6), 849–852.

Van Vugt, M., & Van Lange, P. A. M. (2006). The altruism puzzle: Psychological adaptations for prosocial behavior. In M. Schaller, J. A. Simpson, & D. T. Kenrick (Eds.), *Evolution and social psychology* (pp. 237–261). Psychosocial Press.

Venkatesh, S. (2008). *Gang leader for a day: A rogue sociologist takes to the streets.* Penguin.

Viola, T. W., Niederauer, J. P. O., Kluwe-Schiavon, B., Sanvicente-Vieira, B., & Grassi-Oliveira, R. (2019). Cocaine use disorder in females is associated with altered social decision-making: A study with the prisoner's dilemma and the ultimatum game. *BMC Psychiatry, 19*(1), 211.

Wampold, B. E., & Imel, Z. E. (2015). *The great psychotherapy debate: The evidence for what makes psychotherapy work* (2nd ed.). Routledge/Taylor & Francis Group.

Wang, S. S., Moon, S., Kwon, K. H., Evans, C. A., & Stefanone, M. A. (2010). Face off: Implications of visual cues on initiating friendship on Facebook. *Computers in Human Behavior, 26*(2), 226–234.

Ward, A., & Webster, M. (2016). *Sociality: The behaviour of group-living animals.* Springer.

Waters, S., Edmondston, S. J., Yates, P. J., & Gucciardi, D. F. (2016). Identification of factors influencing patient satisfaction with orthopaedic outpatient clinic consultation: A qualitative study. *Manual Therapy, 25,* 48–55.

Weintraub, S. (2001). *Silent night: The story of the World War I Christmas truce.* Simon and Schuster.

Wheeler, D. L., Jacobson, J. W., Paglieri, R. A., & Schwartz, A. A. (1993). An experimental assessment of facilitated communication. *Mental Retardation, 31*(1), 49–59.

White, L. (1990). *The comforts of home: Prostitution in colonial Nairobi.* University of Chicago Press.

Whitehead, D., & Russell, G. (2004). How effective are health education programmes—resistance, reactance, rationality and risk? Recommendations for effective practice. *International Journal of Nursing Studies, 41*(2), 163–172.

Whitman, M. (1993). *Removing a badge of slavery: The record of Brown v Board of Education.* Markus Wiener.

Wiederman, M. W. (2005). The gendered nature of sexual scripts. *The Family Journal, 13*(4), 496–502.

Wilkinson, G. S. (1984). Reciprocal food sharing in the vampire bat. *Nature, 308*(5955), 181–184.

Williams Institute. (2016). *How many adults identify as transgender in the United States?* https://williamsinstitute.law.ucla.edu/publications/trans-adults-united-states/

Williams, K. D., & Nida, S. A. (2011). Ostracism: Consequences and coping. *Current Directions in Psychological Science, 20*(2), 71–75.

Wilson, J., & Hudson, W. (2013, November 11). *Gun violence in PG-13 movies has tripled.* CNN: Health. http://www.cnn.com/2013/11/11/health/gun-violence-movies/index.html

Wilson, M., Daly, M., & Daniele, A. (1995). Familicide: The killing of spouse and children. *Aggressive Behavior, 21*(4), 275–291.

Woolley, A., & Kostopoulou, O. (2013). Clinical intuition in family medicine: More than first impressions. *The Annals of Family Medicine, 11*(1), 60–66.

World Health Organization. (2019). Rational use of personal protective equipment for coronavirus disease 2019 (COVID-19). *WHO reference number:* WHO/2019-nCov/IPC PPE_use/2020.1

Wortmann, M. (2012). Dementia: A global health priority—highlights from an ADI and World Health Organization report. *Alzheimer's Research & Therapy, 4*(5), article 40.

Xie, G. X., & Lee, M. J. (2008). Anticipated violence, arousal, and enjoyment of movies: Viewers' reactions to violent previews based on arousal-seeking tendency. *The Journal of Social Psychology, 148*(3), 277–292.

Yeo, T. E. D., & Fung, T. H. (2018). "Mr. Right Now": Temporality of relationship formation on gay mobile dating apps. *Mobile Media & Communication, 6*(1), 3–18.

Yeung, H. M., & Hebert, R. S. (2018). End-of-life chemotherapy: A prisoner's dilemma? *BMJ Supportive & Palliative Care, 8*, 58–60.

Yin, R. K. (2009). *Case study research: Design and methods.* SAGE.

Young, J. (1971). *The drugtakers: The social meaning of drug use.* MacGibbon and Kee.

Zahn-Waxler, C. (2000). The development of empathy, guilt, and internalization of distress: Implications for gender differences in internalizing and externalizing problems. In R. J. Davidson (Ed.), *Anxiety, depression, and emotion* (pp. 222–265). Oxford University Press.

Zhang, L., Pan, N., Chen, T., Wang, S., Gu, J., Yang, X., … Gong, Q. (2020). Gender differences in the frequency of aggression in dreams: A meta-analysis. *Dreaming, 30*(1), 1–18.

Zuk, M. (2011). *Sex on six legs: Lessons on life, love, and language from the insect world.* Houghton Mifflin Harcourt.

Index